William Collins and Eighteenth-Century English Poetry

Partial support for this publication
was provided by the Northwestern University
Research Grants Committee.

William Collins and Eighteenth-Century English Poetry

Richard Wendorf

University of Minnesota Press

Minneapolis

187535

Published by the University of Minnesota Press,
2037 University Avenue Southeast, Minneapolis, MN 55414
Printed in the United States of America.

Library of Congress Cataloging in Publication Data

Wendorf, Richard.
    William Collins and eighteenth-century English
poetry.

    Includes index.
    1. Collins, William, 1721-1759 — Criticism and
interpretation. I. Title.
PR3354.W46   823'.8   81-14674
ISBN 0-8166-1058-4   AACR2

The University of Minnesota
is an equal-opportunity
educator and employer.

For Barbara

Contents

Preface

William Collins's career as a poet was extremely brief, almost embarrassingly so. He wrote most of his poetry in three years, from 1744 to 1746; two important later poems date from 1749, but there is no reason to believe that he began any additional poems in the following (and final) ten years of his life. An equally remarkable characteristic of Collins's career is his virtual anonymity as a poet. By this I mean both our scanty knowledge of the figure who actually wrote the poems and the poet's own elusive voice in his work (this in spite of the insistent "I" of many of the odes). It would be fair to say, for instance, that we know as much about Collins as a schoolboy at Winchester in the late 1730s as we do about the suddenly mature poet writing his major odes in the mid 1740s, and in each case we know very little. Collins's other editors would surely agree that the circumstances surrounding the writing and publication of almost every poem are sketchy at best. We may be able to determine *probable* causes and circumstances, but substantive proof, if it exists, has not yet been found. The same is true of Collins's intellectual history. Both the little information we have and the allusive nature of the poetry itself suggest an impressive knowledge of classical and Renaissance literature, contemporary painting and music, and contemporary poetry, philosophy, and critical theory; but here—as elsewhere—we must content ourselves with tentative conclusions. Even Collins's relations with his closest literary friends, Johnson and the Wartons, are far from clear. When we turn to a study of "Collins," in other words, we are primarily confronted by the poems themselves, and they often prove to be complex, elusive, even fragmentary.

Many would argue, of course, that this is the way things should be. But I continue to find it odd that such an unusually small collection of poetry, bereft of the conventional biographical context, should have produced a body of criticism that has often favored biographical speculation and theories about Collins's anxieties as a poet rather than an analysis of the poetry itself or an examination of Collins's development as a writer. Certain limitations on our knowledge are capable of creating fresh and unhampered opportunities for exploration; but the "New Criticism" of the 1940s and 1950s, which might well have found Collins an appropriate subject for close scrutiny and which did in fact produce impressive and original readings of several important eighteenth-century poets, left Collins's poetry virtually untouched. Many of Collins's most interesting poems, "The Manners" and "The Passions" in particular, have still not received the attention they deserve; similarly, the historical contexts that most clearly reveal the immediate environment in which Collins wrote have never been fully explored.

I also find it surprising that so many of Collins's early poems have been neglected by his modern critics. If Collins is indeed an important transitional figure in English poetry (as his critics agree), then surely his development as a poet, especially his struggle to create fresh literary forms, is of considerable interest. I have devoted my third and fourth chapters to this subject, often granting his early poems a fuller reading than might otherwise be justified. I have discovered, moreover, that these poems are not always harbingers of his later work: although the early poems reveal a clear pattern of poetical development (and an awareness on his part of the poet's career), they also disclose an extensive reliance on the poetry of Pope and his contemporaries (which he was soon to reject). Although Collins fully intended, in his mature poems, to forge a revised idiom for lyrical poetry, in his early works he began by paying more studious attention to Augustan poetry than we have previously realized.

Much of what I argue in this book is therefore meant to restore the balance that has been impaired by recent criticism of Collins's work: both by the tendency toward biographical speculation that culminates in the work of Harold Bloom, and by the attempt to place Collins within a general scheme of influence and repression (here I am thinking of the work of Bloom, Paul S. Sherwin, and Thomas Weiskel). I do not mean to dismiss the importance of these approaches, nor the sensitive readings they occasionally have stimulated.

I am surprised, however, that so little attention has been directed toward the poems themselves and their place within the poetical upheaval of the 1740s, and I have consequently taken these as my primary concerns. I do not propose a single thesis that ties Collins's work neatly together. My approach is largely inductive; I attempt to analyze the poems individually and in light of each other, always working toward generalizations—about nature, the irrational, the poet's career—that follow directly from the works themselves. I have tried to keep in mind not only the specialist in eighteenth-century poetry but also the student or teacher who may be approaching Collins's poetry for the first time, and I have therefore appended a short history of recent criticism and scholarship to the final chapter. I hope that the kinds of close readings and historical background I offer will stimulate further interest in Collins in the classroom as well as in professional scholarship.

The following study is a book of criticism, not a critical biography, but I have found it useful to begin with an examination of Collins's madness and of the various biographical and critical myths that have grown around it. No aspect of Collins's work reveals more clearly the ways in which his poetry has been misread, or how his own interests are closely tied to the concerns of an entire generation of writers. Such contexts can provide important perspectives on the growth, variety, and distinctive quality of Collins's poetical voice. In the second chapter, for instance, I attempt to demonstrate the growing desire in the 1740s to embrace a conception of the "poetical character" that was manifestly at odds with the decorum and spirit of Augustan verse. The poetry of Joseph Warton and Mark Akenside offers a surprisingly neglected context for Collins's own speculations on the powers and perils of the creative imagination. At the same time, recent critical emphasis on the arguments or themes of the "Ode on the Poetical Character" (the role of imagination or of Milton) has tended to discourage an investigation of *how* the poem works. I argue that the notorious difficulties of this central ode—in its syntax, imagery, and formal structure—are neither accidental nor perverse. These difficulties are in fact carefully designed so that Collins's readers will also experience the obstacles and frustrations that thwart the ambitious writer. I believe, in other words, that Collins is not simply a poet talking about poetry to other poets. Although he claims specific powers for the poet, much of his work is devoted to analyzing those human qualities--suffering, friendship, ambition, patriotism, love of liberty—that he shares with a far wider audience.

Chief among these human characteristics is the entire range of emotional responses that he considers in the *Odes* of 1746, and in the concluding ode on "The Passions" in particular. As I suggest in the first chapter, the passions have important connections with the irrational, especially with the manner in which Collins "projects" or bodies forth the dangerous emotions in human form; but, as I emphasize in later chapters, this subject is not limited to irrational emotion or to the temperament of the poetical character. Although contemporary criticism drew attention to it, the general psychological nature of Collins's poetry is an essential feature that we have largely lost sight of, especially his intricate externalization and reabsorption of the reflexive passions (pity, hope, simplicity, fear). Collins's ambition in the *Odes* is considerable, far more sweeping, I would suggest, than we have previously believed; and his final ode in that volume, almost entirely neglected by modern criticism, reveals a determination not only to portray the entire spectrum of the emotions, but to adapt that portrayal to musical representation as well. Collins's enthusiasm for music has been almost completely ignored, and yet this lengthy ode (and the late "Recitative Accompanied") demonstrate that Collins was carefully transforming the traditional musical ode of Dryden and Pope so that it would conform to contemporary musical theory.

Closely allied with Collins's investigation of the passions is his exploration of external nature, especially in "The Manners," the "Ode to Evening," and several of the late fragments. These poems reveal a natural landscape that continually eludes our perception and hence any precise characterization. It is a world of obscure forms and evanescent features—one that contrasts sharply with the certain hierarchies of Pope or Thomson—and thus it presents a challenge to the artist who would successfully evoke and capture it. Both of these important odes depict an apprenticeship in which Collins calls upon nature to teach him the arts by which it is to be approached and celebrated, even if it cannot be permanently fixed.

As my opening and closing chapters suggest, I have little sympathy with the persistent view that Collins's poetry is debilitated or limited by his personal misfortunes (especially his problematical madness) or by his reliance on poetical precursors. Several recent studies, Sherwin's in particular, have stressed Collins's limitations (his "deficiencies") as a poet; in this study I emphasize Collins's achievement, limited as it may be. Collins's confrontation with the major figures who preceded him—Spenser, Milton, Pope, Thomson—actually helped produce much of his most successful work. One has only to compare the "Ode on the Poetical Character" with Gray's self-assured acceptance of Milton's mantle in "The Progress of Poesy" to see how Collins's hesitancy and self-consciousness finally created an ode entirely worthy to appear within the English tradition. But Collins's lesser works also demand a much more careful examination. Even if they are only lower branches on what Collins called "the tree of poetry," they nevertheless suggest the range of his poetical voice and help us to understand more fully the distinctive qualities of his finest work.

Portions of this study have appeared in slightly different form in the *Huntington Library Quarterly*, 42 (1979), 91-116, in *Modern Philology*, 76 (1979), 231-39, and in my introduction to the Augustan Reprint Society facsimile edition of Joseph Warton's *Odes on Various Subjects*. I wish to thank the Huntington Library, the University of Chicago Press, and the Augustan Reprint Society for permission to reprint this material.

I have enjoyed generous support of various kinds during my work on Collins, and I take pleasure in recording this assistance here. I am grateful to the American Council of Learned Societies, which awarded me a Research Fellowship for Recent Recipients of the Ph.D., and to Rudolph H. Weingartner, Dean of Northwestern University's College of Arts and Sciences, whose support allowed me to complete this study during a year's leave from my teaching duties. A grant from the Henry E. Huntington Library enabled me to pursue my research within its extraordinarily rich eighteenth-century collections; a summer stipend from the National Endowment for the Humanities afforded me a particularly pleasant interval in which to examine the musical ode in the eighteenth century. A handsome subvention from the University Research Grants Committee at Northwestern greatly assisted the production of this book.

I also take considerable pleasure in thanking those colleagues and friends — Leonard Barkan, William Brennan, Gerald Graff, Robert Mahony, Mary Margaret Stewart, Herbert Tucker, and Scott Westrem — whose shrewd advice has helped me to focus my arguments throughout this study. Marjorie Weiner prepared the manuscript with her customary care. My greatest debts are to Jean Hagstrum, James King, Lawrence Lipking, and Charles Ryskamp, whose generous advice has made this a better book than it otherwise would have been.

William Collins and Eighteenth-Century English Poetry

1

"Poor Collins" Reconsidered

The question of Collins's madness has long posed a dilemma for those who have endeavored to characterize either his life or his work. In its simplest form, this dilemma raises questions that are primarily biographical: when, and to what degree, did Collins suffer from symptoms usually associated with insanity? The biographical problem serves, at the same time, as a focal point for more complex issues concerning the nature of Collins's poetry and his own conception of the poetical character.

The difficulty inherent in a study of Collins's illness lies in the scarcity of material available to us. It would probably be accurate to say that we know less about Collins than we do about any other comparable figure of the eighteenth century. Despite the poet's assurance that "Invenias etiam disjecti membra poetæ," he has come down to us larger in legend than in fact.[1] The following reconsideration of Collins's madness, which endeavors to gather together all the relevant material for the first time, discusses three related problems in some detail. In the first section, the conclusions that have been (and can be) drawn about Collins's illness are balanced against a close narrative of the last ten years of his life; the second section illustrates how these facts have been reworked into influential fictions; and the final section analyzes the ways in which the fictions and half-truths surrounding Collins's madness have influenced the way his poetry has been read.

3

I. Collins in the 1750s

An indication of the scarcity of material concerning Collins's last years can be seen in the efforts of his first scholarly editor, Alexander Dyce, to obtain anecdotes about the poet. Dyce wrote to Henry Mackenzie, the aging "man of feeling," who was a close associate of the dramatist John Home, the recipient of Collins's "Ode to a Friend" ("Ode on the Popular Superstitions of the Highlands of Scotland"). Dyce received this reply from Mackenzie in 1826: "In the present state of my health, writing is not an easy matter to me; but I am anxious not to delay acknowledging your letter on the subject of your proposed edition of Collins. It would gratify me if I could contribute to it; but I do not recollect hearing any anecdotes from Mr. Home, or having any communication with him or any one else, regarding Collins, the close of whose life made the subject rather a distressing one."[2]

Mackenzie's experience seems not to have been unique. Clearly Collins's madness has been, to some extent, the reason for our limited knowledge of his last years: either his seclusion isolated him from those who normally would have seen him and perhaps have written about him, or the possibility of madness itself became a cause for reticence. John Ragsdale, who preserved many facts about his friend's life in London, was forced to bring his account to a hasty close: "I never saw him after his sister had removed him from M'Donald's madhouse at Chelsea to Chichester, where he soon sunk into a deplorable state of idiotism, which, when I was told, shocked me exceedingly; and even now the remembrance of a man, for whom I had a particular friendship, and in whose company I have passed so many pleasant, happy hours, gives me a severe shock."[3] Collins did have friends who saw or heard more of him during his last years, however, and it is to these men—Samuel Johnson, Gilbert White, and Joseph and Thomas Warton—that we are indebted for the few fragments that provide the following sketch of those sad years.

Collins's illness was thought to have begun shortly after the death of his uncle, Colonel Martin, in 1749. In "Some Account of the Life and Writings of Mr. William Collins," published in the *Poetical Calendar* in 1763, James Hampton wrote that Collins's uncle left him a considerable fortune, "which however he did not live long to enjoy, for he fell into a nervous disorder, which continued, with but short intervals, till his death, which happened in 1756. and with which disorder his head and intellects were at times affected."[4] Johnson, who added a character sketch to Hampton's account, remembered the latter part of Collins's life "with pity and sadness": the poet "languished some years under that depression of mind which enchains the faculties without destroying them, and leaves reason the knowledge of right, without the power of pursuing it." With these clouds gathering on his intellect, Collins sought relief in travel through France "but found himself constrained to yield to his malady, and returned: he was for some time confined in a house of lunatics, and afterwards retired to the care of his sister in Colchester, where death at last came to his relief."[5]

This short account by Hampton and Johnson is not entirely satisfactory, even as a rough outline of these years. Their incorrect information concerning both Collins's date and place of death indicates just how out of touch the biographers were with their subject, and this is corroborated by Johnson's letters in the mid-1750s, as we shall see. Johnson's short character of the poet proved, moreover, to be both enigmatic and highly influential. "His morals were pure, and his opinions pious," Johnson began; but, in a characteristic turn, he pointed out that "in a long continuance of poverty, and long habits of dissipation, it cannot be expected that any character should be exactly uniform." Johnson does not have the "temerity to affirm" that "this man, wise and virtuous as he was, passed always unentangled through the snares of life," but he does state "that at least he preserved the source of action unpolluted," and that his faults stemmed from "casual temptation" and not from his principles, which remained unshaken. What Johnson seems to be saying is that his friend was a good and virtuous man, but—as Johnson's contemporaries who had witnessed Collins's frustrations and anxieties in the late 1740s and early 1750s would have known—he was also human. Biographers in Johnson's footsteps, eager to discover clues to Collins's character (and thus to elucidate his later illness), have pounced on the poet's indolence and "dissipation." "Now what is Johnson telling us, or, more interestingly, what is he concealing?" one scholar has asked; "What were the 'long habits of dissipation'?"[6] But, as Birkbeck Hill's footnote points out in his edition of the *Lives*, "dissipation" was defined in Johnson's dictionary as simply "a scattered habit of attention."[7] At this time the word did not mean "a dissolute mode of living," as later biographers have often assumed.

No evidence exists of any early sign of mental illness in 1750, when Collins was apparently at work on a number of different projects. In the spring of that year, the publishers Manby and Cox advertised his "Epistle to the Editor of Fairfax his Translation of Tasso's Jerusalem."[8] In July "The Passions" was performed at the Oxford Encaenia, and in November Collins wrote to William Hayes, who had set the poetry to music, informing him that he had both a revised version of the poem and an ode on "the Music of the Græcian Theatre."[9] Thomas Warton wrote that he "often saw Collins in London in 1750—This was before his illness. He then told me of his intended History of the *Revival of Learning*, and proposed a scheme of a *Review*, to be called the *Clarendon Review*, and to be printed at the University Press, under the conduct and authority of the University."[10]

The first specific evidence we have of Collins's illness dates from 1751. According to Thomas Warton, "About Easter, the next year, I was in London; when being given over, and supposed to be dying, he desired to see me, that he might take his last leave of me: But he grew better, and in the summer he sent me a letter on some private business, which I have now by me, dated Chichester, June 9th, 1751, written in a fine hand, and without the least symptom of a disordered or debilitated understanding."[11] What Warton tells us here of Collins's illness and recovery suggests that the poet's ailment was both physical and severe, although it may have produced symptoms of a disordered understanding. Collins unfortunately seems to have dropped out of Warton's sight until 1754, and it is during this period that he presumably traveled in France. John Ragsdale insisted (in 1793) that "There are so few of his intimates now living, that I believe I am the only one who can give a true account of his family and connections. The principal part of what I write is from my own knowledge, or what I have heard from his nearest relations."[12] Ragsdale did not see Collins after he was removed from the madhouse in Chelsea, nor was he positive of the date of Collins's death, but he does state that when Collins's "health and faculties began to decline he went to France, and afterwards to Bath, in hopes his health might be restored, but without success."[13]

Collins's travels to France and Bath may have lasted until 1753; it was in the following year that he was confined in MacDonald's madhouse (how long we do not know) before being escorted home to Chichester by his sister Anne. The anecdote with which Johnson closes his narrative indicates that he saw Collins at least once during the years 1750–54; more important, it chronicles an encounter that demonstrates Collins's apparent health and lucidity at this time:

> After his return from France, the writer of this character paid him a visit at Islington, where he was waiting for his sister, whom he had directed to meet him: there was then nothing of disorder discernable in his mind by any but himself, but he had then withdrawn from study, and travelled with no other book than an English testament, such as children carry to the school; when his friend took it into his hand, out of curiosity to see what companion a man of letters had chosen, "I have but one book," says Collins, "but that is the best."[14]

Johnson, however, was out of touch with Collins by 8 March 1754, when he wrote to Thomas Warton:

> But how little can we venture to exult in any intellectual powers or literary attainments, when we consider the condition of poor Collins. I knew him a few years ago full of hopes and full of projects, versed in many languages, high in fancy, and strong in retention. This busy and forcible mind is now under the government of those who lately would not have been able to comprehend the least and most narrow of its designs. What do you hear of him? are there hopes of his recovery? or is he to pass the remainder of his life in misery and degradation? perhaps with complete consciousness of his calamity.[15]

Johnson's statement that Collins's mind was now "under the government" of others suggests that the poet was, at this time, still confined in an institution.

We do not know if Johnson's questions elicited a reply from Warton, but Warton did see Collins twice that year. By September Collins seems to have been sufficiently improved for Thomas and his brother Joseph to visit him in Chichester. Thomas relates that he was then living in the cathedral cloisters with his sister: "The first day he was in high spirits at intervals, but exerted himself so much that he could not see us the second."[16] But on that first day Collins showed his friends both an "Ode to Mr. John Hume, on his leaving England for Scotland" and "another Ode, of two or three-four-lined Stanzas, called The Bell of Arragon." This first poem, the "Superstitions Ode," was written much earlier—in 1749 or 1750—and the second poem has not survived, but it is important that we note Collins's interest at this time in showing these poems to his friends. Joseph Warton also had "a few fragments of some other Odes, but too loose and imperfect for publication, yet containing traces of high imagery." Apparently these are the poems preserved in the Warton papers at Trinity College, Oxford, and they too may have been presented to the Wartons at this time. We do know that a revised copy of the Persian Eclogues (to be retitled Oriental Eclogues) was given to the two brothers, presumably also at this meeting in Chichester.

Thomas Warton saw Collins again in November. "In 1754," Warton wrote, "he came to Oxford, for change of air and amusement, where he staid a month; I saw him frequently, but he was so weak and low, that he could not bear conversation. Once he walked from his lodgings, opposite Christ Church, to Trinity College, but supported by his servant."[17] Warton's account is supplemented by Gilbert White's remembrance of Collins at Oxford, "under Merton wall, in a very affecting situation, struggling, and conveyed by force, in the arms of two or three men, towards the parish of St. Clement, in which was a house that took in such unhappy objects."[18] Collins was at this time, Warton added, "labouring under the most deplorable langour of body, and dejection of mind."[19]

After 1754 mention of Collins becomes even more scarce. He was apparently a witness to David Mallet's will in 1755, but nothing is known of their friendship, even before this period.[20] Johnson, who had written to Warton about their friend in December 1754 ("Poor dear Collins —Let me know whether you think it would give him pleasure if I should write to him. I have often been near his state, and therefore have it in great commiseration"), sent an even gloomier letter to Warton in April 1756: "What becomes of poor dear Collins? I wrote him a letter which he never answered. I suppose writing is very troublesome to him. That man is no common loss. The moralists all talk of the uncertainty of fortune, and the transitoriness of beauty; but it is yet more dreadful to consider that the powers of the mind are equally liable to change, that understanding may make its appearance and depart, that it may blaze and expire."[21] James Hampton in fact thought that Collins died in 1756, and even Johnson seemed unsure of the date of his death.[22] But Joseph Warton, who apparently stayed in touch with his friend, seems as late as 1756 to have expected Collins to finish his *History of the Revival of Learning*. In his *Essay on the Writings and Genius of Pope*, published in that year, Warton writes: "Concerning the particular encouragement given by Leo X. to polite literature, and the fine arts, I forbear to enlarge; because a friend of mine is at present engaged in writing, THE HISTORY OF THE AGE OF LEO X."[23] Collins's project, James Hampton wrote, was a "history of the revival of learning in Italy, under the pontificates of Julius II. and Leo X."[24]

In 1757 Collins's revised *Oriental Eclogues* was published by J. Payne, although Collins's responsibility for this edition is a subject of some dispute. Thomas Warton, however, in his *History of English Poetry*, suggests in his references to Collins's extensive antiquarian library that the poet had kept his collection of early books, and that he was willing to talk of literary subjects "not many months before his death." Speaking of Skelton's "Nigramansir," Warton writes that "My lamented friend Mr. William Collins, whose ODES will be remembered while any taste for true poetry remains, shewed me this piece at Chichester, not many months before his death: and he pointed it out as a very rare and valuable curiosity. He intended to write the HISTORY OF THE RESTORATION OF LEARNING UNDER LEO THE TENTH, and with a view to that design, had collected many scarce books."[25]

It is clear that in these final years Collins, retired to the cloisters and nursed by his sister, was less and less capable of vigorous activity. The two remaining accounts of his retirement make it evident, however, that even at this late date Collins was capable of entirely lucid intervals. Thomas Warton, who wrote to Chichester for information concerning Collins's last years, supplied this account:

> In illustration to what Dr. Johnson has related, that during his last malady, he was a great reader of the Bible: I am favored with the following anecdote from the Rev. Mr. Shenton, vicar of St. Andrews at Chichester, by whom Collins was buried. "Walking in my vicarial garden one Sunday evening during Mr. Collins's last illness, I heard a female (the servant I suppose) reading the Bible in his chamber. Mr. Collins had been accustomed to rave much, and make great moanings, but while she was reading, or rather attempting to read, he was not only silent, but attentive likewise, correcting her mistakes, which indeed were very frequent, through the whole of the twenty-seventh chapter of Genesis."[26]

In a previous letter Shenton had told Warton: "Dr Smyth Rector of S^t. Giles in the Fields can probably furnish you with some Anecdotes about Mr Collins, as I know he was very conversant with him about the time his Health & Senses began to fail."[27]

The other story that survives from this period also suggests the kind of painful lucidity Johnson had noted ("is he to pass the remainder of his life in misery and degradation? perhaps with complete consciousness of his calamity"). William Smith, Treasurer of the Ordnance, who had been a fellow of the same chamber at Winchester as Collins, visited his friend in Chichester "twelve or fourteen years" after they had left the college. When Collins saw his old friend he exclaimed, "Smith, do you remember my Dream!" Smith apparently remembered it well:

> [Collins had been] observed one morning to be particularly depressed and melancholy. Being pressed to disclose the cause, he at last said it was in consequence of a dream: for this he was laughed at, but desired to tell what it was; he said, he dreamed that he was walking in the fields where there was a lofty tree; that he climbed it, and when he had nearly reached the top, a great branch, upon which he had got, failed with him, and let him fall to the ground. This account caused more ridicule; and he was asked how he could possibly be affected by this common consequence of a school-boy adventure, when he did not pretend, even in imagination and sleep, to have received any hurt, he replied, that the Tree was the Tree of Poetry.[28]

Collins died in 1759, eight long years after his first illness and premonition of death.

What are we to make of these few biographical fragments? Dr. Daniel H. Fuller, writing an opinion for Bronson's edition of 1898, believed that "the causes of his mental derangement may be found, without doubt, in these congenital characteristics, in the stress of poverty and worry, and perhaps in his dissipation and intemperance."[29] According to Fuller, Collins's chief congenital characteristic was his want of stability of character and seriousness of purpose; his disorder was less of the intellectual faculties than of his emotional nature. Fuller defined Collins's insanity as a form of melancholia "characterized by periods of great mental pain and wild agitation, with more composed intervals in which the patient exhibits much self-control and mental clearness. It is probable that the poet's debilitated physical condition during his last years was due to his mental disease." Whereas Fuller saw Collins's malady rooted within, the outcome of congenital characteristics, Collins's most recent biographer has described it as a violent encounter with an overwhelming religious force. P. L. Carver speculates that Collins was engulfed in a sudden flood of emotion: "I know that I shall be on delicate ground if I mention the Methodist Revival, and the possibility that Collins had been infected by that influence with *le délire biblique*."[30] Carver is indeed on delicate ground: there is no evidence, besides a strained reading of Johnson's and Warton's memoirs, to sustain such speculation.

A recent medical opinion, which takes a closer and more balanced view of the evidence, finds Collins a manic-depressive. Dr. W. B. Ober believes that it is "reasonable to assign Collins's feelings of inadequacy as a major cause of his depression. Whether this emotional state was superimposed on some unknown (at this date unknowable) constitutional predisposition or organic factor is a matter of idle speculation."[31] What Ober neglects to examine, however, is the possibility that Collins's mental distress was either the result of a physical disease or was actually a physical disease that was mistaken for mental illness. The poet's debilitated physical condition during his last years, Fuller wrote, "was due to his mental disease," but a possibility exists that this was simply the other way round. "I would guess from the little evidence we have," Oliver Sigworth argues, "that Collins was intermittently in very great pain, from what cause we cannot now say, but occasionally of such excruciating severity as to cause him to cry out and act irrationally."[32] Collins's first illness, in 1751, does sound like a serious physical collapse, severe enough to convince Collins that he was soon to die; Shenton points to the time "his Health & Senses began to fail." Surely the possibility of a physical cause should not be ruled out, especially in light of the continuing research today into the nature of mental disease. "When the chemical and physiological basis of madness becomes clearer," Matthew Hodgart has written, "a number of phantoms will disappear, and the lives of the mad poets, quite a few of whom lived in the eighteenth century, will have to be reconsidered."[33]

Recent biographical work on Swift and George III indicates how myths of insanity are often exploded—or replaced by more persuasive hypotheses—and it is difficult to see why Collins should be excluded from this process.[34] Johnson, in revising his early sketch for the "Life of Collins" in 1781, qualified his discussion of Collins's illness with this assertion: "His disorder was not alienation of mind, but general laxity and feebleness, a deficiency rather of his vital than intellectual powers. What he spoke wanted neither judgement nor spirit; but a few minutes exhausted him, so that he was forced to rest upon the couch, till a short cessation restored his powers, and he was again able to talk with his former vigour."[35] Johnson's account is indebted to the Wartons, and they, like Gilbert White, saw Collins at his worst.

What remains most certain about Collins's madness is that the little evidence we possess does not support any single explanation. The facts that have been assembled here, however, should clear away certain persistent misconceptions. We can no longer believe the common assertion that Collins died in 1759 "having long been completely insane."[36] In the first place, the length of Collins's illness is uncertain. We know that he was healthy in 1750, and that he recovered from his illness of the following year. He seems to have traveled in search of health in 1752 and 1753 (and, as Johnson suggests, unsuccessfully sought it in the bottle as well),[37] but the first certain signs of any mental troubles are his stay in an asylum and his retirement to Chichester in 1754. We may also conclude that, despite the occasional severity of his ailment, he was not "completely" insane. The evidence points to a disorder of intermittent character. Shenton speaks of Collins's "last illness," which indicates that his disease was apparently remittent. We know that Collins was writing poetry as late as 1750, that he revised his eclogues sometime before 1754, that he was eager to show his uncollected and unfinished poetry to friends, and that his major project, the *History of the Revival of Learning*, was never despaired of by the Wartons. Collins's abilities (and perhaps his interests) seem to have changed during this last decade, but despite these changes, Thomas Warton informs us, he remained actively interested in literature, perhaps even within a few months of his death. These few facts suggest responses more complicated than the explanations they have previously elicited. And, what remains more disturbing, the facts and fictions concerning "poor Collins" have too often and too easily been confounded.

Engraved from an Original Draw.^g by W.Holt.

THE MONUMENT *Erected to the Memory of* WILL.^m COLLINS, in Chichester Cathedral.

Publish'd by J.Sewell. Cornhill. Aug.1.1796.

Plate 1. An engraving of Flaxman's monument to Collins, printed as the frontispiece to the *European Magazine*, 30 (1796).

II. The Growth of the Myth

The transition from fact to fiction seems not to have been a difficult one, and was perhaps facilitated by the general neglect of Collins's poetry until John Langhorne's edition appeared in 1765. The legends about Collins that flourished in the eighteenth and nineteenth centuries were usually the result of facts being ignored or reinterpreted. In most early accounts of Collins's life, for example, the information available to commentators was either reemphasized or embellished. In more influential interpretations, however, Collins's illness in the 1750s was shown to have had its roots in his activities (and inactivity) of the previous decade, or his illness was seen as a product of the poetic temperament itself, yet another proof that genius and madness are near allied.

Reemphasis and embellishment can be seen in accounts like the one in Stephen Jones's *A New Biographical Dictionary* (1794), a concise hodgepodge of facts and opinions culled from Langhorne and Johnson. Johnson noted the reversals of fortune in his "Life of Collins": "Collins, who, while he 'studied to live,' felt no evil but poverty, no sooner 'lived to study' than his life was assailed by more dreadful calamities, disease and insanity." To this Jones added: "He died lunatic."[38] Collins's reason was fervid to the last, Sir Egerton Brydges wrote in 1830, "but it is said that his shrieks sometimes resounded through the cathedral cloisters of Chichester till the horror of those who heard him was insupportable."[39] Occasionally the exaggeration defies all belief, as in the Rev. George Gilfillan's memoir of Collins in his edition of 1854: "Genius is not only a mystery in itself, but equally mysterious in the manner in which it distributes its favours and scatters its fire," he opens his narrative. "Now it sits serene in the blind eyes of a Milton, alone in his obscure chamber, and meditating times to come; and now it pines away in the dull madness of a Collins, or serves to exasperate his misery, as, in a wilder mood, he runs, howling like a dog, through the aisles of Chichester Cathedral."[40] The image seems to have had such an effect on Gilfillan's imagination that even when he attempted to proceed from the facts available to him he repeated his own embellishments: "Sometimes he was very quiet and manageable; at other times he raved, moaned, and ran howling about the aisles like a houseless dog."[41]

A more subtle form of exaggeration lies in the emphasis the sculptor John Flaxman wielded in his monument to Collins, erected within Chichester Cathedral (Plate 1). On the monument, a correspondent in the *Gentleman's Magazine* wrote, Collins "is represented as just recovered from a wild fit of phrensy, to which he was unhappily subject;

Plate 2. Flaxman's pen and wash designs (Nos. 1 and 2) for Collins's monument. Reproduced by permission of the British Museum.

and, in a calm and reclining posture, seeking refuge from his misfortunes in the divine consolations of the Gospel, while his lyre, and the first of his poems ["The Passions"], lie neglected on the ground. Above, are two figures of Love and Pity entwined in each others arms."[42] Considered individually, the facts of Flaxman's portrait are only mildly distorted: Collins is pictured during a period of calm and lucidity, but the "phrensy" from which he has just recovered is problematical, as we have seen; the Bible had in fact become Collins's chief study, but we know that he retained an interest in his own poetry; even the extent of Collins's "refuge" in religion remains unclear. Taken as a whole, Flaxman's monument, though pardonably exploiting our sympathy, neglects the decade of achievement in which Collins has most claim to our respect. The inscription below the portrait, written by William Hayley and John Sargent, complements Flaxman's vision of a "hapless name" that "Solicits kindness with a double claim":

> Tho' Nature gave him, and tho' Science taught,
> The fire of Fancy, and the reach of Thought,
> Severely doom'd to Penury's extreme,
> He pass'd, in madd'ning pain, life's feverish dream;
> While rays of Genius only serv'd to shew
> The thick'ning horror, and exalt his woe.
> Ye walls, that echo'd to his frantic moan
> Guard the due records of this grateful stone.[43]

The irony of Flaxman's vision of the "thick'ning horror" lies in the fact that his monument was based on only the last (and least expensive) of his preliminary designs.[44] While working in Italy, Flaxman sent back to Chichester a series of designs from which Hayley and his patrons were to choose a suitable memorial. They chose the simplest and cheapest of the designs, and the monument was executed accordingly. But in the early pen and wash drawings he prepared in Rome, Flaxman's emphasis was entirely different. Given the scope of his own imagination and Collins's poetry—and not the limitations of his patrons' purse-strings—he designed elaborate visual accompaniments for Collins's ode on "The Passions" by illustrating the central section: "And *Hope* enchanted smil'd, and wav'd Her golden Hair" (l. 38). Flaxman placed Hope in the middle and "Revenge, Anger, Fear, Despair &c retiring on one side, on the other Joy & Mirth led on by Love, heads of Exercise Sport &c amongst the trees" (Plate 2). Flaxman's design was to become the bas relief, which he considered "the principal object of the Monument."

Our interest in Flaxman's study lies both in the close attention he pays to Collins's poetic achievement and in the way he has attempted to characterize it. The sketch of Hope and her fellow passions in fact constitutes a heroic landscape closely allied to the descriptive allegory of Collins's own odes. And Flaxman, working in Rome, seems not only to have drawn on Collins's work but on the poet's sources as well: lurking behind the sketch—in the placement of the allegorical figures and in the use of sweeping movement and contours—are Guido Reni's "The Massacre of the Innocents" and "Aurora," and, in the attitude of the main figure, his "Fortune" and "Mary Magdalen." These works exerted a significant influence on Collins; directly or indirectly, they also seem to have informed Flaxman's work.[45] But in the sculptor's final design, hardened into marble, the retiring, contemplative figure evokes not so much Guido and his creations as it does the "Melancholia" of Dürer and the iconographers.

Other commentators, faced with a similar scarcity of evidence, have attempted to explain Collins's illness by examining his character and behavior in the 1740s. "When poverty overtook him," Gilbert White explains, "poor man, he had too much sensibility of temper to bear with his misfortunes, and so fell into a most deplorable state of mind."[46] But we know that Collins, however distressing he may have found poverty, became ill only after his uncle's inheritance rescued him from his financial worries. Langhorne, however, reported that "fortune had delayed her favours till they were not worth receiving. His faculties had been so long harrassed by anxiety, dissipation, and distress, that he fell into a nervous disorder, which brought with it an unconquerable depression of spirits, and at length reduced the finest understanding to the most deplorable childishness."[47]

Thomas Miller, editing Collins's works in 1846, claimed that "his modesty was his ruin. Like his own creation of Fear, he was afraid 'E'en at the sound himself had made.'"[48] Miller is referring to Collins's period as a literary adventurer in London, when "that disease which terminated so awfully, by overthrowing 'the throne of reason,' must even at this period have been working its silent way, and checking every approach to decision and perseverance which the spirit was willing to make." Gilfillan's explanation is again the most outrageous: comparing Collins's indolence and "dissipation" with Coleridge's, he wonders "whether the cause were not in both the same,—whether Collins, as well as Coleridge, had not been enervated by *opium*."[49] Collins was, Gilfillan continues, "the slave of sensibility, he nursed it in his bosom when it was young, and, when grown, it stung and strangled him."[50] Gilfillan's final image of Collins's mind is adapted from the poet's own "Ode to Liberty": "His mind, originally, was like that 'blended work of strength and grace,' the *Roman Commonwealth*, as described by himself; but, like it, it was broken 'With many a rude repeated stroke.' " [51] Gilfillan's description bears a strong resemblance to Boswell's image of a tormented Johnson, in which the hero's judgment, continually threatened by "apprehensions," is likened to a gladiator in the Roman Coliseum.[52]

In Christopher Stone's view, Collins was simply paying the penalty for years of alternate privation and dissipation;[53] but a more common explanation, embraced by Dr. Ober as well as by Sir Egerton Brydges, is that Collins suffered from an inability to realize his literary hopes. Brydges blames the overthrow of his reason to his being "embittered by a defect of the principal objects of his worldly ambition."[54] "On such an intellectual temperament," Brydges continues, "the extinction of the visions which Hope had painted to him seems to have been sufficient to produce that derangement, which first enfeebled, and then perverted and annihilated his faculties."[55] Brydges's argument may have had its roots in Isaac D'Israeli's *Calamities of Authors*, in which Collins is portrayed as an example of "Literary Disappointments Disordering the Intellect." It cannot be doubted, D'Israeli assures us, "and the recorded facts will demonstrate it, that the poetical disappointments of Collins were secretly preying on his spirit, and repressing his firmest exertions" in the 1740s.[56] To the perpetual recollections of his poetical disappointments "are we to attribute this unsettled state of his mind, and the perplexity of his studies."[57] "And what was the result of his literary life?" D'Israeli asks; "I have heard that he returned to his native city of Chichester in a state almost of nakedness, destitute, diseased, and wild in despair, to hide himself in the arms of a sister."[58] This explanation has recently been qualified by Arthur Johnston, though, who argues that "What we must avoid is reading into his physical illness after 1750 a response to his failure to find a public."[59] Collins is interesting, Johnston insists, not because of his debilitated condition in the 1750s but because he was a strong young poet of the 1740s.

But strong young poets have penalties to pay as well, or so at least the most radical and influential interpretation of Collins's illness would have us believe. Collins's insanity, this legend insists, was a product of the volatile and precarious poetic temperament itself; and Collins's fate is viewed as another example of Wordsworth's dictum in "Resolution and Independence" that "We Poets in our youth begin in gladness; / But thereof come in the end despondency and madness."[60] This interpretation was presented as early as Langhorne's popular edition of 1765. Langhorne begins his memoir with Collins's madness in view:

"The gifts of imagination bring the heaviest task upon the vigilance of reason; and to bear those faculties with unerring rectitude, or invariable propriety, requires a degree of firmness and of cool attention, which doth not always attend the higher gifts of the mind."[61] Langhorne had in fact put forward this thesis a year earlier in two poems that he claimed had "a peculiar reference to the misfortunes of that most ingenious Poet."[62] In the first of two sonnets Collins is warned:

> Of FANCY'S too prevailing power beware!
> Oft has she bright on life's fair morning shone,
> Oft seated HOPE on REASON'S sovereign throne,
> Then clos'd the scene in darkness and despair.

And Langhorne ends his poem with an image borrowed from Collins's "Ode on the Poetical Character": "The casual lover with her charms is blest, / But woe to them her magic bands that wear!"

Later writers are just as explicit in their commentaries. Gilfillan, again romanticizing from fact—here Collins's meeting with the Wartons in Chichester—claims that the "excitement was too much for the feeble nerves of the Poet, and the next morning he could not be seen,—plunged, doubtless, in the dark gulf the deeper that he had for a little emerged from it, and stood on the sunny summit. Alas for the poetic temperament!—that electric wire stretching between heaven and hell,—familiar with all heights and with all depths—with all ecstacies and with all agonies; but ignorant of the intermediate plains of peace," which Gilfillan calls "calm, sober, solid enjoyment."[63]

A much more thoughtful discussion occurs in a neglected essay by Nathan Drake in his *Literary Hours* (1798). Drake's second chapter— "On the Government of the Imagination; on the Frenzy of Tasso and Collins"—draws a distinction between the salutary and the corrupting influences of "Imagination, that fruitful source of the beautiful and sublime."[64] "Should this brilliant faculty be nurtured on the bosom of enthusiasm, or romantic expectation, or be left to revel in all its native wildness of combination, and to plunge into all the visionary terrors of supernatural agency, undiverted by the deductions of truth, or the sober realities of existence," Drake writes, "it will too often prove the cause of acute misery, of melancholy, and even of distraction." Drake illustrates his theory by way of Tasso's life, but finds examples nearer home: "Yet have we had one melancholy instance, and toward the middle of the eighteenth century, where disappointment, operating upon enthusiasm, has induced effects somewhat similar to those recorded of the celebrated Italian. In the year 1756 died our lamented Collins, one of our most exquisite poets, and of whom, perhaps, without exaggeration it may be asserted, that he partook of the credulity and enthusiasm of Tasso, the magic wildness of Shakspeare, the sublimity of Milton, and the pathos of Ossian."[65]

Drake's comparison was taken up by D'Israeli: "None but a Poet can conceive, for none but a Poet can experience, the secret wounds inflicted on a mind made up of romantic fancy and tenderness of emotion, who has staked his happiness on his imagination; and who feels neglect, as ordinary men might the sensation of being let down into a sepulchre, and being buried alive. The mind of TASSO, a brother in fancy to COLLINS, became disordered by the opposition of the Critics, but their perpetual neglect had not injured it less."[66] It is probable that D'Israeli and his fellow interpreters were deeply influenced by Johnson's description of a mind that was employed chiefly upon "works of fiction and subjects of fancy, and by indulging some peculiar habits of thought was eminently delighted with those flights of imagination which pass the bounds of nature."[67] But it is a significant leap from the *Lives of the Poets* to the *Calamities of Authors*. Johnson's life of Collins, like his life of Savage, another unfortunate poet whom he knew well, is a convincing illustration of an argument that runs throughout the *Lives*, that authors are no more likely to avoid misery than the general lot of mankind. "It seems rational to hope," Johnson writes, "that intellectual greatness should produce better effects; that minds qualified for great attainments should first endeavour their own benefit; and that they who are most able to teach others the way to happiness should with most certainty follow it themselves. But this expectation, however plausible, has been very frequently disappointed."[68] Imagination has its dangers, as Johnson well knew, but only a radical interpretation of poetic creativity burdens it with the seeds of its own destruction. The old leech-gatherer, in Wordsworth's poem, was able by "apt admonishment" to spur the poet to resolution and independence of this myth.

III. Collins and the Irrational

If the problem of his madness has shaped our conception of Collins himself, it has exerted an even greater influence on the way we read his poems and, ultimately, on how we characterize his poetic achievement. In its most common form, this interpretation sees Collins as one mad poet among many, an instance not only of the inseparability of genius and insanity but also of the necessary utterance of the truths of unreason in an age of oppressive reason. Witness A. E. Housman, speaking of eighteenth-century poetry: "Who are the English poets of that age in whom pre-eminently one can hear and recognise the true poetic accent emerging clearly from the contemporary dialect? These four: Collins, Christopher Smart, Cowper, and Blake. And what other characteristic had these four in common? They were mad."[69]

This kind of reasoning often issues from fuzzy chronology. To the best of our knowledge, Collins did not write poetry during his illness; the last poems that we can date with any accuracy were written in 1750, and Collins showed no signs of mental illness until 1751, if then. These important distinctions can be made even clearer by comparing Collins's situation with that of Christopher Smart. Like Collins, Smart suffered a series of severe illnesses; and like Collins, he was institutionalized for insanity following these bouts with physical disease. But whereas Collins wrote all of his poetry before his illness and possible madness, Smart wrote all of his major poetry afterwards, much of it while he was still confined to a private madhouse; and thus the character of his poetical achievement is more problematically tied to the nature of his illness or, more precisely, to the nature of his recovery.

But even if they acknowledge these distinctions, Collins's critics have often argued backwards from the disease and depression of the 1750s to the literary career of the preceding decade. If the poet was in fact the victim of madness, they argue, then surely the roots of his malady can be detected in the poetry itself.[70] Despite this argument's anachronistic bent, its insistence that the man and his work are woven of the same stuff has had a significant effect on the way we respond to Collins's poetry, especially to his use of personification.

For Hazlitt it was Collins's madness—with its attendant intensity of feeling—that in fact enabled the critic to praise Collins's poetic merits. Thus, in his *Lectures on the English Poets*, Hazlitt makes a crucial distinction between Collins and Gray: "I should conceive that Collins had a much greater poetical genius than Gray: he had more of that fine madness which is inseparable from it, of its turbid effervescence, of all that pushes it to the verge of agony or rapture."[71] For Nathan Drake, similarly, it was Collins's ability to evoke a sense of belief in the products of his own imagination that portrayed (or betrayed) the madness working within his verse:

His address to Fear,
> Dark Power! with shudd'ring meek submitted thought
> Be mine to read the visions old
> Which thy awakening bards have told:
> And, lest thou meet my blasted view,
> Hold each strange tale devoutly true.

was prompted by what he actually felt, for, like Tasso, he was, in some measure, a convert to the imagery he drew; and the beautiful lines in which he described the Italian, might, with equal propriety, be applied to himself:

Prevailing poet, whose undoubting mind
Believ'd the magic wonders which he sung. [72]

These comments, despite their questionable biographical accuracy, point to features that are indeed part of Collins's poetic achievement. What Hazlitt and Drake did not realize, however, is that Collins's accomplishment here—especially in the emotional intensity of his vision —was not the unique product of an individual's madness but was the aim of an entire generation of poets and theorists.

Part of the problem seems to lie in the nature of personification. We define prosopopoeia by saying that it gives a humanized (usually visualized) form to an abstraction, that it renders the general by means of the particular. Collins, for instance, writes odes on "Liberty" and the "Poetical Character," but (here lies the confusion) he more often writes odes allegorically describing internal, emotional states: fear, pity, mercy, the entire spectrum of "The Passions." Fears and anxieties can be said to take shape (literally) as the poet calls them forth in personified form. The poet and his audience are to believe, moreover, that they actually see the images they contemplate. Thus we might say that the allegorical poet, in addition to projecting images of a fragmented personality,[73] is also guilty of "seeing things" that are not really there (a confusion in his perception of reality).

To Collins's contemporaries, however, the vivid use of this literary device was not thought to be the inevitable product of a disordered mind, but the attainment of only the most gifted poetic intelligence. To give "form, and colour, and action, even to abstract ideas; to embody the virtues, the vices, and the passions; and to bring before our eyes, as on a stage, every faculty of the human mind," Joseph Warton wrote in the *Adventurer*, " . . . may be justly esteemed one of the greatest efforts of the creative power of a warm and lively imagination."[74] It was assumed by almost all contemporary theorists that "only great boldness and intense emotional force could create effective personification, and furthermore that the artistic use of this figure effectively conveyed to the reader the passionate transport of the author."[75] Personification, to be effective, was to be bold, animated, and passionate; in its higher forms, the imagination was to idealize matter itself. Addison claimed that the mind of man "requires something more perfect in Matter, than what it finds there, and can never meet with any Sight in Nature which sufficiently answers its highest Ideas of Pleasantness; or, in other Words, . . . the Imagination can fancy to it self Things more Great, Strange, or Beautiful, than the Eye ever saw."[76] Thus personification was often associated with what Addison (and later Johnson) called "the fairy way of writing," which "gives life to characters that have no existence but what the poet bestows upon them, such as fairies, witches, and abstractions 'under a visible shape.'"[77]

The visible shape these characters took was often in the form of a "vision," the consequence both of intense feeling and of a vivid imagination. In his endeavors "to embody the fleeting forms of mind, and clothe them with correspondent imagery," Mrs. Barbauld wrote in the introduction to her edition of Collins, the poet "is not unfrequently obscure; but even when obscure, the reader who possesses congenial feelings is not ill pleased to find his faculties put upon the stretch in the search of those sublime ideas which are apt, from their shadowy nature, to elude the grasp of the mind."[78] These shadowy forms are most easily grasped when the rational mind is put to sleep, when the poet enters into the veiled world of dream and vision. But the poetry of vision, though it draws on the irrational and may approach the truths of madness, is not necessarily the product of madness itself. Bishop Lowth characterized the poetic language of Collins's generation when he described the language of the passions in the Old Testament. Whereas the language of reason is "cool, temperate, rather humble than elevated, well arranged and perspicuous," the language of the passions is "totally different: the conceptions burst out into a turbid stream, expressive in a manner of the internal conflict; the more vehement break out in hasty confusion; they catch (without search or study) whatever is impetuous, vivid, or energetic. In a word, reason speaks literally, the passions poetically."[79]

A touchstone for Hazlitt and Drake, as well as for recent critics like Angus Fletcher and Harold Bloom, has been Collins's "Ode to Fear."[80] In the poem's opening lines, poetic imagination melodramatically lifts the veil separating the author from the "shad'wy Tribes of *Mind*," the world of cloudy forms that lies within:

> Thou, to whom the World unknown
> With all its shadowy Shapes is shown;
> Who see'st appall'd th' unreal Scene,
> While Fancy lifts the Veil between.

Collins's invocation results in a sudden encounter as Fear obeys his call:

> Ah *Fear!* Ah frantic *Fear!*
> I see, I see Thee near.
> I know thy hurried Step, thy haggard Eye!
> Like Thee I start; like Thee disorder'd fly.

Fear has been drawn forth through vision ("I see, I see . . . "); Fear is "frantic," but so too is the poet, as the hesitation and repetition of his syntax indicate. Both seer and vision partake of that emotional intensity which is the requirement and result of successful personification. In turn, this kinship between the viewer and the viewed helps to "personify" the object: "Like Thee I . . . like Thee [I]. . . ."

But at this point in the poem Collins's claim is unsupported; the poet must vivify his abstraction in the concrete terms of her awful "Train" in the remainder of the strophe. Thus Fear is particularized through a succession of external objects (*"Monsters"*) who join with a "thousand Phantoms . . . Who prompt to Deeds accurs'd the Mind." Danger "stalks his Round, an hideous Form, / Howling amidst the Midnight Storm, / Or throws him on the ridgy Steep / Of some loose hanging Rock to sleep." Vengeance, "in the lurid Air, / Lifts her red Arm, expos'd and bare: / On whom that rav'ning Brood of Fate, / Who lap the Blood of Sorrow, wait." Who, Collins can then rhetorically ask of Fear, "this ghastly Train can see, / And look not madly wild, like Thee?"

In the epode and antistrophe Collins gives Fear a natural history (in the effect she has had on earlier poets), and then translates her to the shores and superstitions of England. Throughout these lines, Fear (a "mad Nymph") continues to be visualized in terms of her own veiled nature: Jocasta is the incestuous queen "Wrapt in thy cloudy Veil"; Fear herself may "shroud in haunted Cell, / Where gloomy *Rape* and *Murder* dwell." It is therefore Collins's duty as poet "to read the Visions old, / Which thy awak'ning Bards have told," a task that leads him ultimately to Shakespeare, "thy Prophet" who "In thy Divine Emotions spoke." It is thus by the agency of vision, dream, cloud, and prophecy that the rational mind, in Collins's poem, is laid to sleep so that the irrational within may be better observed. It is in this throbbing, trancelike state that internal forces are bodied forth, and the author's and reader's imaginations are put upon the stretch to grasp these shadowy truths.

This argument can be placed in clearer focus by comparing the "Ode to Fear" with the conclusion of Thomson's "Summer":

> With inward view,
> Thence on the ideal kingdom swift she turns
> Her eye; and instant, at her powerful glance,
> The obedient phantoms vanish or appear;
> Compound, divide, and into order shift,
> Each to his rank, from plain perception up
> To the fair forms of fancy's fleeting train;

To reason then, deducing truth from truth,
And notion quite abstract; where first begins
The world of spirits, action all, and life
Unfettered and unmixed. But here the cloud,
So wills Eternal Providence, sits deep.
Enough for us to know that this dark state,
In wayward passions lost and vain pursuits,
This infancy of being, cannot prove
The final issue of the works of God,
By boundless love and perfect wisdom formed,
And ever rising with the rising mind.

(ll. 1788-1805)

Thomson's "she" in this passage is Philosophy, whose powers are described as they are embodied in man, the culmination of a carefully developed hierarchy throughout the poem. And yet in spite of the rising action with which this passage closes, the lyrical focus of these lines also emphasizes man's limitations: "But here the cloud, / So wills Eternal Providence, sits deep." Thomson's final lines are almost elliptical: "this dark state . . . cannot prove / The final issue of the works of God, / [Although] By boundless love and perfect wisdom formed. . . ." The season of fire, power, and light concludes with a sense of man's mortal darkness and ultimate powerlessness.[81]

What I find of particular interest in this passage is the language in which Thomson couches his limitations. Clearly "inward view," "obedient phantoms," "the fair forms of fancy's fleeting train," the "world of spirits" and the deep-sitting cloud are also the familiars of Collins's poetry. But whereas Thomson marshals these images to create a sense of the limitations to our knowledge (an inevitable barrier at which the hierarchy of perception-fancy-reason-abstraction must end), in Collins's poetry these same images suggest a starting point, a threshold through which the world within may be glimpsed. The cloud that marks an end to exploring in Thomson is adopted by Collins as a medium through which an uncharted world may be explored. Thomson's hierarchy is similarly inverted: where reason hesitates, imagination usurps. And it is in the act of usurpation that the imagination bodies forth these inward forms.

Harold Bloom's perception in *The Anxiety of Influence* that Collins's personifications function like neo-Platonic "daemons" is therefore appropriate. These daemons, Bloom argues, are half-human visitors from the spirit world (within us), come, like our poetic ancestors, to effect their influence upon us. But in the theory of poetry that Bloom unfolds (in which influence is anxiety, and tradition is repression),

Collins, burdened with the facts and fictions of his "madness," falls easy prey to critical distortion. In the "Ode to Fear," Bloom asserts, "Fear is Collins' own daemon (as Fletcher observes), the more-than-poetic madness that beckons him into the upward fall of Extravagance. . . . Yet at how high a price Collins purchases this indefinite rapture, this cloudy Sublime! For his poem is one with his deepest repression of his own humanity, and accurately prophesies the terrible pathos of his fate, to make us remember him always, with all his gifts, as Dr. Johnson's 'Poor Collins.' "[82] Similarly, in *The Visionary Company*, Bloom argues that "Collins, like Smart or Cowper, is one of the doomed poets of an Age of Sensibility. His personal myth, which intimately allies his art and his life, is one of necessary historical defeat. The cliff on which Milton lay is 'of rude access,' and supernatural beings guard it. No manic seizure will bring Collins there."[83]

Thus Bloom, despite the perceptiveness of his comments on the allegorical image and on the post-Miltonic "counter-Sublime," vitiates his argument about the "Bards of Sensibility" by confusing the genuinely "irrational" in their work with unwarranted and imprecise biographical speculation. Joseph Warton, in his ode "To Fancy," also asks to be laid "by the haunted stream / Wrapt in some wild, poëtic dream"; like Collins he too recognizes the power of the poetic imagination to place him within a "visionary bliss" that will pierce the "bosom's inmost foldings."[84] Like Collins he invokes Fancy's darling—Shakespeare—and, throughout his work, he too educes Milton as his pervasive daemon. Joseph Warton, however, was manifestly sane. Only Collins's poetry, because of the convenient myths of insanity surrounding the poet himself, has been misread and distorted in ways in which similar, if inferior, poetry by Akenside or the Wartons has not.

"Fine madness" and "frenzy," moreover, may be attributes of the prosopopoeia in Collins's poetry, but they are not the kinds of words his friends used to describe his illness. Collins was usually portrayed as suffering from depression or enervation; in spite of the contemporary cult of the poetry of melancholy in this period, there is little hint of the melancholic in his work.[85] His poems, to borrow a distinction from Freud, focus on mourning rather than melancholia.[86] Emotional stress has a particularized cause in Collins's poetry in the loss of a loved object (as in the "Ode, to a Lady," the "Ode, Written in the beginning of the Year 1746," or the "Ode Occasion'd by the Death of Mr. Thomson"); it is not the indefinite communing of Thomas Warton's *Pleasures of Melancholy*, the "Penseroso" of its day. Grief has its bounds, Collins counsels in his "Ode, to a Lady," and it does not necessarily enforce social alienation (the personification that concludes his poem is, significantly, of "social Grief"). Even in the "Ode to Evening," Collins's furthest venture in the pensive mode, Evening's quiet power is shown in her influence over Fancy, Science, Peace (Health in the revised version), and over Friendship as well.

These distinctions, basic as they may be, may yet do something to clarify the ways in which Collins's poetry, like his life, has been misread. My argument is neither that Collins was free of madness, nor that his poetry did not partake of an irrational element associated with insanity in the eighteenth century. We have too little evidence to make any kind of distinction about the nature of his illness (but enough, I hope, to ensure that convenient fictions will no longer suffice). The evidence available to us does suggest, however, that Collins was free of illness—both physical and mental—during the years in which he did write poetry. To approach Collins as a "mad poet" is to create a misrepresentation of his work akin to the exaggerated fictions spun about his life in the nineteenth century. Nor can a retrospective reading of his poetry expect to find in the poems a sure anticipation of his ultimate distress. The irrational is indeed an element in his poetry but, far from representing the product of an individual's alienated and disordered mind, it is characteristic of a major poetic movement. It was Collins's distinction to differ from his contemporaries in degree, but not in kind.

2

The Poetical Character in the 1740s

Collins's contemporary readers would have found striking indications of a new movement in poetry even as they scanned the title-page of his slim volume of poems. The most significant change was not that the poems were entitled "odes," for the ode, in its varying forms, had retained much of its popularity in spite of the century's early preference for epistles and the mock-heroic.[1] A more fundamental change was the author's specification that his odes were written on "descriptive and allegoric subjects." As Langhorne first demonstrated, these two terms were meant to stand in apposition to each other; both derive their force from the essentially pictorial nature of his poetry.[2] Collins's allegorical characters are animated less by action than by descriptive imagery.

The innovation of Collins's *Odes* therefore lies less in form (although we shall encounter his experiments here as well, especially in "The Passions" and the "Ode on the Poetical Character") than in thematic subject, allegorical mode, and poetic style. Collins drew particular attention to this last element by ambitiously selecting a motto from Pindar's *Olympian Odes:* "Would I could find me words as I move onward as a bearer of good gifts in the Muses' car; would I might be attended by Daring and by all-embracing Power!" (IX.80–83). The words Collins found did not entirely please his early readers. Johnson complained that "his diction was often harsh, unskilfully laboured, and injudiciously selected. He affected the obsolete when it was not worthy of revival; and he puts his words out of the common order, seeming to think, with some later candidates for fame, that not to write prose is certainly to write poetry."[3] Thomas Gray's response was nearly as severe, even though he was later to remark that the language of poetry is never the language of the age. Gray wrote that Collins had "a fine Fancy, model'd upon the Antique, a bad Ear, great Variety of Words, & Images with no Choice at all."[4] This pronouncement is certainly true of passages in several of the odes, but Gray neglects Collins's careful choice of allegorical imagery in his finest poems, particularly in those odes in which the poet most insistently calls upon a daring and all-embracing power.[5] A vivid poetic style was essential to the imaginative vitality he meant his volume of odes to convey.

Inherent in this stylistic revolt was a revaluation of much of the descriptive language of the preceding generation. The images of obscurity, darkness, and decline that help portray the cultural collapse within *The Dunciad*, for example, were soon assimilated without these powerful connotations in poems like Edward Young's *Night Thoughts*.[6] We have already seen this process at work in the different uses of cloud imagery in *The Seasons* and the "Ode to Fear": a metaphor of limitation in Thomson's hands is transformed by Collins into a vehicle for renewed discovery. The ironies in this transformation are surely apparent, but so too is the significance of an altered perspective that is now focused within. What we are witnessing, in other words, is not only a substantial change in poetic representation, style, form, and effect, but also a dramatic shift in the way the poet views himself. In the period encompassing Akenside's *The Pleasures of Imagination* (published in 1744) and Gray's "The Progress of Poesy" (completed in 1754), the subject of most of the decade's finest poetry is the poet's reexamination of the sources of his inspiration and creativity. This is the subject of Collins's most powerful and provocative poem, and the focus as well of works by Warton and Akenside that provide the "Ode on the Poetical Character" with its most immediate context.

I. Joseph Warton's *Odes on Various Subjects* (1746)

In the famous "Advertisement" to his *Odes,* Warton spelled out in general terms the form this new poetic of the 1740s would take: a public accustomed to reading *"didactic Poetry alone"* and *"Essays on moral Subjects"* is now asked to accept a *"fanciful and descriptive"* poetry in which *"the imagination is much indulged."* The fashion of moralizing in verse, Warton argues, has been carried too far, and in its place should stand poetry that proves *"Invention and Imagination to be the chief faculties of a Poet."* The following odes would therefore redeem poetry from the lesser forms and preoccupations of the Augustans by diverting it back *"into its right channel."*[7] It was thus natural that Warton should write his *Essay on the Writings and Genius of Pope* to implement these principles; poetry involves an emotional response to a picturesque or literary rather than a social environment.[8] Truly inventive and imaginative poetry, Warton stated, lies in the representation of sensory experience, especially the visual. The basic tenet of the Warton circle was "that poetry ought to be imaginative, that to be imaginative is to be pictorial, and that the pictorial is principally expressed in allegorical personae 'picturesquely' rendered."[9] In his essay on Pope, Warton was to argue that "The use, the force, and the excellence of language, certainly consists in raising, *clear, complete,* and *circumstantial* images, and in turning *readers* into *spectators.*"[10]

A similar claim could be made for much of the inventiveness in the poetry of this period, but in Warton's case we may catch a unique glimpse of how the pictorial influenced the poetic. In a volume entitled Winchester College "Gathering Book" (1739) among the Warton papers at Trinity College, Oxford, is a previously unpublished entry headed "Subjects for a Picture" and "Similes":

> The Solemn Silence of the Pyramids. The Dark gloomy Scenes in Mines. The Fall of the Nile. Distant Noises. Indian Brachmins wandering by their Rivers. Medea's nightly Spells. Meteors in the Night. Griping of a Serpent or a Crocodile. A Lamp in a lone Tow'r. Noises heard at Hell-Gates, that were shut. Extended prospects from Olym[p]us. The Flames of Ætna seen in a dark Night by Strangers. Cassandra calling on Agamemnon, as he was dying. Pangs & Struggles in Drowning. Lapland Witches, Feasts, & Religion. Evening Dances in Arcadia. Serpents fly from the Rattle-Snake. The Effect of an Eclipse on all the animal Creation. Sudden Thunder over a Summer's Day. Sailors Cries at Sea in a stormy Night. Traveller benighted.—Two strong Seas separated by an Isthmus—or two angry Lions by a wide River. The Priest bleeding: Old Men Slaughter'd[.] Loathsom as the twining of a Serpent round one's Body—The Leaving the Spicy Feilds of Arabia, for gloomy Greenland—Praising an unknown Lady to Raphäels painting Galatea. Adonis's Wound for ever bleeding, to continual Sorrow— . . . The Fall of the River Niagara. Œdipus & his Daughters in the *Storm* a fine Subject for a Picture. Woman with Child meeting a devouring Serpent in a Desart.

The relationship between these pictorial scenes and poetry is clear enough from Warton's titles: the images were suitable both as "Subjects for a Picture" and as "Similes" to be used in poems ("Loathsom as the twining of a Serpent round one's Body"). In each case these images would serve as objective correlatives for the emotions felt by the artist and evoked in the reader turned spectator. Taken together, these images served as a poetical quarry for *The Enthusiast*, several of the *Odes*, and pieces like "An American Love-Ode," which was published as his father's work. The effect of these fragments is to reaffirm Joseph's theoretical claims for the transitive status of language: poetry was to re-create the writer's original images—conceived as much as subjects for painting as for poetry—in the imagination of his readers. Language was to serve primarily as the medium between two acts of visual realization.

Jean Hagstrum has pointed out that the crucial difference in descriptive allegory between Thomson and Collins lies in the opposing imaginative processes of the two poets: "In the *Seasons* the persona is introduced to order and animate a natural scene and is itself a personified natural detail. Thomson's details, personified or not, come originally from nature and rise, as it were, to the poetic scene in which they appear. Collins' come originally from the mind and the imagination, and descend, as it were, to the poetic allegory in which they finally appear."[11] Warton's odes are clearly in the Collinsian mode, and yet it is remarkable how swiftly his original conceptions "descend" into the particulars of nature. Fancy, in the opening of the first ode, is invoked as a spirit, as a parent of the Muses, as a guiding force in poetry; but even as Warton addresses her in spiritual form she is clearly associated with the natural world. She is asked to preside over the poet's "artless" songs; her temple is a "turf-built shrine" where the proper offerings are "No murder'd fatling of the flock, / But flowers and honey from the rock." Even before Fancy is pictured, we realize from the poet's posture that she must be sought and celebrated in the world of nature.

This is what we should expect, of course, for the controlling metaphor of the preceding "Advertisement" is also drawn from the natural world. Poetry will be brought back into *"its right channel,"* and Warton is never far from the watery sources of inspiration in his poems. The emotional climax in the ode "To Fancy" occurs when the poet asks Fancy to "lay me by the haunted stream / Wrapt in some wild, poëtic dream." This is the moment when Warton feels most intensely the power of imagination within him, but nature is the vital element in his waking visions as well. Fancy, pictured as the wood-nymph Diana, wields "An all-commanding magic wand" that has power to control the natural world: "bid fresh gardens blow / 'Midst chearless Lapland's barren snow." Fancy's eyes are able to "pierce" the various landscape in much the same way that the poet hopes his verse—like lightning— will pierce "The bosom's inmost foldings." Imagination, moreover, is to be found in natural settings void of human beings: in the desert, the pathless vale, among the rocks,

> 'Midst forests dark of aged oak,
> *Ne'er* echoing with the woodman's stroke,
> Where *never* human art appear'd,
> *Nor ev'n* one straw-rooft cott was rear'd,
> Where NATURE seems to sit *alone*,
> Majestic on a craggy throne. (my italics)

Fancy is to be found where nature rules. Fancy's haunt is difficult of access, like the re-created Eden of Collins's "Ode on the Poetical Character." Warton must ask her the way to her "unknown sequester'd cell," carefully pictured as the harmonious setting of natural elements: woodbines, moss and shells, hawthorns, thickly woven boughs, and the sound of the nightingale. Having found Fancy's seat, the poet is then "wrapt," like Collins's heroines, in a visionary dream, and he awakes to drown—synaesthetically—in a world of sound. The trance is at once natural, supernatural, and poetic. Warton's fusion of the natural setting with the influence of the spiritual deities (Fancy invoked as a genius loci) lies at the heart of the poem.[12] Warton's stream is "haunted" by the spirit of imagination; the stream provides a haunt both to Fancy and to the myriad of water-nymphs who people Warton's other poems.

In the concluding sections of Warton's major ode, imagination leads the poet to a pastoral setting, to the scene of war, to the realm of love, through the unfolding of the seasons, and, in the revised version of the second edition, through Melancholy's sphere as well.[13] Warton calls upon her as a "warm, enthusiastic maid," without whose vital aid he does not dare touch the sacred string of the Pindaric lyre. In the concluding lines he broadens his invocation to include all contemporary poets: "O hear our prayer, O hither come." The controlling "I" of most of the poem now becomes "some chosen swain," animated and filled with Fancy's "unexhausted fire." And in the closing lines he focuses on the Muses themselves, who in spurning frigid art and the "cold critic's studied laws" may yet hope to bid "BRITANNIA rival GREECE."

To the question Warton continually raises in his poem—"Where is Fancy to be found?"—we may now supply an answer: imagination is to be found wherever she leads us, but especially in those naturally picturesque and sublime settings in which our emotions are most directly affected. One of Warton's correspondents understood his question: "How can you ask where *Fancy* [d]wells?" he wrote to him;

"Turn your Thoughts inward. Look but at Home and you'll soon find you need not go so far as Afric or Asia to seek her. But 'tis sometimes artful in Poets, to represent, as a Matter of doubt, what they are most certain of."[14] For Joseph Warton, the haunt of Fancy is not static: she is present in the groves and on the crags, in the brutal and tender passions, in warmth and cold, in light and in shade. Unlike the relatively pessimistic work of Collins, especially the "Ode on the Poetical Character" and the elegy on the death of Thomson, Warton's odes pose opportunities rather than limitations; Fancy may be veiled, but she is nevertheless immanent in the fusion of spirit and nature.

It has often been argued that although Warton clearly stated the revolutionary intention of his odes in the "Advertisement," the theories were in fact more original than the creations.[15] Warton's reliance on the particulars of nature may seem to corroborate this judgment, but it is impossible not to notice the important claims he has placed on his reader's imagination. Thomas Warton proposed similar criteria for judging the new poetry in a fragment entitled "Essay on Romantic Poetry," probably written in 1745:

> The principal use which the ancients made of poëtry, as appears by their writings, was to imitate human actions & passions, or intermix here & there descriptions of Nature. Several modern authors have employed a manner of poëtry entirely different from this, I mean in imitating the actions of spir[i]ts, in describing imaginary Scenes, & making persons of abstracted things, such as Solitude, Innocence, & many others. A Kind of Poëtry which perhap[s] it would not be improper to call a Romantic Kind of Poëtry, as it [is] altogether conceived in the spirit, (tho with more Judgement & less extravagant) & affects the Imagination in the same Manner, with the old Romances.[16]

Thomas's own poems are perhaps the most extravagant examples of this new poetic, and Collins's the most successful; but the primary elements here—spirits, imaginary scenes, personified abstractions—and the primary process—conception in the spirit to affect the imagination—are the innovative characteristics of Joseph's volume of *Odes* as well. In Joseph's poetry, however, these elements often lead us to a realm that is essentially familiar territory. Ode after ode demonstrates the validity of Woodhouse's remark that Warton was "content that the imagination should fly beyond the limits of actual experience" through a series of pleasant fictions. For Collins, however, vicarious experience and fictitious scenes were not enough. Allegorical figures must be produced by an imaginative power that "bears a relation to truth, and can seize on and present the 'idea' of things,"[17] and the poetical character itself must encompass a more radical principle of creativity than can be found in Warton's several odes.

II. Mark Akenside's *Odes on Several Subjects* and *The Pleasures of Imagination*

In the spring of 1745, Joseph Warton wrote to his brother Thomas about a new volume of poetry they had both been reading: "The Odes you speak of I suppose by this you know are Akensides, & some of 'em are extremely insipid & flat. Collins sent them to me with Tancred & Sigismunda."[18] Mark Akenside's *Odes on Several Subjects*, published in March 1745, must have been of great interest to both Collins and Warton, whose disappointment in the volume may in turn have been a stimulus to their own plans to compose odes during this period. Akenside, although their contemporary, was already an established poet: *The Pleasures of Imagination*, published a year earlier, had drawn an admission from Pope that this was "no every-day writer." We do not know what Collins's own reaction to the volume was, but presumably he would have shared the opinion of his close friends. "Which of Akensides Odes are most approved, or are any of 'em approved?" Joseph asked later in his letter to Thomas; "The thoughts to me are generally trite & common. You see by his Advertisement that he thinks to set up for the first correct English lyric poet." Thomas, in his reply, corroborated his brother's opinion: "As to Akenside's Odes I agree with you that they have a vast deal of y^e *frigid*."[19]

Insipid, flat, trite, common, frigid—these are far from the judgments Akenside meant his *Odes* to elicit in his readers, and yet his failure may be inherent in the limitations he acknowledged in the "Advertisement" to his volume:

> The following ODES were written at very distant intervals, and with a view to very different manners of expression and versification. The author pretends chiefly to the merit of endeavouring to be correct, and of carefully attending to the best models. From what the ancients have left of this kind, perhaps the ODE may be allow'd the most amiable species of poetry; but certainly there is none which in modern languages has been generally attempted with so little success. For the perfection of lyric poetry depends, beyond that of any other, on the beauty of words and the gracefulness of numbers; in both which respects the ancients had infinite advantages above us. A consideration which will alleviate the author's disappointment, if he too should be found to have miscarried.[20]

Akenside apparently abandoned these "correct" precepts in several of his ten odes, especially in the sixth ("On the Absence of the Poetic Inclination"), in which he searched for those distinctly different sources that he believed made great poetry possible:

> Where is the bold prophetic heat,
> With which my bosom wont to beat?
> Where all the bright mysterious dreams
> Of haunted shades and tuneful streams,
> That woo'd my Genius to divinest themes?

(ll. 5-9)

The majority of the odes, however, are consistent with Akenside's call for "the beauty of words and the gracefulness of numbers." In the first ode (an "Allusion to Horace," which sets the tone for many of the odes to follow), Akenside points to those models he will *not* use. The graveyard poetry of Young and Blair is quickly dismissed: Akenside's Muse "flies from ruins and from graves, / From ghostly cells and monkish caves / To day-light and to joy" (ll. 34-36).[21] Nor will exotic pastoral provide a model for his poetry. Akenside, perhaps alluding to Collins's *Persian Eclogues*, claims that his Muse will not "tempt the barren waste; / Nor deigns th' ungrateful stores to taste / Of any noxious thing" (ll. 37-39). His is a humbler Muse, "Nor strives by soaring high in air, / Tho' swans and eagles triumph there, / To draw the giddy throng!" (ll. 28-30). Unlike the Pindaric eagle, Akenside's Muse essays a more modest flight:

> From all which nature fairest knows,
> The vernal blooms, the summer rose,
>   She draws her mingled wealth;
> And when the lovely task is done,
> She consecrates a double boon,
>   To pleasure and to health.

(ll. 43-48)

The consecrated blessing, "vernal blooms," and "mingled wealth" of nature are echoes of Thomson's *Seasons*, but Akenside's debt to Thomson is more than merely verbal. Like Thomson, Akenside is able to picture nature in a unified manner that makes moral judgment possible. So, too, Akenside accepts the limitations this vision places upon man, who remains "Secure that health and beauty springs / Thro' this majestic frame of things / Beyond what he can reach to know."[22] And apparently this limitation on man's knowledge imposes a corresponding limitation on the power of poetry. In the ode "Against Superstition,"

Akenside invites a friend to leave the scene "unblest" where his jealousy first became "To groundless fears a prey":

> Come, where with my prevailing lyre
> The skies, the streams, the groves conspire
> To charm your doubts away.

(ll. 40-42)

At first glance Akenside appears to be making significant claims for his poetic prowess: his is a "prevailing" lyre that has Orphic powers to "charm" his audience. The allusion to Orpheus, however, is misleading. Akenside's powers are not actually Orphic; he does not transform ("charm") nature, nor does he press past it. The power of his lyre, in contrast to Orpheus', lies in its ability merely to "conspire" with the skies, streams, and groves. Akenside's poetry prevails over his reader, not over nature itself.

Akenside's art may lack metamorphic power, but the poet nevertheless believed his work to lie within the great tradition of lyric and epic verse. As the title of his poem "On the Absence of the Poetic Inclination" suggests, Akenside believed that he lacked not the ability but the inspiration to write great poetry. Attempting to reclaim his absent Muse, Akenside calls on "The soul of MILTON" to win her back. And, almost at the mention of Milton's name, the predecessor's spirit infuses his follower's:

> O mighty mind! O sacred flame!
> My spirit kindles at his name;
> Again my lab'ring bosom burns;
> The Muse, th' inspiring Muse returns!

(ll. 19-22)

Akenside then remembers the origin of his own early inspiration, when on the banks of the Tyne the Muse "seal'd" him for her own, "Made all her blissful treasures known, / And bad me swear to follow HER alone."

All the Muse's blissful treasures, we may object, are not disclosed in the following odes in Akenside's volume; but in the final ode, "On Lyric Poetry," Akenside again returns to the theme of his poetical inheritance:

> Once more I join the Thespian quire,
> And taste th' inspiring fount again:
> O parent of the Græcian lyre,
> Admit me to thy secret strain —
> And lo! with ease my step invades

> The pathless vale and opening shades,
> Till now I spy her verdant seat,
> And now at large I drink the sound,
> While these her offspring, list'ning round,
> By turns her melody repeat.
>
> (ll. 1-10)

The scene of this first stanza, a "vision" in the tradition of the dramatic masque or of an exotic fable in the *Spectator*, is one that Collins will re-create throughout his work. Once admitted to the Muse's seat, Akenside describes her poetic offspring in the form of a progress piece that includes, stanza by stanza, Anacreon, Alcaeus, and Sappho. The achievement of these lyric poets is such that Akenside may only wonder at the presumptuousness of any newcomer to this train:

> But, O MELPOMENE, for whom
> Awakes thy golden shell again?
> What mortal breath shall e'er presume
> To eccho that unbounded strain?
>
> (ll. 41-44)

The shell will awaken again, of course, for Pindar, but even as the Pindaric eagle soars above the gazing crowd Akenside is forced to ponder his own stature in the lyric tradition:

> While I so late unlock thy hallow'd springs,
> And breathe whate'er thy ancient airs infuse,
> To polish Albion's warlike ear
> This long-lost melody to hear,
> Thy sweetest arts imploy;
> As when the winds from shore to shore,
> Thro' Greece thy lyre's persuasive language bore,
> Till towns, and isles, and seas return'd the vocal joy.
>
> (ll. 53-60)

These lines are consistent with Akenside's claim that the perfection of lyric poetry depends "on the beauty of words and the gracefulness of numbers." In his attempt to reintroduce the ode to an English audience—"To polish Albion's warlike ear / This long-lost melody to hear"—Akenside will employ the lyric's "sweetest arts." And beauty, as he states later in the poem, will be "link'd with virtue's train."

I find Akenside's voice convincing here: he is aware of the force his middle flight will produce, and even more aware of his late entry into this distinguished company. In his conclusion, however, Akenside banishes both self-doubt and his reliance on the Muse's inspiration. In recording his country's patriotic efforts, he argues, he will require neither Theban voice nor Lesbian lyre:

> my prophetic mind,
> Conscious of pow'rs she never knew,
> Astonish'd grasps at things beyond her view,
> Nor by another's fate hath felt her own confin'd.

(ll. 117-20)

We may believe that Akenside is more convincing, and more influential, when he doubts his own belated powers than when he celebrates a transcendent voice. These are the final lines in his volume of odes, and the poetry of the volume itself offers little proof that the poet has indeed grasped at things beyond his normal view. The "prophetic mind" has neither yielded a vision nor probed beyond the natural surfaces of the world celebrated in the previous odes. Akenside's worry, as he confessed in his "Advertisement," was that his effort might "miscarry." I would argue, however, that his plans for the great ode were simply not carried far enough. In adopting Augustan correctness he seems to have thwarted prophetic fire. The seeming shallowness of his emotional response (noted by the Wartons) and the narrowness of his visionary scope appear to have left the intriguing promise of these closing lines unfulfilled.

In spite of Akenside's ambivalence, his hesitancy, his professed correctness, there was much in his work for Collins and Warton to draw upon. The scope of his volume and the diversity of the odes (in subject, meter, and form) must have provided important examples to these young poets, even if they were to reject them. What they clearly did not reject were the questions about poetry that Akenside raised. Our interest in the antecedence of Akenside's work must finally focus on his ability to ask—in the tradition of *An Essay on Criticism*, but in very different form—what poetry is supposed to provide, how it is shaped, and where its sources are to be found. These are themes that were to haunt the poets of the mid-eighteenth century; they are inherent, to a varying degree, in Akenside's slim volume of odes. Other questions, focusing on the poet's role in the act of creation, had been posed in his more important volume of the preceding year.

Akenside's intention in *The Pleasures of Imagination*, as he stated in "The Design" for the poem, was "to give a view of *these* [the pleasures of imagination], in the largest acceptation of the term; so that *whatever our imagination feels from the agreeable appearances of nature, and all the various entertainment we meet with either in poetry, painting, music, or any of the elegant arts, might be deducible from one or other of those principles in the constitution of the human mind, which are here establish'd and explain'd.*" Akenside's scope is professedly wide: he will trace the effects of sensation by examining the constitution of the human mind. Although Akenside sets out to probe the most general of principles, he focuses on the poet, on the individual who feels most intensely. Nature, he argues, does not unveil herself "alike to every mortal eye" (I.79). Some to higher hopes are destined:

> some within a finer mould
> She wrought, and temper'd with a purer flame.
> To these the sire omnipotent unfolds
> The world's harmonious volume, there to read
> The transcript of himself.

> (I.97–101)

The poet is the book of nature's most sensitive reader. He sees there the beauty "which delights / The mind supreme," and in appreciating the beauty of nature and of man, the poet too partakes of "th' eternal joy."

Akenside's claims on behalf of the artist are not modest ones and he, as poet-philosopher, is aware of the dangers and rewards his own artistic exploration holds:

> But the love
> Of nature and the muses bids explore,
> Thro' secret paths erewhile untrod by man,
> The fair poetic region, to detect
> Untasted springs, to drink inspiring draughts;
> And shade my temples with unfading flow'rs
> Cull'd from the laureate vale's profound recess,
> Where never poet gain'd a wreath before.

> (I.48–55)

Akenside's quest is remarkably similar to Joseph Warton's in the ode "To Fancy," and presumably Warton had Akenside's poem clearly in mind when he began writing his ode in 1745. Both poets propose a search for Fancy's seat, and both externalize her power—and her mysteriousness—in nature itself. This procedure is crucial for Akenside because his argument, drawing on the work of Locke and Addison, specifies that imagination is primarily "a power of observation, and consequently a faculty of physical rather than intellectual experience. . . . he shows a mind closely dependent on the world of sensible objects for its ideas."[23]

And yet if the poet, like other men, is dependent on the world around him, he is also especially empowered to make sense of that world's complexities:

> Such are the various aspects of the mind—
> Some heav'nly genius, whose unclouded thoughts
> Attain that secret harmony which blends
> Th' æthereal spirit with its mould of clay;
> O! teach me to reveal the grateful charm
> That searchless nature o'er the sense of man
> Diffuses, to behold, in lifeless things,
> The inexpressive semblance of himself,
> Of thought and passion.

(III.278–86)

This passage is among the most significant in the poem. Akenside envisions the creative artist—not God—as the center of this world.[24] The artist, allied with heaven and possessing "unclouded" thoughts, will mediate the harsh divorce between spirit and matter.

The artist is, of course, not only an observer of nature but a creator as well.[25] He may "behold, in lifeless things, / The inexpressive semblance of himself," but he also possesses the power to breathe life into those objects. The climax of Akenside's poem therefore focuses on the imaginative process as the artist begins to produce images that mirror the external world. The opening section of Akenside's description is both physiological and a close paraphrase of Theseus' speech in *A Midsummer Night's Dream*:

> By degrees the mind
> Feels her young nerves dilate: the plastic pow'rs
> Labour for action: blind emotions heave
> His bosom; and with loveliest frenzy caught,
> From earth to heav'n he rolls his daring eye,
> From heav'n to earth. Anon ten thousand shapes,
> Like spectres trooping to the wizard's call,
> Fleet swift before him.

(III.380–87)

As these ghostly shapes appear, the artist (with his magic powers) "compares / Their diff'rent forms; now blends them, now divides; / Inlarges and extenuates by turns; / Opposes, ranges in fantastic bands, / And infinitely varies" (III.391–95).[26] This reshaping is not an act of distortion. The imaginative process is described as it works on the observed materials of nature. Eventually it is able to reorder experience from the seeming chaos in which it lies:

> Lucid order dawns;
> And as from Chaos old the jarring seeds
> Of nature at the voice divine repair'd
> Each to its place, till rosy earth unveil'd
> Her fragrant bosom, and the joyful sun
> Sprung up the blue serene; by swift degrees
> Thus disentangled, his entire design
> Emerges.
>
> (III.398–405)

As the artistic product is fashioned, so the artist's stature as a second creator, under God, becomes clear: "A while he stands, and with a father's joy / Contemplates." The artist breathes the fair conception into its proper vehicle "with Promethéan art," a perception and phrasing clearly adapted from Shaftesbury's contention that the artist is "a second *Maker*; a just Prometheus under Jove."[27]

This, then, is Akenside's account of the pleasures of the imagination as the poet strives to re-create the world around him with his "heav'nly genius." Little attention has been paid, however, to the "pleasures" in Akenside's passage that are derived from sexual as well as heavenly sources. If the artist is heavenly inspired, so too his animation is sexually engendered, as Akenside's language demonstrates. The conjured phantoms emerge from "the womb of earth" and the "ocean's bed"; the dark abyss "Pours out her births unknown." Order dawns when the rosy earth unveils her fragrant bosom; the artist, as creator, breathes forth "The fair conception." And, as Akenside makes clear, it is with a "father's joy" that the artist contemplates his work. Thus the creative act is not only an imitation of God's original creation, but one that is characteristically human as well. The "pleasures" of imagination are divine inasmuch as the artist partakes of God's own creative powers and shares his "eternal joy"; but they are terrestial as well, and tie him intimately to the sensual world in which he lives.[28] Even Akenside's final tribute to the poet's achievement is veiled in this ambiguity. The artist has created an imitation that rivals God's original:

> Thus Beauty's palm
> Betwixt 'em wavering hangs: applauding love
> Doubts where to chuse; and mortal man aspires
> To tempt creative praise.
>
> (III.424–27)

Like the presumptuous Pindar in the ode "On Lyric Poetry," the artist here "aspires" to a loftier realm. Akenside's verb in this last line, used in both of its contemporary senses, compounds man's audacity: his "attempt" to re-create nature and thus win the praise reserved for the Creator himself is, ultimately, a compelling "temptation."

We may, of course, overemphasize Akenside's boldness and originality in these passages by isolating them from the poem as a whole. Akenside specifies in "The Design" that these creative powers "seem to hold [only] a middle place between the organs of bodily sense and the faculties of moral perception," and much of the poem is traditionally Thomsonian in its morality and view of nature. But those sections that most hold our attention today, both because of the quality of their poetry and the force of their argument, were surely of great importance in fashioning the new poetics of the 1740s. Akenside's decision to pose poetry itself as the theme of his work—to describe and celebrate the power and vitality (and even the "lateness") of the poet—was instrumental in determining the form and subject of much of the poetry of the ensuing decade. In the climate of Akenside's work, and most probably in these very passages, Collins's own "Ode on the Poetical Character" was nourished.

III. Collins's "Ode on the Poetical Character"

The poetry of Warton and Akenside may set the scene for the "Ode on the Poetical Character," but little in their work prepares us for the complexity, boldness, and difficulty of Collins's poem. The ode remains Collins's most exciting, original, and controversial work; on this point, at least, his critics agree. But how radical are the claims Collins makes for the divine origin of the poetical imagination? Much recent critical writing has focused on this question, and specifically on the figure of the "rich-hair'd Youth of Morn." But there is considerable agreement among critics as well. Most acknowledge that the ode is about the nature of *the* poetical character and of true poetry, about the success and failure of specific kinds of poetry and poets, about the belatedness of mid-eighteenth-century writers, about their ambitions and jealousies, their possibilities and limitations. Most critics also agree that there is a structural imbalance in the poem. Where no structural resolution exists, there can be little sense of fulfillment. And yet if Collins's readers cannot disregard the deep pessimism of the ode, they must also acknowledge the poem's energy, the forceful "enthusiasm" that the poem itself—by calling Fancy the "lov'd *Enthusiast*"—defines as imaginative vitality.

With this much critical attention, however, the ode continues to elude full explication. Working within different contexts and with widely differing purposes, readers have often concurred in denying the ode a full and detailed reading. In some respects, the poem *as* poem still remains unexplored. Attempting to educe its meaning, we too often disregard what the language of the poem ought to prompt us to conclude. Critics appear to have missed or to have discounted much of Collins's linguistic playfulness in the ode, his serious jesting.[29] Similarly, the characteristic forms of difficulty in the poem have never received full analysis. Collins's ode focuses on the difficulty of writing great poetry; also, and appropriately, it is a poem of considerable difficulty. The obstacles in structure and language that mold our experience in reading the poem are also our surest guides to its ultimate meaning.

The ode's first stanza (the strophe) opens with an analogy that is at once both grand and casual. The grandeur derives in part from the analogy's first term, the legend of the "magic Girdle" of chastity related by Spenser in the fourth and fifth books of the *Faerie Queene*. Collins makes it a twice-told tale:

> One, only One, unrival'd Fair,
> Might hope the magic Girdle wear,
> At solemn Turney hung on high,
> The Wish of each love-darting Eye;
> Lo! to each other Nymph in turn applied,
>   As if, in Air unseen, some hov'ring Hand,
> Some chaste and Angel-Friend to Virgin-Fame,
>   With whisper'd Spell had burst the starting Band,
> It left unblest her loath'd dishonour'd Side;
>   Happier hopeless Fair, if never
>   Her baffled Hand with vain Endeavour
> Had touch'd that fatal Zone to her denied!
>
> (ll. 5-16)

Collins retells Spenser's tale of Amoret and Florimel and adds his own emphasis: in his hands it is a legend about chastity and, especially, a tale of aspiration and ambition. Despite the declaration that "One, only One, unrival'd Fair" might hope to wear the magic garment, the girdle is nevertheless "applied" to several nymphs, each desirous of the "fatal Zone." The girdle is desirable because of its beauty, its exclusiveness, its sanctity, and its magical powers. The language of the strophe stresses the garment's sacred and elusive nature, particularly in terms of height: it is "hung on high" at a "solemn" (sacred) tournament. The "hov'ring Hand" in "Air unseen" that protects the prize from unqualified contestants belongs to "Some chaste and Angel-Friend to Virgin-Fame." Even Spenser's "School" of poetry (l. 3) is "above" the others "blest." The consequences of an illegitimate quest for the girdle are correspondingly (and literally) degrading. A whispered spell will "burst" the "starting" band from the unqualified aspirant's side. The uplifted "Wish of each love-darting Eye" will depart the "hopeless Fair." She will become "unblest," her body "loath'd [because] dishonour'd." Her hand, which first applied the magic girdle to her "Side," is now "baffled," her endeavor "vain," the zone "fatal" and "to her denied."

The strophe's grandeur is thus a result of Collins's conception of the sanctity of this legendary quest. But the strophe actually opens on a casual, even playful note:

> As once, if not with light Regard,
> I read aright that gifted Bard,
> (Him whose School above the rest
> His Loveliest *Elfin* Queen has blest.)

Although the tone of these lines is off-hand, their function within the stanza is crucial. They both initiate the controlling analogy of the strophe ("As once," adapted from Akenside's *Odes*)[30] and immediately disrupt it. Instead of proceeding directly in his analogy, Collins digresses on the nature of his sources. He speaks not only of Spenser but of his entire school, and thus immediately raises the important issues of imitation and tradition within the poem.[31] Spenser is introduced as "that gifted Bard," but he is not named. The nature and extent of his "gift" (from divine, poetic sources) are not questioned here, as the poem opens, although eventually they must be measured against the sources of Milton's power. Critics have repeatedly attacked Collins for ironically reading Spenser's poem "with light Regard," but the mistake lies in the conflation within Collins's note, not in the text itself. The poem will eventually corroborate the poet's claim that he has "read aright," a phrase crucial to the ode in the sense that its own task lies, in part, in correctly interpreting the poetry of the past. The effect of this earlier poetry on the present is never far out of sight in the poem: Spenser's "*Elfin* Queen" is not only a creation in his allegorical poem but a presence in this ode as well.[32] Spenser's character becomes a Muse who "blesses" his poetic successors, among whom Collins—in adapting Spenser's legend in the strophe—must be counted.

Much of this foreshadowing in the first few lines is complexly plotted, even if casually delivered. All of it is, of course, an aside, a digression from even the first term of the analogy, still to be announced. These first sixteen lines, few of which actually contribute to the literal progress of the analogy, initiate much of the reader's confusion. In skeletal form, the argument of the strophe may be quoted as follows:

> As once (1)
> One, only One, unrival'd Fair, (5)
> Might hope the magic Girdle wear, (6)
> At solemn Turney hung on high, (7)
> The Wish of each love-darting Eye; (8)
> Lo! to each other Nymph in turn applied, (9)
> It left unblest her loath'd dishonour'd Side. (13)

The following lines (14–16) function as an interjection. We might object that even lines 7–8 are actually an informative aside, another digression that suggests the indirection of Collins's argument (the analogy itself is an indirect form of proceeding) and points to the difficulty that is carefully plotted into our experience of reading the poem.

We might reasonably expect that much of the suspense of the analogy will be resolved when we reach the second term, but difficulties persist here as well:

> Young *Fancy* thus, to me Divinest Name,
> To whom, prepar'd and bath'd in Heav'n,
> The Cest of amplest Pow'r is giv'n:
> To few the God-like Gift assigns,
> To gird their blest prophetic Loins,
> And gaze her Visions wild, and feel unmix'd her Flame!
>
> (ll. 17-22)

Just as once the girdle of chastity was worn by one, only one, unrivaled nymph in Spenser's legend, so another magic garment—this one in the gift of Fancy, and symbolizing poetic inspiration—is also assigned to few of the competing aspirants. Again Collins's explicit argument is minimal and his digressions essential. The language of height and aspiration, introduced in the opening lines of the strophe, is finally resolved here. Young Fancy is, to the poet, a "Divinest Name," esteemed above those of Spenser's Florimel or Amoret, or even the angelic friend of the first legend. Fancy is prepared and bathed in heaven; her cest is of "amplest Pow'r," overshadowing the girdle of chastity. It is, Collins concludes, a "God-like Gift" that will enable the bearer to gird his "blest prophetic Loins," to gaze at Fancy's visions and feel, unmixed, her flame.

In short, the second term of Collins's analogy literally supersedes the first, creating a loftier myth to be embodied in the poem's central statements. Must the first term therefore be forgotten, dismissed as a mere bridge to this more important stage in the ode? The experience of Collins's critics suggests that this first legend cannot be dismissed, that it remains a powerful presence throughout the poem. Much of the critical controversy actually centers on the relationship between these two terms. The first legend provides a myth of chastity; the second, one of literary attainment. The second myth enlarges the sacred nature of the girdle of chastity in explicit terms: it is to be awarded by a goddess bathed in heaven, itself a godlike gift to be worn above blest, prophetic loins. Must the poet of the second myth therefore embody the virtues of the chaste nymph of the first? Is moral purity a requirement of aspirants to the poetical character? This is the argument of Wasserman, who points as well to the "sainted growing Woof" (of the second stanza) from which "The dang'rous Passions" keep "aloof."[33] Contingent with this reading is the possible fate that the first legend poses for the illegitimate aspirant: "Happier hopeless Fair, if never / Her baffled Hand with vain Endeavour / Had touch'd that fatal Zone to her denied!" And this is, of course, the fate suggested in the poem's closing lines.

But such an argument, plausible as it appears, neglects the nature of the analogy. The second term is said to resemble the first, but it is not necessarily ruled by it. Just as Collins's is a loftier myth than Spenser's, so its elements have been enlarged as well. Part of the invigorating power of this imaginative gift is surely sexual: Fancy is pure, but her visions are "wild."[34] The poet experiences them "unmix'd" by any other elements, but what he feels is her "Flame." Moreover, the poet who "girds" the cest is capable of blest prophesying through his "Loins," and here Collins's playful ambiguity performs an important role. "Loins," pronounced "Lines," is an exact rhyme with "assigns." The pun is traditional and crucial: sexual prowess is an inherent part of the poetic process or, to put the argument another way, blest prophetic loins produce blest, prophetic lines. The central pun, strategically placed within the poem, reiterates Akenside's suggestion of the creator as procreator. Literary and sexual creation lie within the same vision of the poet, within the same word. The playfulness of the sexual innuendo concludes the strophe in the same spirit of carefully constructed jesting in which it began. The reader's difficulties are never entirely resolved: just as we had, at first, to await the resolution of the suspended analogy, so now we must continue to hold the two terms in an unsteady tension.

The poem's second stanza, the epode or "mesode," presents difficulties of a different kind. The obstacles here lie not in the mode of arguing (although the entire stanza comprises only one sentence), but in the argument itself. Collins has often been called obscure; is the obscurity of this argument thematically functional as well?

> The Band, as Fairy Legends say,
> Was wove on that creating Day,
> When He, who call'd with Thought to Birth
> Yon tented Sky, this laughing Earth,
> And drest with Springs, and Forests tall,
> And pour'd the Main engirting all.
>
> (ll. 23-28)

Collins's own legend, begun in the preceding stanza, is now extended; the band of poetic inspiration is given not an analogous framework (as in the strophe), but a history of its own. But whose "Fairy Legends" are these? They are obviously of Collins's invention, and yet they suggest that even a myth about the birth of poetic inspiration has its own literary context. Much of Collins's myth is adapted, of course, from Scripture: the poet focuses on "that creating Day" (the fourth) following God's formation of the heavens and the earth. Wasserman has interpreted this passage as a neo-Platonic "double" creation—first in idea ("Thought") and then in fact—but this argument, plausible as it may be, is not necessary.[35] By also drawing upon Milton's account of the creation in *Paradise Lost* (VII.339-86), Collins specifically points to the later formation of the sun and the creatures it rules. The poet's perspective, seemingly omniscient, is really mortal: he paints creation beneath "Yon tented Sky" but above "this laughing Earth." The imagery of this first phase repeats the secular descriptions of clothing in the strophe: the sky is described as "tented," the earth "drest" with springs, the oceans "engirting" the land much as the magic girdle encompasses nymph and poet.[36] Although the scene is laid in heaven, it points to earth.

In the first lines of the mesode, then, the poet describes God's creation of the world; in the succeeding lines we learn that God performs this task by an act of Fancy:

> Long by the lov'd *Enthusiast* woo'd,
> Himself in some Diviner Mood,
> Retiring, sate with her alone,
> And plac'd her on his Saphire Throne,
> The whiles, the vaulted Shrine around,
> Seraphic Wires were heard to sound,
> Now sublimest Triumph swelling,
> Now on Love and Mercy dwelling;
> And she, from out the veiling Cloud,
> Breath'd her magic Notes aloud:

And Thou, Thou rich-hair'd Youth of Morn,
And all thy subject Life was born!

(ll. 29-40)

Fancy, as pictured in the strophe, appears only in her traditional role as the human faculty of "Imagination" and she is extolled much as Warton and Akenside had already celebrated her. Although her purity is emphasized, the extent of her divine kinship is revealed only in the mesode. Here we learn that she is God's "lov'd *Enthusiast*" and that in a contemplative moment he places her on his "Saphire Throne." Collins is both echoing his sublime sources in *Paradise Lost* and conveying an image of Fancy that is tied to the figure of "Sapientia," divine wisdom. Fancy is both personified as a woman and presented as one of God's attributes. Read in fully allegorical fashion, therefore, this passage describes God retiring with Wisdom to create the youth of morn. The creation is itself an imaginative act—the supreme act of imagination—and yet Fancy is more than a human faculty, although related to it: she embodies the wisdom from which both God and the poet derive their creative power.[37]

Such a reading of this central passage repudiates any sexual or quasisexual union of God and Fancy that results in the birth of the poet. As Northrop Frye states this more radical interpretation, "not only does the poet in his creation imitate the creative power of God, but [he] is himself a son of God and Fancy, a 'rich-hair'd youth of morn' associated with the sun-god, like the Greek Apollo, a prophet and visionary of whom the last exemplar was Milton."[38] Or as Harold Bloom describes this scene: "God rested from his labors, but in the company of his spouse, Fancy, who long had wooed him. On this day, 'in some diviner mood,' God takes her. Amidst the triumphal music, Fancy breathes her magic notes aloud, and the poet as Orc, or Apollo, is born."[39] But does God "take" Fancy? Is she his "spouse"? Is the offspring of their "retirement" the poet or merely the sun? These questions continue to engage most readers, and answers capable of convincing both sides in the controversy are difficult to find. Although Fancy is described as a wooer of God, and herself loved by him, she is clearly not his spouse. There is also no real need for God to "take" her: she, as an *"Enthusiast"* and as an attribute of God, is already possessed by him. God is imagined in a "Diviner Mood," much as Fancy, in the first stanza, was hailed by the poet as a "Divinest Name." And this diviner mood, accompanied by the music of the spheres, results in the creation of the physical world: both the ruling sun and his "subject Life." On the other hand, God and Fancy clearly form a couple, male and female, who retire "alone." The music dwells both on triumph and on "Love and Mercy." The couple is "veiled" from our view as Fancy breathes her "magic Notes" and the youth is born. Thomas Weiskel is prompted to comment that "If this doesn't suggest sexual union I don't know what does."[40]

But, as Weiskel also suggests, the problem lies not in the interpretation of the lines themselves but in our ability to read metaphor (a generalization we may expand to include allegorical personifications and the structure of the allegorical ode). Not all readers insist that the poem describes an actual sexual union between God and Fancy. Bloom characterizes it as quasisexual: "The beauty of Florimel becomes transformed into the bright world of Fancy by a consummation analogous to sexual completion."[41] By extension, then, the consummation celebrated here echoes the sexual innuendo of Akenside's description of the poetic process. Man, in his limited imitation of God as creator, partakes of a sensuous pleasure similar to that of sexual activity. Collins reverses this perception as well: the poet, even as he pictures God in the process of creating the world, lends that portrait a distinctly human perspective. God creates the world with the aid of his divine wisdom; in allegorically portraying this internal action, the poet must rely on recognizable external action (even nuances of it) in order to describe this supreme act of the imagination. The sexual overtones indicate the poet's necessarily human point of view; they also suggest the emotional ambivalence he feels as he contemplates, in this stanza as well as in the first, the moral purity of the creator.

Similarly, the "rich-hair'd Youth of Morn" of the succeeding lines surely represents the sun (its concrete referent) and a series of more suggestive associations. The passage's literal reading is fairly clear: the youth of morn is the sun itself (the "bright-hair'd Sun" of the "Ode to Evening"), ready to rule over the subject life below it. The youth makes his appearance, moreover, at the exact midpoint of the ode, the traditional locus for the introduction of the sun.[42] The figure for the sun is a personification, however, and as a personified male the sun is most closely associated with the god Apollo. Collins's descriptions of the sun are in fact indebted to Spenser's in the *Faerie Queene*: "And *Phœbus* fresh, as bridegrome to his mate, / Came dauncing forth, shaking his deawie haire: / And hurld his glistring beames through gloomy aire" (I.v.2.3-5). Thus the sun is associated here both with God's creation of the universe and with his creation of the poet's cestus, for Apollo is the god of prophecy, poetry, and music. Apollo is therefore a fit personage to preside with the other characters in Collins's scene while the magic woof of poetry is woven. Apollo is not the poet himself (the Apollonian poet of Frye's argument), nor is he, strictly speaking, even an exemplar of the poetical character. But he is clearly associated with the poet even if he is himself a god, descended from the gods. In his personified form, he functions appropriately as a mediator between the heavenly and the mortal: he supplies the poet with a sense of possibility; he inspires the poet, lending him his imaginative spark. That Collins had such a middle-ground figure in mind is corroborated by his close borrowing from a passage in Sir William Temple's "Of Poetry," an essay repeatedly echoed in Collins's work. In his description of Apollo, Temple speaks of "that Cœlestial Fire which gave such a pleasing Motion and Agitation to the minds of those Men that have been so much admired in the World, that raises such infinite images of things so agreeable and delightful to Mankind. . . . [it] is agreed by all to be the pure and free Gift of Heaven or of Nature, and to be a Fire kindled out of some hidden spark of the very first Conception."[43] Fancy's flame, her heavenly gift of imagination, the first conception—each is a significant aspect of Collins's myth fashioned from Temple's suggestive essay. Temple's argument, like Collins's, is not that the poet is (or is capable of becoming) an Apollo, but that he is inspired by such a figure, that he is capable of sharing the remains of this divine spark.

To read Collins's description more literally than this is to deny the force of his metaphor; but to read the figure of the rich-haired youth as the poet himself is to err in the opposite direction. The figure of Apollo hovers behind the literal image of the sun, suggestive of both the physical referent and one of its many associations—lyric poetry. To insist that he must be read as only sun or only poet is to collapse the richness of the personification and to violate the spirit and terms of Collins's poetry. The very nature of personification is one of suggestive fluidity, an ambiguity that enables the poet to join the general and the particular, the animate and the inanimate, the mortal and the divine.[44] The personified figure, by definition, cannot be pinned down; it refuses to be reduced to any one of its several terms. The difficulty in reading Collins's figure is thus an obstacle in our interpretation of his other works as well, and much the same kind of confusion has produced unsatisfactory interpretations of similarly complex characters: Evening, Fear, Fancy herself.

Some of the difficulty in this passage is thus characteristic of most of Collins's mature work, but part of it is particularly contrived. How, for example, are we to judge the force of the conjunctive "And" when Collins tells us that " . . . Thou, Thou rich-hair'd Youth of Morn / And all thy subject Life was born"? Does the "And" denote a relationship of cause and effect between Fancy's warbling and the appearance of the earth, or merely a temporal relationship (the preceding lines begin "Now . . . Now . . . And")? Or, to put the argument another way, is Fancy's role—as she breathes her magic notes aloud—one of simple accompaniment to God's creative act or is it instrumental in a more active sense? The ambiguity is an essential part of the act of creation itself, which remains a literally clouded subject. What happens behind "the veiling Cloud" where God and his Fancy have retired alone? The language suggests a union of a specific kind, but the veil is never actually lifted; contrary to what Weiskel argues, the primal scene is never viewed. Collins's reticence is telling: even in an analysis of the original creation (or first conception, as Temple put it), the engendering act remains a powerful mystery within Collins's myth.

The conclusion of the mesode marks the creation of the poet's cestus:

> The dang'rous Passions kept aloof,
> Far from the sainted growing Woof:
> But near it sate Ecstatic *Wonder*,
> List'ning the deep applauding Thunder:
> And *Truth*, in sunny Vest array'd,
> By whose the Tarsel's Eyes were made;
> All the shad'wy Tribes of *Mind*,
> In braided Dance their Murmurs join'd,
> And all the bright uncounted *Pow'rs*,
> Who feed on Heav'n's ambrosial Flow'rs.
> Where is the Bard, whose Soul can now
> Its high presuming Hopes avow?
> Where He who thinks, with Rapture blind,
> This hallow'd Work for Him design'd?
>
> (ll. 41-54)

In his sound commentary on the poem, Roger Lonsdale argues that "God created the world (ll. 23-8) by an act of Fancy (ll. 29-40) and in this way the poetic imagination was born (ll. 41-50)."[45] The sun, earth, and attendant figures appear as a consequence of God's creative act, but "the sainted growing Woof," the poet's cestus, is still in the process of being created. The type of the poetical character emerges from the creation of the poetical band of imagination, not from the figure of the "rich-hair'd Youth of Morn." The poem continues to work by analogy, and the language of the original analogy in the strophe is echoed in the imagery of clothing: the sainted "Woof," Truth in his "Vest," the "braided Dance" of the shadowy tribes. "The dang'rous Passions" keep aloof, but the emergence of the cestus is nonetheless witnessed by a rich and disparate band of characters, contrasted by the imagery of darkness and light. "Ecstatic *Wonder*" listens to the deep, applauding thunder, whereas Truth is in "sunny" vest arrayed. The "shad'wy Tribes of *Mind*" join their murmurs even as "bright" uncounted powers feed on the nectar of heaven.

The mesode closes with an interjection: where is the presumptuous poet who, having witnessed the birth of this hallowed work, can think it designed for him? The speaker's assumption is that the poet's soul already has "high presuming Hopes"; can the poet now "avow" them? The "now" refers both to the temporal scheme of the ode—now, after witnessing the creation of the poet's sacred cestus—and to the age in which the ode is written. Who, in any age, the poet asks, can successfully entertain these presumptuous aspirations? Collins's answer, fully fleshed in the concluding stanza, is implicit here: only a poet with "Rapture blind," only a bard in the loftiest tradition of inspired, prophetic utterance. Both literally and figuratively, of course, this "blind" rhapsody points to the example of Milton.

The final stanza, the antistrophe, opens with no apparent transition from the preceding lines in the poem:

> High on some Cliff, to Heav'n up-pil'd,
> Of rude Access, of Prospect wild,
> Where, tangled round the jealous Steep,
> Strange Shades o'erbrow the Valleys deep,
> And holy *Genii* guard the Rock,
> Its Gloomes embrown, its Springs unlock,
> While on its rich ambitious Head,
> An *Eden*, like his own, lies spread.
>
> (ll. 55-62)

The transition is implied, however, for the Eden Collins portrays is modeled closely on Milton's description of the garden in *Paradise Lost*; and Milton, as the closing lines of the mesode suggest, is the poetic predecessor whose example the contemporary poet must confront. The difficulties of these lines are not as celebrated as those of the first two stanzas, but they are just as considerable. The tangled syntax and suspension of grammatical sense (the verb appears near the end of the final line) mirror the "disruptive" difficulty of Collins's analogy in the strophe. Collins's poetry here makes for difficult reading, and in the difficulty lies part of the passage's thematic statement: reaching a poetic Eden is hard work, a difficult attainment. Descriptions of this physical garden, which is built upon a Parnassian or Olympian height, function as descriptions of Collins's poetry—piled up, of rude access, tangled, shadowy, guarded, locked, and only finally spread before the reader.

The difficulties in this passage, however, are also part of the poet's Miltonic inheritance: as in Milton's description of Eden, the reader's progress is continually mired in poetic obstacles.[46] We, too, must labor to reach this happy rural seat:

> So on he fares, and to the border comes
> Of *Eden*, where delicious Paradise,
> Now nearer, Crowns with her enclosure green,
> As with a rural mound the champain head
> Of a steep wilderness, whose hairie sides
> With thicket overgrown, grottesque and wilde,
> Access deni'd; and over head up grew
> Insuperable highth of loftiest shade,
> Cedar, and Pine, and Firr, and branching Palm,
> A Silvan Scene, and as the ranks ascend
> Shade above shade, a woodie Theatre
> Of stateliest view.
>
> (IV.131–42)

Collins's mountain is more threatening, his garden less sexually inviting than Milton's, but the perspective remains the same. It is Satan who comes as an interloper to "attempt" the climb and "tempt" the inhabitants, not yet fallen. Collins's poet, on the other hand, arrives at an Eden peopled not by Adam and Eve but by the poetic efforts of Milton himself:

> I view that Oak, the fancied Glades among,
> By which as *Milton* lay, His Ev'ning Ear,
> From many a Cloud that drop'd Ethereal Dew,
> Nigh spher'd in Heav'n its native Strains could hear:
> On which that ancient Trump he reach'd was hung.
>
> (ll. 63-67)

Like the envious Satan in Milton's epic, the contemporary poet must challenge this Eden's inhabitants. Collins's mountain is rich and ambitious; its steeps, jealous. The extent of Collins's jealousy of Milton's achievement can be gauged by the manner in which the predecessor is first introduced: "An *Eden*, like his own, lies spread." This other Eden is simply referred to as "his": to the jealous mind there can be only "him." This is how Collins has already constructed his initial confrontations with the other creators in the poem, Spenser and God; neither is called by name in the poem itself.

Collins's scene in the poem's antistrophe does not therefore merely reflect an Eden like Milton's. The very example of Milton's achievement places this contemporary effort in a historical context; the postlapsarian has succeeded the genuinely innocent garden.[47] Collins cannot create an Eden without Milton in it, composing his own poetry, listening (as his successor cannot) to the music of the spheres. Even this suggestion is richly ambiguous: Milton hears heaven's "native Strains" as they are filtered through the "Cloud that drop'd Ethereal Dew," but both he and the cloud are "Nigh spher'd in Heav'n." Again, both music and cloud are pictured at the center of the creative scene.[48] Milton, imagined among these fancied glades, has successfully imitated God's creative action in the mesode; he has partaken of as much of the divine as a mortal may dare.

The successor's envy, his jealousy, even his fears can thus be understood. But these are characteristics of Milton himself, of the title's ideal "poetical character." Milton aspired to the "ancient Trump" of prophetic poetry (hung, like the band of chastity, above the aspirant), and it was granted to him. He too was ambitious, a reacher, and his achievements were exceptional. Do these possibilities still exist for the belated poet? Milton's is described as an "Ev'ning Ear," an echo of the poet's account of his method of composition in *Paradise Lost*. But the adjective also suggests the temporal progress of the poem toward darkness, in which "ev'ry future View" is "curtain'd close":

> Thither oft his Glory greeting,
> From *Waller*'s Myrtle Shades retreating,
> With many a Vow from Hope's aspiring Tongue,
> My trembling Feet his guiding Steps pursue;
> In vain— Such Bliss to One alone,
> Of all the Sons of Soul was known,
> And Heav'n, and *Fancy*, kindred Pow'rs,
> Have now o'erturn'd th' inspiring Bow'rs,
> Or curtain'd close such Scene from ev'ry future View.
>
> (ll. 68-76)

Even as Collins retreats from Waller and the lighter forms of poetry ("Myrtle Shades" that include the school of Pope as well), his own trembling (metrical) feet follow Milton's "Glory" in vain. The poet may depict the bleakness of the poetic future with a Miltonism, but the vision remains no less bleak: "Such Bliss to One alone, / Of all the Sons of Soul was known."

Collins borrows his concluding metaphors from Spenser and from the theater. The inspiring Spenserian "Bow'rs" have now been overturned by Heaven and Fancy, the kindred powers from whom the poet (like God) receives his imaginative gift. Each "Scene" in the poet's drama is now "curtain'd close"; no prophetic vision awaits the poet, no final prospect is afforded his reader. Like Collins, we experience a tantalizing glimpse of another world; like a dramatic audience, we wish to preserve that view, but the future lies outside our control.

The poem's structure underscores this bleak conclusion. The traditional structure of the ode is based on the choric strophe, antistrophe, and epode of Greek tragedy. The chorus moves—literally and thematically—one way, then another, and only finally in resolution. Collins, however, has subverted the form: the epode, instead of resolving the conflicts in the other stanzas, stands between them as they balance each other out. No sense of final progression is possible. The stanzas, like Collins's syntax and analogies, are stalled, interrupted, admitting little sense of final resolution. The structure within the strophe and antistrophe also works to the same purpose. The secular emphasis in the strophe is followed by a much shorter sacred passage as the strophe ends; in the antistrophe, however, the extended sacred prospect is concluded by a brief and disappointing secular view.[49]

The structured futility of the ode is only a final breakdown within the poem. Built into each stanza is a distinctive mode of difficulty that also threatens a breakdown or interruption of the reader's progress in the ode. The strophe begins with a narrative that is repeatedly interrupted. Playfully and maddeningly, the "As if" of the opening lines not only introduces the poem but controls it. Much of the power of the ode—what Collins's contemporaries would perhaps have called the poem's sublimity—lies in its suggestiveness, in the metaphorical force of the poet's "As if." The opening analogy works by suggesting (but not insisting on) similarities; the tension between the analogy's two terms is never explicitly resolved. Similarly, the complex, suggestive figures of the mesode—including the cloudy act of creation—and the syntactical problems of the antistrophe reinforce our sense of struggle within the ode. And in our struggle, we also experience the difficulties of the poet as he attempts to claim a lost divinity, to control the difficult elements of his art. The confusion throughout the poem is thematically deliberate; the poem is cloaked in obscurity even as the poet calls for light.[50]

The most disquieting confusion within the poem remains the ambivalent nature of the major personifications, which prefigure the fade-outs and fluid dissolutions of Wordsworth.[51] But here too lies the transcendence at which the poet aims. Spenser's "*Elfin* Queen," we should recall, is both Spenser's creation and an agent within Collins's poem, a Muse-like figure who blesses Spenser's successors. The magic girdle of the first stanza is both an emblem of chastity (and therefore awarded to the chaste) and an effective force (the cause of chastity remaining intact). Much the same argument can be made for each of Collins's major creations in the ode. The rich-haired youth is both a physical object, the sun, and a figure replete with symbolic associations that tie it to the poet's magic girdle, yet to be fully spun. The poetic cestus is both a prize awarded to the true poetical character and an endowment that makes poetical achievement possible. Milton's Eden in *Paradise Lost* engenders a new creation (Collins's Eden), in which Milton appears as the principal character. Each of these created figures acts in turn as a creative agent, an appropriate element within a poem described as "an allegory whose subject is the *creative imagination* and the poet's passionate desire for its power."[52] Moreover, like Longinus' *Peri Hupsous* or Pope's *Essay on Criticism*, Collins's poem is a representation of its own argument: "Whose *own Example* strengthens all his *Laws*, / And *Is himself* that great *Sublime* he draws."[53] The difficulties and creative elements within the ode represent, in concrete form, the poet's passionate consummation of his imaginative powers. Collins, in a mode never fully realized by Warton and Akenside, is able to make his poetic claims part of his own poetry.

And like Akenside (in his *Odes*) and Gray (in "The Progress of Poesy") he discovered what was to become a major Romantic theme: the admission of difficulty, even of futility in writing poetry, often enables the poet to create a vehicle that may, if only fitfully, reach these paradisal heights.

3

Shaping a Career

At one point in the composition of the *Aeneid*, Virgil intended to open his epic poem not with the familiar "Arma virumque cano" but with an acknowledgment of the poems—*Eclogues* and *Georgics*—he had already sung: "I am he who once tuned my song on a slender reed, then, leaving the woodland, constrained the neighbouring fields to serve the husbandmen, however grasping—a work welcome to farmers: but now of Mars' bristling arms and the man I sing. . . ." These experimental lines, which reflect Virgil's consciousness of the shape of his own literary career, established an influential pattern for poets (particularly English poets) writing in his wake.[1] By attempting to make a carefully structured artistic work of his own life, Pope in fact left the clearest model of the shape of the poet's career. Pope informed Joseph Spence that in an early epic work he "endeavoured (says he, smiling) in this poem to collect all the beauties of the great epic writers into one piece. There was Milton's style in one part and Cowley's in another, here the style of Spenser imitated and there of Statius, here Homer and Virgil, and there Ovid and Claudian." Spence asked him whether "It was an imitative poem then, as your other exercises were imitations of this or that story?" and Pope replied, "Just that." Pope also told Spence that "My next work after my epic was my *Pastorals*, so that I did exactly what Virgil says of himself:

> Cum canerem reges et proelia, Cynthius aurem
> Vellit, et admonuit; 'pastorem, Tityre, pinguis
> Pascere oportet ovis; deductum dicere carmen.' "

56

[When I was fain to sing of kings and battles, the Cynthian plucked my ear and warned me: "A shepherd, Tityrus, should feed sheep that are fat, but sing a lay fine-spun."] [2]

Collins's early work suggests that he placed himself firmly within this traditional mold and that he adopted Pope as his poetic master. His early lyrics are poetical exercises, his *Eclogues* a convenient starting point for more serious work, and his epistles an attempt to reach the heroic strain. The emphasis throughout recent criticism of Collins's poetry has rested on the influence of Milton, who is seen as a usually debilitating figure in the young poet's development.[3] But this emphasis on Milton has almost entirely obscured the influence of Pope, who remained an imposing "precursor" even after his death in 1744. All of Collins's poems written before the *Odes* of 1746—the lyrics, *Oriental Eclogues*, epistle to Hanmer, many of the Drafts and Fragments, and even the Shakespearean elegies—are consciously imitative of Pope's lyrics, *Pastorals*, progress pieces, elegies, and epistles. This early dependence on Pope in turn suggests why Milton had such an ambivalent effect on Collins: liberation from one master enforced an even more dangerous bondage to another. As Christopher Ricks has suggested, the struggle to escape the influence of the father may lead to an eventual identification with the poetic grandsire.[4]

Milton thus represented a traditional source of inspiration for Collins that would enable the emerging poet to reject Pope's enormous influence in the mid-1740s. We have already seen the nature of that rejection in Warton's famous "Advertisement" to his *Odes* and in Collins's "Ode on the Poetical Character." The poems written before 1746, on the other hand, provide a portrait of Collins mastering the traditional literary forms as he attempts to find a suitable poetic voice. But the process of imitation contains its own inherent tensions. Always at the back of the young poet's mind is the traditional advice so powerfully encapsulated by Johnson: "No man ever yet became great by imitation"; a writer's work "must contain in itself some original principle of growth."[5] Collins's early poems reveal his paradoxical struggle to create imitations that are distinctly his own.

I. Early Lyrics

Even Collins's earliest surviving poems suggest the consciously imitative nature of his poetry and his career. The "Sonnet" and the verses addressed "To Miss Aurelia C—r, on her Weeping at her Sister's Wedding" are both schoolboy efforts, written while he was at Winchester

College and published separately above pseudonyms in the *Gentleman's Magazine* in 1739.[6] Neither lyric has received much attention. "To Miss Aurelia C——r" has been reintroduced only recently into the canon of the poet's works, but even the "Sonnet"—long acknowledged to be Collins's—has provoked little critical scrutiny. The few critics who discuss this early poem have been both puzzled and impressed: the sonnet is not only an excellent imitation but a "perfect achievement," and yet it reveals "a sensibility overweighted from the beginning by a precious literary instinct"; the poem displays a pitch of aesthetic acuteness that seems to have little relation to actual experience.[7] Its tightness suggests the richness of the metaphysicals, and yet it is difficult to account for Collins's knowledge of the metaphysical school; was he reading widely at this early date, or was he influenced here, as in so many other areas, by his school-fellow Joseph Warton?[8] We may resolve these perplexities, however, if we place the poem in its proper context. Collins's "Sonnet" is indeed an imitation, but of a peculiar kind: the poem has as its source not a metaphysical lyric but yet another imitation. Collins was reading widely, even during his days at Winchester, but his reading was entirely predictable. Collins was stimulated by Pope, whose influence dictated not only the kind of poetry he would write but the preciosity and "perfection" of the work as well.

Collins's "Sonnet" is modeled on one of Pope's early lyrics, written in 1701 and published among the *Poems on Several Occasions* of 1717.[9] This is an interesting point in itself for it suggests that as the young poet searched for a poetic voice he turned not only to the age's dominant figure but, in particular, to that poet's own youthful efforts. Pope entitled his work "Verses in imitation of Cowley: By a Youth of thirteen." Collins's clearest source is the first of these imitations, "Weeping," a three-stanza lyric modeled in turn on one of Cowley's poems in *The Mistress*.

Cowley's "Weeping" consists of a series of four related conceits. In the first stanza, Cowley's speaker delivers both a compliment and a warning: his mistress appears so beautiful even in her distress that *"ill Fortune"* may wish to dress herself permanently in this sorrowful guise.[10] The playful comparison of tear and eye is developed further in the next stanza. The speaker, claiming that each tearful drop reflects his mistress's eyes, broadens his conceit by introducing the mythological Narcissus, pictured here as the *"Baby"* (the human figure reflected in a glistening eye) who gazes into the flood below him.[11] The tearful flood then suggests the weather conceit of the third stanza: the speaker extols the combination of *"Sun-shine and Rain together"* and searches for the source of these streaming tears in his mistress's forehead, "that pure *Hill* of *snow*." This frigidity then becomes the focus of the final stanza, in which the speaker laments the coldness (or indifference) of his mistress, whose tears now most resemble hail. By the poem's conclusion, Cowley has traced his water imagery through its various courses (tears, ocean, flood, rain, fountain, stream, distilled water, and finally hail) and has suggested through these transformations both his own temperament and that of his mistress. The coldness of the final stanzas also reveals the distance between these lovers, and explains why this lyric presents a description of a woman weeping rather than an address directed to her.

Pope's lyric is an imitation of Cowley's style and a variation on his subject. Pope's Celia is also a sorrowful beauty; her eyes, even when filled with tears, still shine brightly.[12] In fact, Pope argues, these tears act as necessary filters ("mists") that allow us to gaze on a source of radiance greater than the sun. Pope's conceits follow easily enough from Cowley's; his only variation is the brisk introduction of a mythological figure at this point (the sunny Apollo first rising from the ocean). Pope's second stanza is an elaboration of the weather motif in Cowley's third and fourth stanzas; here too the speaker admires the combination of contrasting natural forces ("soft show'rs" and "blasting lightnings"). Only in his final stanza does Pope introduce the figure of the "baby," pictured here not as a Narcissus admiring his own shape in the tearful pool but—consistent with the figure of Apollo in the first stanza—as a Phaeton drowned in his attempt to consume the earth in fire. Like Cowley, Pope proceeds by association; but whereas Cowley's progression traces a development in attitude, Pope's simply provides three different but equally striking ways of viewing a weeping woman's charms. Pope extends the conceits of his model, but his Celia is neither a distant nor a cold mistress. The thirteen-year-old poet is obviously on firmer ground in complimenting his mistress than in portraying amorous strife.

The context of these two poems suggests that Collins would at least have known Pope's imitations of the metaphysical school, even if he was not yet familiar with Cowley's own work. Pope, of course, may have led Collins back to Cowley, but it is clear that Pope was the more important figure. In imitating Pope, Collins was obviously imitating Cowley as well, but in a sense the entire question of the influence of metaphysical poetry on Collins's early career is misdirected. The crucial model for the youthful Collins was the youthful Pope; the early imitations of Cowley and Waller, which Pope annotated with his age at the time of their composition, provided an explicit stimulus to the young Collins's own poetry. This in part explains both the limitations and perfections of Collins's earliest work: if the "Sonnet" is judged a "perfect achievement," then that achievement lies in gradual literary refinement (of both Pope and Cowley). And in this perfection lies its limitations: Collins's poem, like Pope's, represents the mastery of a literary genre; it does not necessarily represent the poetic synthesis of an emotional experience.

Collins's "Sonnet" contains striking resemblances to Pope's lyric, but there are important differences as well:

> When *Phœbe* form'd a wanton smile,
>> My soul! it reach'd not here!
> Strange, that thy peace, thou trembler, flies
>> Before a rising tear!
> From midst the drops, my love is born,
>> That o'er those eyelids rove:
> Thus issued from a teeming wave
>> The fabled queen of love.

Collins's is a further condensation of Cowley's lyric; it is in fact a "sonnet" only in the contemporary sense of a "small poem." But in spite of the poem's extreme brevity, Collins is able to fashion an appealing meditation on the workings of the heart. The speaker's response in the first stanza is one of mild astonishment; he realizes that although Phoebe's playful smile has been unable to move him, his soul's peace "flies / Before a rising tear!" The speaker is startled at the moment when he first discovers his mistress's beauty and he is intrigued by its paradoxical cause, which is not the willful force of the smile but the helplessness of the tear. These tears then appear more forceful in the second stanza (they "rove" over her eyelids) as the speaker explicitly states that his "love is born" in this one brief moment.

The final lines of the poem suggest, however, that this moment does not embody a unique psychological phenomenon: "Thus issued from a teeming wave / The fabled queen of love." The birth of the speaker's love is similar to the timeless birth of Venus, the queen of love, pictured here as she emerges from the "teeming" (breeding) wave. Just as tears have become waves, so too the fluctuations of the individual heart are viewed in the broader perspective of the eternal birth of beauty and love. Collins draws the mythological parallel not as a mere illustration but as a psychological explanation: he accounts for individual experience by evoking an eternal moment that we all recognize. The sonnet's argument, both simple and short, insists on pushing towards myth: Collins's conjunction is "thus"; his Venus is the "fabled" queen of love. This particular moment is also part of the eternal, this particular beauty also part of our general conception of beauty in women. Like Pope, Collins provides compliment through conceit; unlike Pope, he also dramatizes a moment of psychological insight. But even if Collins's subject is actually closer to Cowley's than to Pope's, his stylistic debts are unmistakably clear. The "Sonnet" represents a final stage in a process of refinement, and the young poet appropriately signed his work "Delicatulus."

Collins's other lyric of 1739, "To Miss Aurelia C——r," echoes several of Pope's early imitations of Waller but eludes any specific context. This poem is, like the "Sonnet," both sweet and ingenious; it also manages to tease us through its gentle humor. James Hampton was surely right in claiming that this short poem "discovers a genius, and turn of expression, very rarely to be met with in juvenile compositions."[13] Like its companion piece, "Aurelia" is fashioned from metaphysical conceit, mythological extension, and the language of paradox:

> Cease, fair *Aurelia*, cease to mourn;
>   Lament not *Hannah*'s happy state;
> You may be happy in your turn,
>   And seize the treasure you regret.
> With *Love* united *Hymen* stands,
>   And softly whispers to your charms,
> "Meet but your lover in my bands,
>   "You'll find your sister in his arms.

The subject of this poem is a separation that must be both justified and resolved. Aurelia is asked to cease mourning her sister Hannah's marriage; she too will find happiness in her turn, and seize the treasure she now regrets. But what is the "treasure" Aurelia "regrets"? Is it Hannah, lost through marriage, or the joys of marriage itself, which her sister will experience first? Does Aurelia grieve at the loss of a happiness she has already shared or envy a happiness she has not yet enjoyed?

Collins elaborates Aurelia's ambiguous loss in the second quatrain. In a mythological tableau, Hymen consoles the weeping sister with the paradoxical assurance that when she marries she will find her sister—in Cupid's arms. But how, exactly, will Aurelia find her sister by marrying a lover of her own? Collins suggests that one love will replace the other: she will discover in marriage the happiness her sister already enjoys and find a happy state much like the one she has already known. Collins's tone here is also double-edged. The poem both compliments Aurelia (Hymen will softly whisper to her "charms") and catches the petulance of her tearful despair (she laments the loss of her sister's companionship and yet envies that sister's happiness). Collins skillfully implies the selfishness of Aurelia's distress in his punning consolation: if she will "cease" to mourn, she may yet "seize" the treasure for herself. Separation is temporary; through her union with a lover she will understand why her sister so eagerly embraced conjugal joys, and the mythological figures (Hymen "united" with Cupid) reinforce this theme. In spite of these assurances, however, Collins's playful ambiguity remains: Aurelia will be granted what she wishes (happiness), but the poet politely calls it by a different name ("your sister").

These two early pieces are considerable achievements in a minor way, even if Collins was later, in the "Ode on the Poetical Character," to retreat "From *Waller's* Myrtle Shades." The "Sonnet" alone prompts Sigworth to speculate that "had there been many poets writing thus, the 1730's might be remembered for lyrics as well as for Pope."[14] Collins nevertheless seems to have realized that there was little room for real poetical success here, even if this is where one began. A broader canvas and a more sustained poetic form were clearly needed. Ambition prompted Collins to complete a larger work while he was still at Winchester; a sense of the poet's career led him to find his model once again in Pope.

II. Pastorals

Collins's *Oriental Eclogues* represent a calculated compromise between tradition and innovation. On the one hand, Collins fashioned his first major work in the pastoral genre, a literary form endowed both with a rich heritage and with a reputation as the appropriate starting point for an aspiring poet. On the other hand, Collins lent this traditional genre an innovative twist by translating the action of the poem to the fashionable orient, which had been recently depicted in Thomas Salmon's *Modern History: Or, The Present State of All Nations.* The tension between these two contending forces can be seen in the similarities and differences between the *Eclogues* and Collins's principal model for his poem, Pope's *Pastorals* of 1709. Both works comprise four eclogues, each set during a different time of the day (morning, noon, evening, and night). But Pope's eclogues are also focused on the four seasons of the year, whereas Collins creates a corresponding variety in his poems by considerably changing the scenes. Pope's pastorals, moreover, are English eclogues; like Spenser in *The Shepheardes Calender,* Pope attempts to translate Greek pastoral scenes to his own country. Collins, however, exactly reverses this process by translating the scenes of his poems to a more exotic setting than even the original Greek eclogues could provide.

Collins's *Eclogues* also differ from Pope's in their thematic emphasis. At the heart of both works lies the tribute pastoral poetry traditionally pays to the power of time, but the two poems suggest different ways of viewing the nature of temporal change. Pope's approach is essentially Christian. As Martin C. Battestin has argued, "The essence of pastoral, as Pope understood, is the recognition of the Fall and of our desire to repudiate the wretched legacy of Adam."[15] Progress brings with it both individual mortality and a larger, mythic pattern of history. Pope views the artist as the sole agent of permanence and ideal beauty within this temporal flux: "The subject of the *Pastorals* is the nature, the mystery, the efficacy of Art itself, viewed in relation to those correlative concepts with which the artist is most nearly concerned: the meaning of Time and Nature in a fallen world."[16] Thus Pope's "Spring" is a spirited dialogue that resolves tensions through the harmonizing power of song: art—symbolized both in Daphnis' bowl and in the counterpoint of Pope's poetry—serves as an emblem of permanence appropriate to an innocent, golden age. "Summer" depicts an age of silver, of dissatisfied maturity; the innocent amours of "Spring" have now grown older; the music of pastoral song has turned elegiac. Eventually, in "Winter," Pope portrays time's ultimate triumph over ideal beauty in our laggard age of iron. But, as Battestin reminds us, the *Pastorals*, unlike *The Dunciad*, were not intended to end in decay. Pope's "Messiah," a "sacred eclogue," was meant to serve as a conclusion to the four secular eclogues; the true transforming power is Christ's, not the poet's, whose efforts are only illusory. Pope ultimately views Christ as the shepherd who will make the golden world a reality.

Collins's pastorals, on the other hand, are entirely secular. His *Eclogues* are not concluded by a "Pollio" or "Messiah," nor do they stress the redemptive power of art. Instead Collins suggests something that lies between these extremes: the values that nourish and protect a civilized society. These values are called "Virtues" in the first eclogue and are represented in the marriage of love and valor in the third. The threats to these values are embodied in the human greed of the second eclogue and in the invading Tartar of the fourth. Collins establishes his own counterpoint in the poem by pairing the eclogues with and against each other, but common to all are the recurring images of waste. The true seat of a cultivated life, Collins suggests, lies somewhere between the desert and the court.

But to summarize Collins's *Eclogues* in this manner is to do them a partial injustice. As we strive to detect a historical pattern embedded in the work, we still may manage to slight the poem by ignoring its equally artful surface. Pope concluded in his prefatory "Discourse" that pastorals should be "delightful,"[17] and Collins echoes his master in part of the original motto he chose for his poem: "But let us for the moment waive these solid advantages; let us assume that entertainment is the sole end of reading." Collins's own pleasure in his work can be seen in the *"rich and figurative"* language and *"Elegancy and Wildness of Thought"* that he ascribes to the Persians in his preface. The *"naturally Strong and Nervous"* style of the English will here be foresaken by Collins, who playfully portrays himself as the "translator" of these "original" eclogues. The *Eclogues* themselves are often uneven in quality, and much of our interest in the poem is prompted by Collins's ambitious attempt to fuse delicate and sensuous language with traditional Augustan concerns. And these concerns, of course, are never actually far from the poem's surface, as the continuation of Collins's Ciceronian motto indicates: "Let us assume that entertainment is the sole end of reading; even so, I think you would hold that no mental employment is so broadening to the sympathies or so enlightening to the understanding."[18]

The first eclogue opens with a morning oration by Selim, who delivers "the Shepherd's Moral" in a valley near Baghdad:

> Ye *Persian* Maids, attend your Poet's Lays,
> And hear how Shepherds pass their golden Days:
> Not all are blest, whom Fortune's Hand sustains
> With Wealth in Courts, nor all that haunt the Plains:
> Well may your Hearts believe the Truths I tell,
> 'Tis Virtue makes the Bliss, where'er we dwell.
>
> (I.1-6)

The temporal setting of Collins's scene is somewhat ambiguous: Selim speaks in the present tense of "how Shepherds pass their golden Days," but he speaks to characters who need instruction in the art of living. The golden days appear to characterize the duration of the shepherds' watch rather than the age in which they live. Unlike Pope, Collins opens his pastorals on a note of loss—"Not all are blest"—and then proceeds to intimate the dangers to be found in the following eclogues. "Wealth in Courts" describes Abbas's situation in the third eclogue, Hassan "haunts" the desert in search of fortune in the second eclogue, and Agib and Secander are fugitives from the plains in the fourth. The moral of Selim's tale is essentially Johnsonian: "'Tis Virtue makes the Bliss, where'er we dwell." Collins emphasizes an active, forceful virtue that cannot be found in the natural environment of a pastoral world; Selim teaches "the Swains that surest Bliss to find, / What Groves nor Streams bestow, a virtuous Mind" (I.11-12).

The backdrop of Selim's lessons, however, is certainly not austere; here we are granted our first glimpse of the rich sensuousness of these pastoral scenes:

> When sweet and blushing, like a Virgin Bride,
> The radiant Morn resum'd her orient Pride,
> When wanton Gales, along the Valleys play,
> Breathe on each Flow'r, and bear their Sweets away:
> By *Tigris'* wand'ring Waves he sate, and sung
> This useful Lesson for the Fair and Young.
>
> (I.13–18)

Collins's portrait of the sweet and blushing sun and the breathing, possessive gales blends the five senses in a vision that is both sensual and innocent. The gales are "wanton" only in the sense of being "playful"; the rich landscape suggests an unspoiled, Edenic setting for Selim's song. And yet the song itself stresses a spoilage that has already occurred in this pastoral world. Selim delivers necessary advice: "Ye *Persian* Dames, he said, to you belong, / Well may they please, the Morals of my Song" (I.19–20). The central portion of Selim's song contains a carefully structured transition from the superficial beauties of the world to the moral reserves that lie within us:

> The Morn that lights you, to your Loves supplies
> Each gentler Ray delicious to your Eyes:
> For you those Flow'rs her fragrant Hands bestow,
> And yours the Love that Kings delight to know.
> Yet think not these, all beauteous as they are,
> The best kind Blessings Heav'n can grant the Fair!
> Who trust alone in Beauty's feeble Ray,
> Boast but the Worth *Balsora's* Pearls display;
> Drawn from the Deep we own their Surface bright,
> But, dark within, they drink no lust'rous Light:
> Such are the Maids, and such the Charms they boast,
> By Sense unaided, or to Virtue lost.
>
> (I.23–34)

Selim's maids are bathed in flattery and synaesthetic delight: the sun's warming rays are "delicious" to their eyes; flowers are designed to please the maids, and kings to love them.

But these are not the "best kind Blessings Heav'n can grant the Fair." Beauty, if trusted alone, emits only a "feeble Ray." Selim constructs a parable from the pearls drawn from the Persian Gulf. Employing conventional Augustan antithesis, he directs the maid's attention from

the pearls' surface brilliance to their inner darkness, and he concludes
by reversing his original synaesthesia: "dark within," the pearls "drink
no lust'rous Light." Such are the maids—and the charms they boast—
who are lost to virtue or guided only by "Sense." And in the following
lines Selim unleashes an even harsher attack on superficial beauty in
which the senses, especially heat, are now seen to lead the maids astray.
Selim's emphasis on "ruling"—"Who seeks secure to rule . . . "
(I.39)—is especially interesting, for in the following eclogues Collins
will suggest the importance both of ruling oneself (Hassan is ruled by
greed rather than common sense) and of ruling others (Abbas rules
and is ruled; Agib and Secander flee a country poorly ruled by its protector).

Where then are these virtues found? Selim briefly paints a portrait
of a different kind of reign:

> Blest were the Days, when Wisdom held her Reign,
> And Shepherds sought her on the silent Plain,
> With Truth she wedded in the secret Grove,
> Immortal Truth, and Daughters bless'd their Love.

(I.43–46)

Selim underscores what is already implicit in his tale: a true golden
age is past, but its virtues may still be practiced in the pastoral world
we call our own. The days of Wisdom's reign were truly blest, but the
blessings remain in our dutiful obedience to unaging values. The allegorical tableau, soon to become such an important element in Collins's
poetry, emphasizes the unspoiled value of these virtues. We can detect
Collins's own emphasis in his revision of this passage, in which "The
fair-eyed Truth" of the first edition became "Immortal Truth" in the
revised edition of 1757. Collins may have thought "fair-eyed" to be
an inappropriate epithet for a male deity,[19] but it is also clear that the
poet meant to stress the immortal nature of Truth, even amid the flux
of a later age.

In the final stanzas of the first eclogue, Selim urges a reunion of
beauty and truth. The maids and "Virtues" are urged to seek each
other out; Peace and Plenty—the offspring of Truth and Wisdom—will
assist in leading the maids to other virtues. Most of these virtues have
been "Lost to our Fields," but "The dear Deserters shall return again"
(I.51–52). These "Deserters" are literally desert-dwellers whom we
have exiled from their native plains. Their return, Selim promises, will
signify a new golden age, a new growth symbolized by the balmy,
soothing shrub that will now grace the shepherds' shores. But also present, and more important, are the individual virtues Collins personifies

in his first full-fledged allegorical invocation: sweet Modesty will lead
the train of virtues that includes Faith, Meekness, Pity, and Love. In
an extended passage, Collins creates an early model for the important
allegorical portraits of subsequent poems:

> With Thee be Chastity, of all afraid,
> Distrusting all, a wise suspicious Maid;
> But Man the most; not more the Mountain Doe
> Holds the swift Falcon for her deadly Foe.
> Cold is her Breast, like Flow'rs that drink the Dew,
> A silken Veil conceals her from the View.
>
> (I.57–62)

We may question Selim's advice (most of Collins's commentators have),
but not its apparent effect:

> The Maids of *Bagdat* verify'd the Lay:
> Dear to the Plains, the Virtues came along,
> The Shepherds lov'd, and *Selim* bless'd his Song.
>
> (I.70–72)

Collins's second eclogue involves a dramatic shift from the pleasant
valleys of Persia to the terrors of the desert: "In silent Horror o'er the
boundless Waste / The Driver *Hassan* with his Camels past." The desert,
a wasteland void of the virtues "Dear to the Plains," functions as an appropriate setting for Hassan's interior monologue. The midday sun provides a spotlight effect on the merchant who is torn by the conflicting
forces of greed and security. The desert, Collins indicates, is a world un-
suitable to man: "The sultry Sun had gain'd the middle Sky, / And not
a Tree, and not an Herb was nigh" (II.7–8). But the desert is Hassan's
by choice; he grieves with his camels for the green world they have lost:

> Here, where no Springs, in Murmurs break away,
> Or Moss-crown'd Fountains mitigate the Day:
> In vain ye hope the green Delights to know,
> Which Plains more blest, or verdant Vales bestow.
>
> (II.23–26)

But the merchant's choice is not irrevocable; he may yet be able to
reject the false values symbolized by the desert: "Yet Money tempts
us o'er the Desert brown, . . . Full oft we tempt the Land, and oft
the Sea, / And are we only yet repay'd by Thee?" (II.35–38). Collins,
like Akenside, employs "tempt" in both its senses: wealth is pictured
as a powerful temptation that goads us to attempt a hazardous enterprise (here a form of moral trial). The conflict, however, involves more

than a struggle of the will. The desert supplies literal dangers that are envisioned in Collins's first full portrait of fearful apprehension:

> What if the Lion in his Rage I meet!
> Oft in the Dust I view his printed Feet:
> And fearful! oft, when Day's declining Light
> Yields her pale Empire to the Mourner Night,
> By Hunger rous'd, he scours the groaning Plain,
> Gaunt Wolves and sullen Tygers in his Train:
> Before them Death with Shrieks directs their Way,
> Fills the wild Yell, and leads them to their Prey.
>
> (II.51–58)

Collins's sketch of the lion's train, which should be paired with Modesty's entourage in the first eclogue, allows the young poet a much needed imaginative freedom. Hassan's fears show Collins attempting to extend the range of emotional experience, much as he was later to do successfully in the *Odes*.[20]

But there is success here as well, particularly in Hassan's vision of his nightly horrors:

> At that dead Hour the silent Asp shall creep,
> If ought of rest I find, upon my Sleep:
> Or some swoln Serpent twist his Scales around,
> And wake to Anguish with a burning Wound.
>
> (II.61–64)

These lines are as curiously elliptical as any in the odes. The silent asp may indeed injure the camel-driver as he sleeps, but equally nightmarish is the asp's entrance into Hassan's dreams. Another serpent may "wake [him] to Anguish with a burning Wound," but the omission of the direct object also suggests that the serpent will wake itself to anguish. Hassan's wounds are, of course, self-inflicted; and he has chosen to make himself, like the serpent, a creature of the desert. Collins nicely frames the ambiguous nature of these fears; he does not feel himself bound by Pope's assertion in his "Discourse" that the poet must "use some illusion to render a Pastoral delightful," which consists in "exposing the best side only of a shepherd's life, and in concealing its miseries."[21] In Collins's eclogue, escape from the desert's sun and sleep is to be found within, and Hassan finally asks deliverance from the burdens of greed:

> Thrice happy they, the wise contented Poor,
> From Lust of Wealth, and Dread of Death secure;

They tempt no Desarts, and no Griefs they find;
Peace rules the Day, where Reason rules the Mind.

(II.65–68)

If Hassan will allow himself to be ruled by reason rather than by unhealthy ambition, he will share the security of the pastoral world and
the love of the "tender *Zara.*" "O! let me teach my Heart to lose its
Fears," he cries, "Recall'd by Wisdom's Voice, and *Zara*'s Tears" (II.83–
84). Hassan, like Selim's maids, must learn to recognize the virtues
that haunt the plain.

Collins's third eclogue prolongs the theme of virtuous love. Like the
first eclogue, it consists of a song designed for the instruction of
women. The scene is a forest; the time, evening. Emyra sings of "the
pleasing Cares of Love" in a setting not unlike Selim's:

In *Georgia*'s Land, where *Tefflis*' Tow'rs are seen,
In distant View along the level Green,
While Ev'ning Dews enrich the glitt'ring Glade,
And the tall Forests cast a longer Shade,
What Time 'tis sweet o'er Fields of Rice to stray,
Or scent the breathing Maze at setting Day.

(III.1–6)

The shepherdess Abra lives in the kind of green world Hassan returns
to at the conclusion of the preceding eclogue, a pastoral scene that lies
between the hazardous desert and the towers of Tefflis, glimpsed "In
distant View." Emyra stresses Abra's ties to nature: she tends the
flocks, leads her companions in native dances, and fashions a flowery
chaplet for her hair. Into her peaceful world "Great *Abbas* chanc'd
that fated Morn to stray, / By Love conducted from the Chace away"
(III.21–22). The sultan Abbas is led by music from one hunt to another: Abra, implicitly the victim of the chase, is ruled by Abbas and
by fear. And as her royal lover leads her from the plain to his court,
Abra (in an ironic twist of the Orpheus legend) looks behind her at
the joys she must relinquish:

Yet still her Crook and bleating Flock remain:
Oft as she went, she backward turn'd her View,
And bad that Crook, and bleating Flock Adieu.

(III.30–32)

In the continuation of Emyra's song, however, we learn that the
nature of "ruling" in the lovers' relationship is soon reversed. Amid
"the Blaze of Courts," Abra continues to fix "her Love, / On the cool

Fountain, or the shady Grove." Her transformation into a Georgian sultana is only superficial; like the fabled models of Selim's song, she retains the essential innocence of her mind. She is allowed to join her former companions on the plain, and her initial fear of Abbas turns to love. The tempering character of the cool fountain and shady grove have their effect in turn on Abbas, who soon thinks "of Crowns and busy Courts no more." Together Abra and Abbas re-create the peace and happiness of the golden age; his union of "The Lover's Myrtle, with the Warrior's Crown," of the court with the bucolic countryside, inspires the first celebration of the present moment in the *Eclogues*: "Oh happy Days! the Maids around her say, / Oh haste, profuse of Blessings, haste away!" (III.69–70).

These blessings, however, are short-lived, and Collins's final eclogue portrays the dangers that threaten even the happiest of realms. The opening lines of the fourth eclogue are entirely consistent with the conclusion of Emyra's song, but the sudden transition in the third line indicates the plight of the Circassian fugitives, Agib and Secander:

> In fair *Circassia*, where to Love inclin'd,
> Each Swain was blest, for ev'ry Maid was kind!
> At that still Hour, when awful Midnight reigns,
> And none, but Wretches, haunt the twilight Plains;
> What Time the Moon had hung her Lamp on high,
> And past in Radiance, thro' the cloudless Sky:
> Sad o'er the Dews, two Brother Shepherds fled,
> Where wild'ring Fear and desp'rate Sorrow led.
> Fast as they prest their Flight, behind them lay
> Wide ravag'd Plains, and Valleys stole away.
>
> (IV.1–10)

"Awful Midnight" rules the nightmarish flight of the two shepherds, who are led by Fear and Sorrow from their native fields. Their pastoral existence has been ravaged; even the valleys, which steal away from the shepherds as they climb Circassia's mountains, have been stolen from them by the invading Tartars. Agib and Secander exchange their apprehensions in a dialogue similar to Hassan's monologue in the second eclogue: "Still as I haste, the *Tartar* shouts behind," Agib cries, "And Shrieks and Sorrows load the sad'ning Wind." Collins's final eclogue depicts a situation in which the "hastening" of the previous pastorals now becomes a literal necessity. Selim advised his audience to "hasten" toward virtue (I.47–48); Hassan asked "Why heed we not, whilst mad we haste along, / The gentle Voice of Peace, or Pleasure's Song?" (II.41–42); Abra's companions sang of a golden age: "Oh haste, profuse of Blessings, haste away!" But these exiled shepherds, in contrast even to Hassan, have no choice but to hasten in their lonely flight.

The blessings of their unhappy land "tempt the Sword," and they can no longer rely upon their ruler to preserve them:

> Far off in thoughtless Indolence resign'd,
> Soft Dreams of Love and Pleasure sooth his Mind:
> 'Midst fair *Sultanas* lost in idle Joy,
> No Wars alarm him, and no Fears annoy.
>
> (IV.35–38)

Secander's lament naturally reminds us of the idle joys of the third eclogue, and Agib wisely warns his neighbors of the barbarian threat: "Some weightier Arms than Crooks and Staves prepare, / To shield your Harvests, and defend your Fair" (IV.61–62). The playful imitation of the shepherd's life will not do; Abbas will have to exercise his warrior's skill in defending his country's joys. Emyra, in the third eclogue, had asked that we "Let those who rule on *Persia*'s jewell'd Throne, / Be fam'd for Love, and gentlest Love alone" (III.65–66), but the horrors of the final eclogue indicate that love is not enough; rulers must take their shepherding in earnest.

The terrors of this midnight scene are only made worse by the shepherds' remembrance of the peaceful world they have lost. The invading Tartar serves as the personification of those barbarous forces that threaten a cultivated society, and Collins appropriately emphasizes the "native Deserts" in which he is bred. The second and fourth eclogues stress the arid, forsaken world that lies so precariously near the pastoral scene; but in the other eclogues as well we are forced to recognize the desert that lies within. Collins's first major work ends on the same despairing note of flight and darkness that characterizes his more mature poetry: "Th' affrighted Shepherds thro' the Dews of Night / Wide o'er the Moon-light Hills, renew'd their Flight."

The deep pessimism of this final eclogue suggests how far Collins has deviated from Pope's *Pastorals*. The ravages of time are clearly greater, the security and values of the pastoral life more precarious. In his edition of Pope, Joseph Warton wrote that Salmon's *Modern History* prompted Collins to lay the scenes of his own poem in Persia, "as being productive of new images and sentiments."[22] But Collins's revisions suggest that the cultivation of new images and sentiments alone did not produce a work that was substantially original, even if it often diverged from its model. "In his maturer years," Warton continues, "he was accustomed to speak very contemptuously of them, calling them his Irish Eclogues, and saying they had not in them one spark of Orientalism."

Collins's change in the title from "Persian" to "Oriental Eclogues" suggests the more limited claim he intended to make for his poem, and his textual revisions suggest a continual attempt to escape the early influence of Pope. Collins's description of the pearls in the Persian Gulf indicates the direction of this revision:

> Who trust alone in Beauty's feeble Ray,
> *Balsora*'s Pearls have more of Worth, than they;
> Drawn from the Deep, they sparkle to the Sight,
> And all-unconscious shoot a lust'rous Light.

> (I.29–32, 1742 edn.)

> Who trust alone in beauty's feeble ray,
> Boast but the worth Balsora's pearls display;
> Drawn from the deep we own their surface bright,
> But, dark within, they drink no lust'rous light.

> (I.29–32, 1757 edn.)

Collins's entire passage in the first eclogue is indebted to Clarissa's speech in Canto V of *The Rape of the Lock*, and we should particularly note the similarity between the 1742 text ("sparkle to the Sight . . . shoot a lust'rous Light") and the conclusion of Clarissa's address: "Beauties in vain their pretty Eyes may roll; / Charms strike the Sight, but Merit wins the Soul" (V.33–34). Collins's revision signals a departure from Pope's model and provides a richer image as well (one, as we have already seen, that reverses the synaesthetic effect of earlier lines). Collins's revision also appears to mirror changes James Thomson made in later editions of *The Seasons*. In the early texts of "Summer" Thomson wrote: "At thee the ruby lights its deepening glow, / A bleeding radiance grateful to the view" (ll. 147-48, 1727-38 edns.); but the text of 1744 reads: "At thee the ruby lights its deepening glow, / And with a waving radiance inward flames." Thomson's addition of a line in 1744 ("The lively diamond drinks thy purest rays," l. 142) is also closely paralleled in Collins's revision. Thomson, who was one of Collins's closest friends in the late 1740s, appears to have exerted his own influence on Collins even as the poet attempted to reduce his original debt to Pope.

Collins's *Oriental Eclogues* finally transcend the limited territory of Pope's *Pastorals*, and of pastoral poetry in general. Collins's emphasis on the cultivation of wisdom, virtue, and knowledge borders on the domain of Virgil's *Georgics*; and his ultimate focus on the forceful preservation of society suggests the extended scope of Virgil's epic.

But even these concerns tie Collins to the themes of Pope's poetry in general, if not specifically to his *Pastorals*. Collins's link to the Augustan tradition is implicit in the motto he chose for the second edition of his work, selected from the *Georgics*: "And when on us the rising Sun first breathes with panting steeds, there glowing Vesper is kindling his evening rays" (I.250–51). Collins quotes a lesson in geography, occasioned by Virgil's speculations on the path of the sun. Collins, like Virgil, stresses the distance between two poles: one area grows light as the other darkens, but the sun that arrives and departs is the same (England and Persia, Collins implies, have their similarities as well as their differences). Collins's parallel is traditional, his perspective essential to the Augustan vision that linked English culture to its classical models. Similarly, Collins's emphasis on corruption and decay, on the precarious preservation and translation of culture, is also the focus of Dryden's "Mac Flecknoe" and Pope's major Horatian satires (and, ultimately, *The Dunciad*). The *Oriental Eclogues* demonstrate Collins's careful assimilation of Augustan poetry; the epistle to Hanmer indicates what Collins could achieve in a formal imitation of those models.

III. An Epistle to Hanmer

Collins's *An Epistle: Addrest to Sir Thomas Hanmer, On his Edition of Shakespear's Works* is his first occasional poem, but the occasion itself—and the poet's motives for quickly revising his poem—are shrouded in mystery. This poem was clearly intended to celebrate the publication of Hanmer's monumental edition of Shakespeare, often called the "Oxford edition" because it was printed by the university press and its publication supervised by several university figures. Collins graduated from the university on 18 November 1743, and his poem, advertised for December of that year, carried the date-line "*Oxford, Dec. 3. 1743.*" But apparently Hanmer's edition was not issued until 1744, and thus it seems probable that Collins's epistle actually anticipated this important Oxford event. Collins's motivation for praising Hanmer and his (mediocre) edition is not clear, but it is possible that Collins either was courting Hanmer's patronage as he left Oxford for London, or was hoping that his role in an important university event would bolster his chances for a fellowship there.[23] If so, he was successful in neither enterprise. The *Epistle* was subsequently revised and then reissued in May 1744, and the nature of Collins's changes in the poem suggests that these hypotheses are probably accurate. Collins is no longer as deferential to Hanmer in the revised edition; his poem is "Addrest to Sir Thomas Hanmer," not "Humbly Address'd." Gone too is the early focus on Oxford, especially the fanciful myth of the "fair *Isis*" in ll. 9-28 of the first edition. Hanmer is no longer viewed as the "One perfect Mind, which Judgment calls its own" (l. 20, 1743 edn.), but, more justly, as a capable curator, a "gen'rous Critic" of Shakespeare's works.

Other changes in Collins's text reflect a new stylistic and thematic emphasis. Several revisions free Collins's lines of unnecessary repetition, but others reveal his attempt to avoid images and diction too clearly indebted to Pope. In l. 63, for example, Collins substituted "*Smiles* and *Graces*" for "Loves and Graces," which, in the 1743 edition, closely mirrored Pope's "In these gay Thoughts the Loves and Graces shine" ("Epistle to Miss Blount, With the Works of Voiture," l. 1).[24] These revisions announce a new sense of independence in the final version—independence both from a neglectful patron and from a poetic model—but the *Epistle* remains an essentially derivative work. The structure of the poem is drawn from the traditional progress piece and *translatio studii*; its specific models can be found in the progress of scholarship in *An Essay on Criticism* and the progress of Dulness in *The Dunciad*.[25] The *Epistle* is, by its nature, a public work, intended to address a public figure on an important occasion. Hanmer had been Speaker of the House of Commons during the Protestant succession on the death of Queen Anne, and throughout the poem Collins stresses the double role Hanmer plays as a cultural guardian and public servant. But Collins's revisions in the final version also alert us to the double nature of his own poem: the *Epistle* addresses important cultural issues that are the concerns of a broad and anxious audience, and yet it manages to become a personal poem as well. Embedded within the larger design of the poem is the distinctive voice of the poet himself, now really heard for the first time. Significantly, the *Epistle* of 1744 was the first work to which Collins allowed his name to be fixed.

The opening lines of the poem indicate Collins's public and private subjects:

> SIR,
> While born to bring the Muse's happier Days,
> A Patriot's Hand protects a Poet's Lays:
> While nurst by you she sees her Myrtles bloom,
> Green and unwither'd o'er his honour'd Tomb:
> Excuse her Doubts, if yet she fears to tell
> What secret Transports in her Bosom swell:
> With conscious Awe she hears the Critic's Fame,
> And blushing hides her Wreath at *Shakespear*'s Name.
>
> (ll. 1-8)

The sense of the first four lines is fairly simple. The patriotic Hanmer, the protector of Shakespeare's works, is destined to bring "happier Days" to the beleaguered Muse of poetry; while Hanmer nurses Shakespeare's lays, the Muse will see her own myrtles bloom, unextinguished by Shakespeare's death. And yet the Muse is hesitant to communicate her doubts and "secret Transports"; awed by Hanmer's reputation, she unobtrusively hides her wreath "at *Shakespear*'s Name." These last four lines, however, are confusing, and seem not to follow directly from the opening lines of the poem. What secret transports must the Muse conceal, and why must she blush as she offers her tribute to Shakespeare? These questions can be answered only if we notice the change Collins makes in the nature of the Muse. In the first four lines she is the Muse of poetry, but in the following lines she is the more particularized Muse of the youthful poet, himself singing Shakespeare's and Hanmer's praises.[26] The Muse, in other words, becomes self-conscious as the poet himself enters the poem. The secret transports belong to Collins; they suggest the effects Shakespeare's works have upon him, effects perhaps inappropriate in a public poem. And thus Collins, blushing at his own temerity in raising this private tribute, quietly fashions his poem (the Muse's "Wreath") as much for Shakespeare as for Hanmer. The poet will render tribute to Hanmer, of course, but the wreath is carefully laid in its appropriate place.

Collins's bold strategy quickly establishes the double portrait embedded in the entire work. Just as Collins celebrates the new life that will be brought to Shakespeare's works—and poetry in general—by Hanmer's edition, so he also focuses attention on his own role in that revivifying and celebratory process. The emphasis in the first lines is on rebirth and new beginnings: Hanmer is "born" to bring "happier Days" to poetry; he will in turn "nurse" Shakespeare's works while the Muse's myrtles "bloom, / Green and unwither'd" over the dramatist's honored tomb. But it is possible to read these lines as a portrait of Collins as well; is not the poet of this work, if only in a lesser way, "born to bring the Muse's happier Days"? And does not Hanmer's patriot hand protect both Shakespeare's work and the youthful poet of this composition? Hanmer appears to have become a patron in spite of himself: the rebirth of Shakespeare's reputation provides an opportunity, an occasion in both a public and private sense, for Collins's own poetic beginnings.

But if Collins's self-conscious portrait of himself signals a new perspective in his poetry, the subject of the *Epistle* reflects the characteristic concerns of his earlier works, especially the *Oriental Eclogues*. Hanmer is destined to bring about "happier Days" (a motif we already have seen in Collins's pastorals), and the corresponding imagery for this event (the blooming myrtles) is pastoral as well. This vital relationship between culture and cultivation is stressed in the following lines of the poem:

> Hard was the Lot those injur'd Strains endur'd,
> Unown'd by Science, and by Years obscur'd:
> Fair Fancy wept; and echoing Sighs confest
> A fixt Despair in ev'ry tuneful Breast.
> Not with more Grief th' afflicted Swains appear
> When wintry Winds deform the plenteous Year:
> When ling'ring Frosts the ruin'd Seats invade
> Where Peace resorted, and the Graces play'd.

(ll. 9-16)

Collins likens the neglect of Shakespeare's works to a musical untuning of the cultural sphere; a responsive ("tuneful") audience has survived, but the strains themselves, "injur'd" because "obscur'd," are no longer heard. The succeeding metaphor provides an elaboration of this dilemma, in which the neglect of Shakespeare resembles the fall of nature, especially the natural world of pastoral poetry. By analogy, Shakespeare's works are likened to "the plenteous Year" now deformed by wintry winds and to "ruin'd Seats" now invaded by lingering frosts. The metaphorical connection between culture and cultivation, moreover, reflects Collins's quickening grasp of poetical technique. In the first edition this relationship is explicitly (and baldly) stated in a rather Popean couplet: Fancy asks whether Science will "still resign / Whate'er is Nature's, and whate'er is mine?"

In the poem's second stanza, Collins delineates the process by which culture is nurtured and then translated from one region to another:

> Each rising Art by just Gradation moves,
> Toil builds on Toil, and Age on Age improves.
> The Muse alone unequal dealt her Rage,
> And grac'd with noblest Pomp her earliest Stage.

(ll. 17-20)

These heavy Augustan lines pull us up short, for they reveal a view that exempts literature from the general progression (and improvement) of the arts. The Muse of poetry bestowed her inspiration ("Rage") in an unequal manner, blessing most "her earliest Stage," a supple pun that points both to the Greek theater and to the original "stage" of artistic development. Collins's description of these early masterpieces—especially Euripides' *Hippolytus* and Sophocles' *Oedipus Tyrannus*—

emphasizes the vitality and human suffering captured in their "speaking Scenes"; it also anticipates his projected ode on the music of the Grecian theater, begun but never finished at the close of his career.

In the following stanzas of the poem, Collins outlines the westward translation of dramatic art through Europe. Rome almost rivaled Greece in comedy, "But ev'ry Muse essay'd to raise in vain / Some labour'd Rival of her *Tragic* Strain." The phrase "in vain" should be familiar to us: it is repeatedly voiced by Secander in the fourth of the *Oriental Eclogues*, and it is Collins's own response at the conclusion of the "Ode on the Poetical Character." Again Collins couches his statement of cultural disintegration in imagery derived from the cultivation of nature: "*Ilissus*' Laurels, tho' transferr'd with Toil, / Droop'd their fair Leaves, nor knew th' unfriendly Soil." The imagery continues in Collins's description of drama's sojourn through medieval and Renaissance Italy: Cosimo de' Medici protected the exiled Muses in "th' *Etrurian* Shade," and the Provençal troubadours furthered their journey along "*Arno*'s Stream."

These are certainly not artistic improvements, and yet Collins suddenly admits an exception to this general literary decline in the next stanza. Heaven, true to its "various" nature, has fashioned in Shakespeare's works a final "beauteous Union" of the imaginative vitality and just proportions of classical drama and Italian poetry. But even the mention of Shakespeare's achievement does not entirely remove the general specter of a stifled progress in dramatic art; Shakespeare's works, in fact, underscore the less successful attempts that follow:

> Yet ah! so bright her Morning's op'ning Ray,
> In vain our *Britain* hop'd an equal Day!
> No second Growth the Western Isle could bear,
> At once exhausted with too rich a Year.

> (ll. 51-54)

The bounty of Shakespeare's harvest has exhausted England's natural resources; the "plenteous Year," promised in l. 14, has been realized, and the brilliance of the day's first rays has eclipsed all succeeding efforts. Ben Jonson "Too nicely . . . knew the Critic's Part"; Fletcher's work merely "warms the Female Mind." As in Greece, so in England; the Muse's "earliest Stage" produces the most vibrant and enduring art:

> But stronger *Shakespear* felt for *Man* alone:
> Drawn by his Pen, our ruder Passions stand
> Th' unrivall'd Picture of his early Hand.

> (ll. 64-66)

Collins's portrayal of Shakespeare's vitality and endurance is one that he will repeat throughout his career: like the Greek tragedians who produce "speaking Scenes," Shakespeare is able to combine the verbal and painterly arts in "Th' unrivall'd Picture of his early Hand." And like the dramatists who depict "Each changeful Wish of *Phædra's* tortur'd Heart" (l. 22), Shakespeare also portrays man's essential passions, the emotional character of human nature.

And yet, even as he approaches his central characterization of Shakespeare, Collins pauses in a digression on French drama in the hands of Corneille and Racine:

> With gradual Steps, and slow, exacter *France*
> Saw Art's fair Empire o'er her Shores advance:
> By length of Toil, a bright Perfection knew,
> Correctly bold, and just in all she drew.

> (ll. 67-70)

These lines are themselves "correct" and "just," their slow tempo and Augustan phrasing embodying a slackening in both dramatic progress and the progress of the poem. These lines remind us of the difficulties of poetic succession, but they do not necessarily dictate a pessimistic conclusion to the poem.[27] Collins emphasizes the artistic pitfalls of seventeenth-century England and France even as he celebrates Shakespeare's achievements, but Collins's motive for citing these dangers so early in the poem lies both in emphasis and in dismissal. The clearly symmetrical structure of the poem seems not to have been noticed. Collins, in an intriguing strategy that rivals the boldness of the opening lines, has structured his poem in two parts. The revised version of 1744 contains 148 lines; Collins breaks off his discussion of literary disappointments and decline exactly halfway through the poem. The second half of the poem begins with a new progress through the scenes of Shakespeare's works; an increased momentum leads us finally to a rediscovery of his dramatic principles and a resurgence of his powers in the combined elements of contemporary art. The instructive "But" that begins l. 75 heralds a new direction in the poem; if the *Epistle* is temporarily halted, it still manages to begin anew in a manner reminiscent of the poem's opening lines. Shakespeare's successors are thus discussed and dismissed before the poet turns to his extended vision of Shakespeare's achievements; the digressions point to real dangers, but they also allow the ensuing poem to proceed in a manner that is entirely triumphant. The *Epistle* rises in its "triumphal form" exactly at its midpoint in order to continue and conclude in a celebratory mode.[28]

Collins's praise of Shakespeare is twofold. On the one hand, Collins celebrates Shakespeare's ability to delineate human nature: "He alone to ev'ry Scene could give / Th' Historian's Truth, and bid the Manners live" (ll. 77-78). On the other hand, he emphasizes the effect Shakespeare's work has on its eighteenth-century audience, especially an audience of painters and poets. Collins himself enters the poem as a writer suddenly aroused by the force of Shakespeare's art: "Wak'd at his Call I view, with glad Surprize, / Majestic Forms of mighty Monarchs rise" (ll. 79-80). Collins becomes an observer within his own poem, and his stance and diction anticipate his vision of Milton's works in the "Ode on the Poetical Character": "I view that Oak, the fancied Glades among, / By which as *Milton* lay . . . " (ll. 63–64). Collins calls on Shakespeare to "take thine Empire o'er the willing Breast! / Whate'er the Wounds this youthful Heart shall feel, / Thy Songs support me, and thy Morals heal!" (ll. 102-104). To a certain extent, Collins asks us to gauge Shakespeare's greatness by observing his influence on the sensibility of artists who are his poetic inheritors.

Collins also asks us to judge the force of Shakespeare's work in its inspiration of the sister arts:

> There ev'ry Thought the Poet's Warmth may raise,
> There native Music dwells in all the Lays.
> O might some Verse with happiest Skill persuade
> Expressive Picture to adopt thine Aid!
> What wond'rous Draughts might rise from ev'ry Page!
> What other *Raphaels* Charm a distant Age!
>
> (ll. 105-110)

The following stanzas have been called "a gallery of imitative verse-portraits," but this description is only technically true.[29] Collins pays tribute to Shakespeare first by suggesting the inspiration his plays will bring to modern painters, and then by attempting, in his own lines, to suggest these pictorial effects. Collins's imitation is not a simple one, for it must manage to convey a sense of the pictorial as well as the dramatic nature of Shakespeare's work. And Shakespeare's plays, Collins emphasizes, are themselves imitative works that imaginatively strive to capture the nature of reality: "Where'er we turn, by Fancy charm'd," Collins claims, "we find / Some sweet Illusion of the cheated Mind," an observation derived from Milton, whose Comus hurls his "dazling Spells into the spungy ayr, / Of power to cheat the eye with blear illusion" (ll. 154-55). At their best, Collins's portraits approach the fashionable, self-conscious artistry of the masque. His lines are strongly iconic; they seem to be modeled on an imagined painting.[30] Sources for Collins's portraits have in fact been discovered in the engravings in Rowe's edition of Shakespeare (1709 and 1714), with which Collins was surely familiar.[31] But clearly Collins also draws on the pictorial suggestiveness of Shakespeare's scenes; in Collins's hands, "dramatic action has become frozen gesture and arrested motion."[32]

Collins chooses to illustrate scenes from the history plays—*Henry V, Richard III, Julius Caesar,* and *Coriolanus*—and from the pastoral comedies. His choices are entirely appropriate. The historical scenes focus our attention on the passions; Coriolanus, for example, is pictured at a moment of extreme personal crisis as he confronts his wife and mother: "O'er all the Man conflicting Passions rise, / *Rage* grasps the Sword, while *Pity* melts the Eyes" (ll. 131-32). But these portraits of the "Majestic Forms of mighty Monarchs" also emphasize the patriotism and preservation of a national culture that already have been praised in the poem. Collins eventually views Shakespeare within this context when he asks the dramatist to "take thine Empire o'er the willing Breast!" The pastoral scenes, by contrast, stress the powers of Fancy:

> Oft, wild of Wing, she calls the Soul to rove
> With humbler Nature, in the rural Grove;
> Where Swains contented own the quiet Scene,
> And twilight Fairies tread the circled Green:
> Drest by her Hand, the Woods and Vallies smile,
> And Spring diffusive decks th' *enchanted Isle.*
>
> (ll. 95-100)

Spring now replaces the "wintry Winds" and "ling'ring Frosts" of the first stanza. Filled with allusions to *A Midsummer Night's Dream* and *The Tempest,* these lines create a pastoral world that is restored here through the illusive powers of Shakespeare's art.

Collins's poem closes without a halted progress or Dunciadic decline. The poet stresses Hanmer's importance as a curator by likening his efforts to Pisistratus' preservation of Homer's scattered works, and he concludes by invoking a new alliance among the sister arts:

> Thus, gen'rous Critic, as thy Bard inspires,
> The Sister Arts shall nurse their drooping Fires;
> Each from his Scenes her Stores alternate bring,
> Blend the fair Tints, or wake the vocal String.
>
> (ll. 133-36)

Collins's projected rejuvenation of the arts is more ambitious, I think, than has previously been realized: he calls both for the assistance of pictorial art and, as he has already suggested in the poem (l. 106), for the artistry of music as well. This union of the arts is, as we shall see, an ideal that finally finds full expression in "The Passions" and in Collins's last, unfinished poem, but it is intimated as early as 1744. The *Epistle* clearly stands at an important transition point in Collins's career. Formally a traditional verse-epistle, the poem nevertheless suggests Collins's attempts to push beyond the limitations of Augustan poetry. Collins prefers Shakespeare's originality and native vitality to the correctness of his successors, and he is not afraid to consider himself an important voice in the resurgence of this creative force. But these are all, finally, suggestions and tendencies within a work that is itself essentially traditional; we must look elsewhere for the ultimate transition between Collins's early poetry and the great odes of 1746.

IV. Elegies and Epistles

The interval between the publication of the *Epistle* in December 1743 and the publication of the *Odes* three years later would seem to represent a crucial period of poetic development for Collins, but the poems that we can confidently assume to have been written during this period reveal little clear direction towards the major odes. It may be that, with the exception of the draft of an ode "To Simplicity," Collins destroyed his working manuscripts of the odes, or of poems that clearly anticipate the odes. John Ragsdale suggests as much in his account of Collins at work:

> To raise a present subsistence he set about writing his *Odes*, and having a general invitation to my house, he frequently passed whole days there, which he employed in writing them, and as frequently burning what he had written, after reading them to me. Many of them which *pleased me*, I struggled to preserve, but without effect; for pretending he would alter them, he got them from me and thrust them into the fire.[33]

The few drafts of poems that escaped the fire during these three years are largely imitative efforts, closely resembling the format and focus of the *Epistle*. But surviving with these verse-epistles are three additional poems that, though they are obviously imitations, also demonstrate Collins's attempt to broaden his poetic range.

Collins included "A Song from Shakespear's *Cymbelyne*. Sung by Guiderus and Arviragus over Fidele, suppos'd to be Dead" in the second edition of the epistle to Hanmer. Collins's first elegy is a delicate replacement of Shakespeare's "Fear no more the heat of the sun," and later in the century it was occasionally substituted for the original lament in performances of *Cymbeline*. In many ways this poem anticipates the much briefer "How Sleep the Brave" and the more ambitious (and more personally moving) elegy on Thomson. Collins opens the poem by picturing "fair FIDELE's grassy Tomb," where "Soft Maids, and Village Hinds shall bring / Each op'ning Sweet, of earliest Bloom, / And rifle all the breathing Spring." Fidele's death marks a fusion of natural elements; nature is appropriately brought to one who was herself a maid "of earliest Bloom," prematurely "rifled" from this evocative landscape. Guiderius and Arviragus protect her tomb with a song of exorcism: no wailing ghosts, withered witches, or goblins will endanger her grassy plot; instead, "The Female Fays shall haunt the Green, / And dress thy Grave with pearly Dew!"

Collins, in a maneuver that marks much of his later poetry, also provides the song with a double perspective. The elegy combines a spatial close-up of the lamented maid (to whom the elegy is now directly addressed) and a broader temporal perspective (suggested by the insistent future tense) that reveals the consolations that await her:

> The Redbreast oft at Ev'ning Hours
>   Shall kindly lend his little Aid:
> With hoary Moss, and gather'd Flow'rs,
>   To deck the Ground where thou art laid.
> ·
>
> Each lonely Scene shall thee restore,
>   For thee the Tear be duly shed:
> Belov'd, till Life could charm no more;
>   And mourn'd, till Pity's self be dead.
>
> (ll. 13-16, 21-24)

Fidele's memory will be perpetuated by an appropriately evocative "Scene"; the creatures of nature—both high and low—will remain faithful to one whose very name signifies loyalty and service. The entire poem is focused on the powers of "charm," a pun Collins had already used in the short lyric to "Aurelia C——r." Fidele's memory will be protected by a charming scene that evokes tears in those who view it. Guiderius and Arviragus will, at the same time, contrive charms to protect the maid from the nightmare world of the dead. We, in our turn, will love Fidele as long as we live ("till Life could charm no more"); and Fidele herself, merely "suppos'd to be Dead," remains charmed by a powerful potion.

A "Song. The Sentiments borrow'd from Shakspeare" provides an instructive foil for the virtues of Collins's first elegy. The alternating rhythm of this balladlike lament produces a monotonous singsong poorly suited to Collins's elegiac voice. The poet's concerns remain the same; once again he envisions a premature victim—"Young Damon of the vale"—whose death is lamented in an appropriate manner by the natural elements:

> Pale pansies o'er his corpse were plac'd,
> Which, pluck'd before their time,
> Bestrew'd the boy like him to waste,
> And wither in their prime.
>
> (ll. 9-12)

But Collins is obviously uncomfortable with the narrative style of the ballad, and the final stanza is particularly and uncharacteristically weak. Although Collins claimed that the sentiments were borrowed from Shakespeare, Lonsdale has helpfully pointed out that the song is derived not only from Ophelia's mad-scene (in the fourth act of *Hamlet*) but from David Mallet's popular ballad *William and Margaret* (1723) as well. This additional source suggests some of the complexities raised by Collins's imitations. In each poem Collins directs our attention to an original text, but in each case the elegy itself is as closely derived from contemporary sources as it is from a Shakespearean original. The "Song from Shakespear's *Cymbelyne*" is clearly modeled on Pope's "Elegy to the Memory of an Unfortunate Lady"; both poems consistently echo James Hammond's *Love Elegies*, published in 1743.[34] We may wish to read these early elegies as poems that emphasize our natural, human bonds as strongly as they suggest the development of a personal, elegiac voice in Collins's career.[35] But we must also emphasize the essentially derivative nature of these early works, which are imitative not only in their diction and format, but in their "sentiments" as well. Perhaps Collins's greatest success in the "Song from Shakespear's *Cymbelyne*" lies in his ability to create freshness and delicacy in a poem that is thickly encrusted with allusions to its various sources.

Also dating from this period is a poem "Written on a paper, which contained a piece of Bride Cake given to the author by a Lady." The title refers to the custom of placing a piece of wedding-cake beneath one's pillow in order to dream about one's lover during the night. Collins's poem, perhaps prompted by an actual incident, begins as a conventional occasional piece. Like many of Cowper's brief poems (and even the opening of *The Task*), this lyric attempts to lend a sense of grandeur to an otherwise trivial event:

> Ye curious hands, that, hid from vulgar eyes,
> By search profane shall find this hallow'd cake,

> With virtue's awe forbear the sacred prize,
>   Nor dare a theft for love and pity's sake!

(ll. 1-4)

The inflated language sets the appropriate tone of artificiality and mock-heroic protestation for the poem; the humble bride-cake soon becomes a "precious relick," intended "by love to charm the silent hour, / The secret present of a matchless maid." Collins's language is consistently playful: the poet/lover will be "charmed" to sleep by the "matchless" (unwed) maid. And the donor, because she is a woman, will impart "pains that please" along with her charms. The "nice" ingredients of the bride-cake are blended by "The *Cypryan* queen" herself: "With rosy hand the spicy fruit she brought / From *Paphian* hills, and fair *Cythera's* isle" (ll. 13-14).

Collins's transformation of the actual occasion of the poem eventually produces a full mythological tableau, but the final stanzas reveal another kind of transformation in which the focus returns to the poet himself, attended by allegorical figures but nonetheless alienated by his amorous anguish and the effects of pride, scorn, and ardor:

> *Sleep*, wayward God! hath sworn while these remain,
>   With flattering dreams to dry his nightly tear,
> And chearful *Hope*, so oft invok'd in vain,
>   With fairy songs shall soothe his pensive ear.
>
> If bound by vows to friendship's gentle side,
>   And fond of soul, thou hop'st an equal grace,
> If youth or maid thy joys and griefs divide,
>   O much intreated leave this fatal place.
>
> Sweet *Peace*, who long hath shunn'd my plaintive day,
>   Consents at length to bring me short delight,
> Thy careless steps may scare her doves away,
>   And grief with raven note usurp the night.

(ll. 21-32)

Collins closes by addressing the possessors of those "curious hands" that opened the poem. His visitors are asked, in the name of friendship, to leave the poet to the consolations of oblivious sleep, and the poet finally ushers his intruders (including us) out of the poem. Collins's predicament is overstated, his language highly allusive and overblown, but the poem nevertheless manages to close in a powerful and convincing fashion. Critics from Langhorne to the present day who have lamented Collins's supposed neglect of love in his poetry have surely

•

overlooked these lines, which anticipate the major odes and later fragments in their diction, allegory, and anguish.

The six verse-epistles written in 1744-45 provide less anticipation of the major odes than they do a sustained reflection of the epistle to Hanmer. Each fragment is written in heroic couplets; each takes art—usually literature—as its subject; and each may have had its origin as an occasional piece (the fourth fragment, addressed to the publisher Jacob Tonson, suggests an attempt to snare a patron). Not until the seventh fragment ("The Moon with dewy lustre bright / Her mild Æthereal radiance gave") do we find a significant break in the subject and form of Collins's drafts and, interestingly, these changes occur simultaneously.[36] Our interest in these early fragments lies primarily in the portrait they reveal of Collins as a young author. The first two drafts demonstrate his interest in drama: the first denounces the "wild pomp" and "Idle reign" of the Restoration stage; the second, of joint authorship, appears to represent a dialogue between a financial backer and an ambitious producer. The third fragment expresses Collins's enthusiasm for James Harris's treatise on the sister arts, and foreshadows (as we shall later see) the poet's attempt to fuse poetry, painting, and music in "The Passions." The following fragment praises Tonson and the long line of English poets who have been published on his family's press. The fifth epistle addresses a fastidious critic who deprecates the literature of the present age, and the sixth offers a cultural itinerary to a friend about to embark on a tour of Italy.

The concerns of these six poems are also central to the epistle to Hanmer: the welfare of the English stage, the relationship between poetry and its sister arts, and a sense of the immense inheritance to be enjoyed and emulated by contemporary poets. The Drafts and Fragments reveal the broad range of knowledge Collins has already attained, but they also suggest a view of literary history far less mature (and far more comfortable) than that posed in the major odes. The problem of imitation is in fact the subject of the fifth fragment, the epistle addressed to a narrow critic. The circumvention of past achievements seems far less difficult for the youthful poet than for his friend, the "Chast Athenian":

> Ah where on Thames shall Gentle Dodsley find
> The Verse contriv'd for so correct a Mind?
> Or How shall Hayman trembling as you gaze
> Obtain one breath of such unwilling praise?
> Go Then in all unsatisfied complain
> Of Time's Mistake in Waller's desprate strain

> For Ah untimely cam'st Thou forth Indeed
> With whom Originals Alone succeed!
> Go as Thou wilt, require the bliss denied
> To call back Art and live e'er Carlo died.
>
> (ll. 29-38)

Lonsdale has justly noted that Collins's conventional exposition of the sister arts here, his respect for Addison, Rowe, and Waller, and his caution about the possibility of original genius in the modern writer "all point to an early stage in the formation of Collins's thinking about literature and practice as a poet."[37] Clearly Collins did not consider the "bliss denied" to him during these formative years, and yet the poems themselves do not suggest the ways in which he was to fashion his own literary achievement. Neither in this epistle nor in the others—nor in the elegies and occasional piece—can we find the crucial fusion of elements that seems so suddenly to have enabled him to create the odes of 1746. For a clearer understanding of Collins's development of a mode that contains in itself "some original principle of growth" we must turn to the odes themselves.

4

The Odes *of 1746*

The publication of the *Odes on Several Descriptive and Allegoric Subjects* in December 1746 marks a crucial turning point in Collins's poetic development. His early poetry reveals how carefully he patterned his own career on classical and neoclassical models, but the poems in this slim volume indicate how sharply his work finally diverges from conventional patterns and standard (epic, or at least mock-epic) forms.[1] Collins's mature poetry clearly takes a different direction (a different *"channel,"* as Warton put it) from Pope's, and yet, as we have already seen, the transition itself is difficult to pin down. What remains most clear is the distinctive fusion of elements that made the evolution of the *Odes* possible in Collins's career: the subject matter of the odes—poetry itself and the various human situations it depicts—is drawn from the verse-epistles; the generalized and polished form of the ode is derived, at least in part, from the early lyrics; and the personal voice of the odes is adapted from the epistle to Hanmer and the elegies. Johnson's "original principle of growth," so difficult to distinguish in the imitations, finally finds its proper roots in this fusion of early tendencies, in the development of personified figures, and in the collaborative ferment that Warton seems to have brought to Collins's career.

I. The Growth of the Ode

Joseph Warton's letter to his brother, in which he announces his collaboration with Collins in a joint poetic venture, indicates that both young poets had already written odes independently before they met in late May of 1746: "I wrote out for him my Odes, and he likewise communicated some of his to me. . . . You will see a very pretty one of Collins's, on the death of Colonel Ross before Tournay. It is addressed to a lady who was Ross's intimate acquaintance, and who by the way is Miss Bett Goddard."[2] Warton's account suggests that their exchange may have been lopsided: Collins communicated only "some of his" poems. It would be helpful if we knew which odes these were (and how many others had already been written), but Warton's letter at least indicates that the "Ode, to a Lady" was not the only poem Collins was able to write out for his friend. Warton, for his part, seems to have had his volume of odes well in hand by the time of their meeting; but we cannot be certain that they all had been written by this date, nor that they were not extensively revised after Warton had read Collins's work. We do know, however, that Warton was working on his ode "To Fancy" earlier in the year, and it is possible that Collins's draft poem "To Simplicity," which is initially addressed to Fancy, may have been influenced by this poem.[3] The amount of information concerning this important period in Collins's career is scanty, but what evidence we do have focuses our attention on poems in which we can clearly see the evolution of the ode: the "Ode, to a Lady" and its subsequent revisions, and the "Ode to Simplicity" and its predecessor, Fragment 9.

The "Ode to a Lady, On the Death of Col. Charles Ross, in the Action at Fontenoy. Written May, 1745" was published in Dodsley's *Museum* on 7 June 1746. The date of its publication, barely a fortnight after Collins's meeting with Warton, suggests that he had the poem in fairly polished form when he showed it to his friend (and that he may well have written it in May of the preceding year, as the title states). The battle of Fontenoy had been fought on 11 May 1745; the Duke of Cumberland, directing the allied forces, had been defeated by the French. Among the casualties was Capt. Charles Ross who, although he probably was not one of Collins's friends, was an "intimate acquaintance" of Elizabeth Goddard, whom Collins may have met in the small village of Harting, north of Chichester.[4] Collins substantially revised the poem for its inclusion in the *Odes* of December, and made further changes when it appeared in Dodsley's *Collection* in 1748. Thomas Warton also pointed out that he had seen Collins's original manuscript of the poem, and it too varied in some respects from the first printing in the *Museum*.[5] These numerous revisions, especially the alterations made after the first printing, cast an in-

teresting light on Collins's struggle to create a workable form for the ode.
The "Ode, to a Lady" opens in grand, mythological terms:

> While, lost to all his former Mirth,
> *Britannia*'s Genius bends to Earth,
>   And mourns the fatal Day:
> While stain'd with Blood he strives to tear
> Unseemly from his Sea-green Hair
>   The Wreaths of chearful *May*.
>
> (ll. 1-6)

Collins begins to describe the lady's loss by picturing the lament of
the entire English nation. The mythic figure of "*Britannia*'s Genius"
has, like us, been caught off guard by Ross's death. Normally a festive
creature, especially in "chearful *May*," the wreathed Genius must suddenly tear the amorous garlands from his hair as he prepares to mourn
his nation's loss. His annual preoccupation with love and renewal, reflected in his laurels and green hair, provides an ironic counterpoint
to the soldier's death and the lady's lament. Collins turns to the lady
herself in the poem's second stanza, where the continued use of personification reminds us of the extended range of his lament. Prompted
by pity and remembrance, the lady muses on her soldier's fate while
her active imagination, relentless and unkind, keeps the nightmarish
image of "the bleeding Friend" sharply in view.

The spectre of the bleeding Ross serves as a transition to the third
stanza, in which Collins describes the countryside where the soldier
is buried and offers his first words of consolation:

> By rapid *Scheld*'s descending Wave
> His Country's Vows shall bless the Grave,
>   Where'er the Youth is laid:
> That sacred Spot the Village Hind
> With ev'ry sweetest Turf shall bind,
>   And Peace protect the Shade.
>
> (ll. 13-18)

Although the "descending Wave" accentuates the soldier's descent
and the roaring catastrophe that has engulfed him, it also marks a
"sacred Spot" hallowed by his death, consecrated by a grateful nation,
and tended by the local hind. Ross's final resting place, though vague,
is made familiar for the lady's sake; it crowns a rural scene in which
Britannia's Genius would find himself at home. Peace protects the
shade that cloaks the grave, and the shade that lies within it.

The following stanza promises consolation of a different kind:

> Ev'n now, regardful of his Doom,
> Applauding *Honour* haunts his Tomb,
>   With shadowy Trophies crown'd:
> Whilst *Freedom*'s Form beside her roves
> Majestic thro' the twilight Groves,
>   And calls her Heroes round.

> (ll. 19-24, *Museum* text)

The previous stanza predicted what *would* happen; here the poet emphasizes events that are already taking place. "Ev'n now" Honor haunts his tomb and Freedom glides through this twilight world. And Freedom, as she calls her heroes round, offers her own consolation in the following lines: "The warlike Dead of ev'ry Age, / Who fill the fair recording Page, / Shall leave their sainted Rest" and pay appropriate tribute as they "hail the blooming Guest" (ll. 25-27, 30). The poet consoles the lady by predicting that Ross will in time ascend to the ranks of these early heroes, "half-reclining" on their disused spears.

But in the final two stanzas Collins appears to admit that even these consolations may not be enough. If, in her constant sorrow, the lady can only see Ross as a fallen victim, if her unkind imagination continues to paint distressful scenes that the poet's "pictur'd Glories" cannot displace, then at least she will be able to find consolation in a faithful and attentive Muse who will keep her "gentlest Promise" with "social Grief." The poet's imagination may not rival the productions of a grieving mind, but it may offer, in its "sad repeated Tale," an appropriate tribute to Ross that will keep his memory alive. The poem itself serves as an enduring commemorative when a nation's vows and Honor's "shadowy Trophies" fail.

The "Ode, to a Lady" surely marks a new direction in Collins's poetry. The poem is more of an occasional piece than the early elegies and more intimate and direct than the early epistles, and in this fusion of elegiac and epistolary elements we can finally discern the characteristic form of Collins's odes. At the same time, the characteristic structure of Collins's mature odes seems lacking in this first version of the "Ode, to a Lady." The poem lacks a specific focus that binds the diverse elements together, a central personification that controls the action and imagery. Collins's revisions of the ode, completed before its republication in the *Odes* in December, however, suggest just this kind of development. At the heart of these revisions is an expansion of the central allegorical figures in the ode. The poem's fourth stanza, in which Honor and Freedom haunt the tomb in the first version, is focused in its revised form on a tearful Honor, now pictured as a masculine figure who calls "his Heros round." Freedom now enters the poem in three additional stanzas that expand Collins's roll-call of the "warlike Dead of ev'ry Age." And although her entrance occurs later than in the original version, she dominates the ode's "pictur'd Glories":

> But lo where, sunk in deep Despair,
> Her Garments torn, her Bosom bare,
>   Impatient *Freedom* lies!
> Her matted Tresses madly spread,
> To ev'ry Sod, which wraps the Dead,
>   She turns her joyless Eyes.
>
> Ne'er shall she leave that lowly Ground,
> Till Notes of Triumph bursting round
>   Proclaim her Reign restor'd:
> Till *William* seek the sad Retreat,
> And bleeding at her sacred Feet,
>   Present the sated Sword.

(ll. 37-48)

These stanzas, as many of Collins's critics have pointed out, are poetically disappointing, but they serve a double purpose: Collins extends his vision of British heroes to the present day by inciting the Duke of Cumberland to victory and peace, and he also provides a central personification (in Freedom) that defines the value of warlike action. The argument he presents to the lady in the ode remains unimpaired, but the revisions more clearly emphasize the context of valor and freedom in which Ross's death must be viewed. Ross's death is as significant here as in the earlier version, but it is subsumed by the central figure of Freedom, who now provides a mythic parallel to the Genius of the opening lines. The revisions show that Collins is striving toward a more generalized conception of action in the ode; in its ultimate form this action will displace individuals entirely and will, as in the "Ode, Written in the beginning of the Year 1746," replace them with the abstract "Brave, who sink to Rest, / By all their Country's Wishes blest!"

We can isolate a similar structural and thematic tightening by comparing Collins's Fragment 9, "To Simplicity," with the "Ode to Simplicity" that appeared in his volume of odes. In spite of its title, the draft of an ode "To Simplicity" opens with an address to Fancy, who is the first of Collins's allegorical figures to dominate an entire poem. Collins views her as a neglected bride, "betrayd" and "cheated" so long by artists that she now weds her heart to the mere "Toys and

Pageant" of art. Although she was once the "Thrice Gentle Guide" of the three exalted arts, she has long since abandoned chaste thought for more common triumphs. Collins asks her, in the following stanzas, to relinquish her "enfeebling dreams" and to return in all her ancient strength: "bid our Britain hear thy Græcian Song" (l. 12). He fashions a mythological tableau that emphasizes her Greek origins and her association with ancient tragedy, and he reminds her, in the fourth stanza, of her didactic powers. At this point in the fragment, however, we begin to notice Collins's shift in focus: the figure he addresses is still Fancy (the creative imagination), but his stress now falls on the specific attributes (simplicity of thought and expression) she has lost.

The closing stanzas of the poem attempt to define the quality of simplicity more fully. In painting, the traditional collaboration of the understated graces of art with the "impassion'd line" of "Feeling Nature" has been deserted in favor of "wild Excess" and "wild design." In the poet's own domain ("'midst my Cave in breathing Marble wrought"), Simplicity is asked to preside over the speaker's heart, charm his sight, and prompt his temperate thought. The poet, in turn, will create an appropriate tribute for the figure he has successfully invoked:

> And when soft Maids and Swains
> Reward my Native Strains
> With flow'rs that chastest bloom and sweetest breathe
> I loveliest Nymph Divine
> Will own the merits thine
> And round thy temples bind the modest wreath.
>
> (ll. 37-42)

Collins finally proposes a revival of ancient simplicity and strength, and, as in the epistle to Hanmer, he will place his wreath at its proper shrine. But only in the deftly concealed pun on "temples" does he suggest any complexity or ingenuity in his visualization of this goddess. The words Collins chooses to describe this maid—gentle, simple, modest, soft, sweet, chaste, temperate, and yet impassioned—show the nature of the classical art he wishes to revive, but the relentless repetition of the descriptive diction and the eventual shift in focus suggest that the fragment survives in a far from finished state. Just as telling, perhaps, is the absence of a sustained objective correlative that would unify the various qualities Collins invokes.[6] Collins's finished ode resolves this central deficiency, however, by presenting an allegorical figure that is carefully fleshed out in the poem's nine stanzas.

Collins draws upon two different forms of allegory to describe Simplicity in the ode: the first, second, fifth, and eighth stanzas highlight aspects of the idea of simplicity through analysis; the third, fourth, sixth, and seventh stanzas celebrate historical manifestations of this personified quality by example.[7] (This two-edged technique, we should add, lies at the heart of most of Collins's mature work.) To a certain extent, however, these allegorical practices merge in each stanza, and it may prove more profitable for us to approach the allegorical structure of the ode by sensing the intricate balance of the stanzas. The first four stanzas define Simplicity by embodying this quality in a central allegorical figure and her background. The first stanza presents her genealogy; the second describes her clothing; the third emphasizes the Greek culture and tragic poet (Sophocles) with which she is intimately associated; and the fourth ties her to the Grecian countryside, the site of political freedom. These stanzas anticipate Collins's vigorous invocation of his goddess in the central stanza of the poem. The first two stanzas, moreover, are directly addressed to Simplicity, and actually anticipate this later invocation ("O Thou . . . to Thee I call!"); the third and fourth stanzas specify the qualities and powers by which this invocation is to be made ("By all the honey'd Store . . . By old *Cephisus* deep . . . "). Collins's cry for an infusion of the goddess into his own life and works follows in the fifth stanza, the central scene of the poem and, appropriately, the point at which he will emphasize the ordering power of this goddess. The final four stanzas depict Simplicity's progress and decline, the antagonism of the poet's contemporaries, and his own desire to bring about the infusion of Simplicity that he had first called for in the center of his poem.

The comparative structural unity of the ode is also reflected in the increasingly complex nature of Collins's allegory. In the fragment Collins defined Simplicity (or Fancy) merely by voicing her qualities and tentatively suggesting her cultural context. In the "Ode to Simplicity," however, we must unravel the intricate fabric of the poem to isolate her specific qualities. In the fragment, for instance, Collins briefly pictures Fancy as an infant lying on the shores of her native Greece, quietly learning the ways by which her own "persuasive Ease" can substantiate the powers of Wisdom and Truth. In the final ode, Collins presents a full portrait of Simplicity's origins:

> O Thou by *Nature* taught,
> To breathe her genuine Thought,
> In Numbers warmly pure, and sweetly strong:
> Who first on Mountains wild,

> In *Fancy* loveliest Child,
> Thy Babe, or *Pleasure's*, nurs'd the Pow'rs of Song!

(ll. 1-6)

These lines suggest Simplicity's important role as a mediator. She learns her first lessons directly from Nature, and supplies them in turn to Fancy (and imagination, Collins hints, may perhaps be the actual offspring of this goddess).[8] Both the relationship between Fancy and Simplicity and the nature of Simplicity itself are made more specific here. Simplicity in art finds its original in Nature; it then becomes the "genuine Thought" derived from the object of contemplation, and finally finds expression in simple verse ("Numbers warmly pure, and sweetly strong").[9] The elaboration of Simplicity's genealogy helps define her specific attributes and establishes the process by which simplicity in art is realized. The musical mode of instruction suggests the early stages of this artistic development and provides an important link with the inspiration (literal breathing) that the poet will call for in the central and final stanzas. In the fragment Collins considers music as a separate discipline and simply groups it with the other arts ("Thrice Gentle Guide of each exalted Art!"), but in the ode he fashions a myth that reveals music to be an essential element of Simplicity's power.

Collins's description of his goddess's appearance points to a similar sophistication of poetical statement in which Simplicity's attributes are embodied in the symbolic nature of her dress:

> Thou, who with Hermit Heart
> Disdain'st the Wealth of Art,
> And Gauds, and pageant Weeds, and trailing Pall:
> But com'st a decent Maid
> In *Attic* Robe array'd,
> O chaste unboastful Nymph, to Thee I call!

(ll. 7-12)

The goddess's clothing suggests the classical restraint and beauty of ancient art; her apparel, like the language of poetry, lacks any unnecessary adornment. She appears to us as a "decent" (suitable) maid, and her clothing reflects her natural beauty. There is, as Crider notes, a measure of primitivism in Collins's portrait: Simplicity is depicted as a quality of Fancy in her earliest manifestations; she shuns the "Wealth of Art" and models her heart on the spirituality of the hermit.[10] In particular, she disdains the fustian costumes of the drama ("Gauds, and pageant Weeds, and trailing Pall"), which now replace, in more concrete fashion, the slackly sketched "Toys and Pageant" of the fragment. The vague Greek landscape of the unfinished ode "To Simplicity," moreover, is given a sharper focus in the incantation by which the poet invokes his goddess. Collins explicitly links "*Hybla's* Thymy Shore" and the lovelorn nightingale with Sophoclean tragedy (and implies that Simplicity first found a poetic utterance in his verse). In the fourth stanza, the Boeotian river Cephisus provides another appropriate haunt for Simplicity. Milton, in his tenth sonnet, had decried "that dishonest victory / At *Chæronéa*, fatal to liberty" (ll. 6-7), which was won by Philip of Macedon on the banks of this river. Collins's description of the river's "enamel'd Side" where "holy *Freedom* died" subtly alludes to Milton's poem and anticipates the corresponding decline of Simplicity depicted in the later stanzas of the poem.

In the central stanza of the ode, however, Collins attempts to invoke this goddess's still vital powers:

> O Sister meek of Truth,
> To my admiring Youth,
> Thy sober Aid and native Charms infuse!
> The Flow'rs that sweetest breathe,
> Tho' Beauty cull'd the Wreath,
> Still ask thy Hand to range their order'd Hues.

> (ll. 25-30)

Collins's plea is more extensive than has been realized. The poet asks Simplicity to become part of him, to be "infused" into his "admiring Youth." The focus is primarily literary, as the metaphor of the culled flowers suggests; but Collins also requests that ancient simplicity become an essential part of him, that sobriety and artless ("native") charms adorn his life as well as his poetry. He calls for a fusion of his spirit with Simplicity's that will lead, in turn, to an increased ability on his part to inspirit her qualities in his own sweet and breathing lines. The quality Collins stresses lies in Simplicity's power to order nature as well as to interpret it. Beauty may cull the sweetest flowers, but she still relies upon Simplicity to arrange "their order'd Hues." Simplicity lies in the ordering of disparate parts into a unified, organic whole, but Collins's description of this power also applies to the ordering of one's "admiring Youth." Simplicity, Collins emphasizes once again, is a mediating force; its design can be seen in the artistic artifact, in the object it represents, and in the artist who interprets and expresses this design.

Collins specifically links this artistic vitality with political freedom. The sixth and seventh stanzas of the ode suggest that Simplicity pertains to a state of mind necessary for the production of great poetry, and that this attitude is nurtured and sustained by freedom, a quality akin to naturalness and spontaneity.[11] This assumption pervades the entire volume of odes and helps explain why Collins so often adopts historical situations as the subject or background for his work: political liberty and individual freedom provide the essential climate for an unfettered imagination. And yet the final two stanzas of this ode insist once again that imaginative exuberance must rely upon classical restraint; Freedom nourishes Fancy, but Fancy and Freedom both rely on Simplicity's ordering powers:

> Tho' Taste, tho' Genius bless,
> To some divine Excess,
> Faints the cold Work till Thou inspire the whole.
>
> (ll. 43-45)

The road of excess may well lead to the palace of wisdom, but—in Collins, at least—it does not do so without the chaste warmth that Simplicity provides. Simplicity is not in itself a limiting force; it is, in fact, an essential element in the sublime ("Thou, only Thou can'st raise the meeting Soul!"). Simplicity is not dissociated from genius and divine excess; it simply controls them.

In the final stanza of the poem, Collins contents himself with a more modest achievement:

> Of These let others ask,
> To aid some mighty Task,
> I only seek to find thy temp'rate Vale:
> Where oft my Reed might sound
> To Maids and Shepherds round,
> And all thy Sons, O *Nature*, learn my Tale.
>
> (ll. 49-54)

This is clearly not the attempted sublime of the "Ode to Fear," the "Ode on the Poetical Character," or "The Passions," but it helps define the alternative voice of the "Ode to Evening" and "How Sleep the Brave." Collins's conclusion here is not unlike the final stanza of his fragment, but it insists, more forcefully than does the earlier poem, on the skillful structuring that must inform even the most temperate and humble of poetical works. The qualities of simplicity, fully pictured in the ode and directly invoked in the central stanza, are finally "infused" in the poet's own productions. Even these modest works, if properly fashioned and performed by an inspired piper, will find an appreciative audience in those who share the poet's concern for simplicity of thought and expression.

II. Structure and Personification

The final versions of the "Ode, to a Lady" and the "Ode to Simplicity" reveal the kind of poetic unity Collins wished to create in each of his allegorical odes. The transition from the early poems should now be clear: the digressions and independent scenes in the *Oriental Eclogues* and the *Epistle* have become poems in their own right, each focusing on an abstract quality and animated by a central personification. The originality of Collins's personification lies at the heart of his contribution to allegorical poetry; the richness and vitality of his central figures enable him to forge a unified and self-sufficient form that relies on imagery rather than conventional allegorical action for its success.[12]

The first ode in Collins's volume, the "Ode to Pity," displays this structural cohesiveness with considerable skill. Collins carefully paired the "Ode to Pity" with the "Ode to Fear": both poems analyze the emotions Aristotle said were raised and purged in tragedy. Collins intended to translate and provide a commentary on *The Poetics* in 1744 or 1745, and he in fact draws on Aristotle's treatise in a footnote to the poem.[13] This first ode suggests the aesthetic subjects raised throughout the collection and, just as important, provides Collins's readers with an introduction to the kind of poetry to be found in the ensuing odes.

The "Ode to Pity" has often been singled out as Collins's "purest" or archetypal ode by those who emphasize the poem's characteristic invocation, descriptions, and development as well as its similarities—in voice and structure—to traditional forms of prayer.[14] This emphasis on the religious quality of the speaker's supplication is clearly justified by the opening lines of the ode, where the personified figure is endowed with magical powers and addressed as a goddess:

> O Thou, the Friend of Man assign'd,
> With balmy Hands his Wounds to bind,
> And charm his frantic Woe:
> When first *Distress* with Dagger keen
> Broke forth to waste his destin'd Scene,
> His wild unsated Foe!
>
> (ll. 1-6)

Pity appears to man as his guardian and nurse; she has been "assign'd" to him long ago, when distress first entered his world. She is an enchanting figure, able to "charm" and distract us from our "wild unsated Foe" even if she cannot restore our "destin'd Scene." This "Scene," moreover, suggests the dramatic (perhaps melodramatic) setting of the entire stanza, and Pity, of course, functions within this theatrical setting both as a conventional emotional quality and as Aristotle's tragic pity, closely linked with dramatic catharsis.[15]

The spectacle we witness involves only two characters—the poet and the goddess he invokes—but the invocation in turn reveals another dramatic scene, enacted within the speaker, as he attempts to conjure up this figure and her attendant train. The speaker, of course, attempts to describe and analyze this elusive quality by giving it external form; but the extraordinary vividness of Collins's initial personification almost causes us to forget that he is actually describing an intricate emotional process. The depiction of Distress, for instance, closely resembles passages in the *Oriental Eclogues* (especially the laments of Hassan and Agib), but Collins's emphasis here is on an internal and not an external threat. Distress breaks forth from within us; his "Dagger keen" is felt as he escapes his captivity. In his portrayal of "the Friend of Man," Collins may have had in mind the figure of the Good Samaritan, whose balm was indeed applied externally; but the "Wounds" that Pity binds, we must remember, are associated with emotional, not physical, distress.[16]

The ode's invocation is followed by a formal obsecration:

> By *Pella*'s Bard, a magic Name,
> By all the Griefs his Thought could frame,
>   Receive my humble Rite:
> Long, *Pity*, let the Nations view
> Thy sky-worn Robes of tend'rest Blue,
>   And Eyes of dewy Light!
>
> (ll. 7-12)

We have encountered this form of magical incantation before in the "Ode to Simplicity"; here Collins entreats his goddess to receive his humble rite by invoking an earlier favorite—Euripides—who in a footnote to the poem is styled the "Master of the tender Passions." The obsecration is succeeded by the long-admired portrait of Pity, depicted in synaesthetic language and in an attitude that suggests the iconographic forms of Ben Jonson's masques.[17] These descriptive lines also introduce the formulaic statement that furnishes the prayer with its particular power. Collins hopes to project the past into the future: he invokes the suffering Euripides portrayed in his tragedies to ensure Pity's unbroken reign ("Long, *Pity,* let the Nations view . . . "). Collins's invocation is based on a traditional form of prayer: "Even as thou didst of old, so do also now."[18] This prayer, moreover, is closely linked to the traditional theme of cultural and political progress. The third and fourth stanzas depict this historical progress in highly condensed form, but the principle is as deeply embedded here as it is in the "Ode to Liberty." The playwright Otway serves as an intermediate figure between Pella's bard and Collins himself. Pity, together with her *signa* of wren, myrtle, and doves, has already revealed herself to the infant Otway in Collins's native Sussex; surely she can be induced to appear again.[19] The manifestations of Pity in past literary and cultural history are therefore part of the progress theme that runs throughout the odes, and they are related, in turn, to the nature of the prayer that lends the odes their structure.

The pattern of prayer is continued in the poem's fifth stanza, which has been characterized as the presentation of need and consequent wish for the goddess to dwell within the suppliant, and even as a formal religious offering:[20]

> Come, *Pity*, come, by Fancy's Aid,
> Ev'n now my Thoughts, relenting Maid,
>   Thy Temple's Pride design:
> Its Southern Site, its Truth compleat
> Shall raise a wild Enthusiast Heat,
>   In all who view the Shrine.
>
> (ll. 25-30)

Pity will finally be evoked by means of Fancy; she now appears as an imaginative presence, the original model for the artful and religious shrine the poet will erect (like Euripides) in his own "Thoughts." Although Collins's images are not specific, "Picture's Toils" (l. 31) are apparently devoted to a portrayal of "each disastrous Tale" of ancient tragedy in a gallery echoing the expressive pictures of the epistle to Hanmer. In particular, the imaginative luxuriance of the shrine's southern wall is said to raise a "wild Enthusiast Heat" in viewers who, as in the "Ode to Simplicity," come with a "meeting Soul."[21]

Collins's final stanza indicates that this is a temple in which the poet himself can live:

> There let me oft, retir'd by Day,
> In Dreams of Passion melt away,
>   Allow'd with Thee to dwell:
> There waste the mournful Lamp of Night,
> Till, Virgin, Thou again delight
>   To hear a *British* Shell!
>
> (ll. 37-42)

The comparison of this passage with the formal dedication at the end of a prayer is especially suggestive, for the poet not only expresses his sacred declaration to Pity but literally gives himself up (devotes himself) to this emotional force.[22] This devotion approximates virtual dissolution: he will "melt away" into the dreams of passion he has created within the splendors of his temple. But Pity's shrine, after all, is located in the poet's mind. In these lines Collins hopes to suggest his own psychological readiness; he has prepared himself to receive this goddess's "indwelling" by erecting that dwelling himself and placing himself within it. There he will await the goddess's return, which is associated not only with a resurgence of pity but with the restoration of a poetry of pathos.

Collins's final dedication to Pity also borrows heavily from "L'Allegro" and "Il Penseroso," and the organization of Milton's companion poems reveals yet another structural pattern that lies behind these odes.[23] But these structural elements are closely entwined, as we have seen. The central figure of the ode is depicted pictorially; Collins places her in a heroic landscape while also drawing on the iconographical nature of the masque. Her personified train of attributes and companions in turn suggests the animating principles of the poetical progress, a progress that appears in the ode as an element of prayer and in the mode of the Miltonic setting. In the "Ode to Pity," as well as in the other poems, the unfolding of the masque, pageant, prayer, or progress involves the dramatic presentation, confrontation, and resolution of these emotional forces. To speak of one pattern in the odes is to invoke all of them.

I nevertheless wish to isolate the dramatic structure of the ode in order to focus on the complexity of Collins's personifying process. Crider has noticed how often Collins opens his odes by creating a dramatic scene in which the speaker and personification eventually exchange roles: "In Collins' odes the personification is no longer a means but an end, the focal point of the whole, invoked and supplicated as 'Thou,' an object which is also a subject and before which the poet feels himself an object." The poet therefore becomes an actor in his own drama: "In the progress piece the poet typically addresses his audience about an object. Collins speaks not to his audience but to the personification, while the audience looks on and overhears."[24]

I find the implications of this argument especially intriguing. Crider's description of the relationship between the poet and his audience echoes John Stuart Mill's dictum that lyric poetry is not "heard, but overheard,"[25] and suggests a change in point of view that distinguishes Collins's poetry from the epistles, progress pieces, and didactic poetry of his immediate predecessors. But how is the poet able to dismiss his audience so completely? Clearly the confrontation between the speaker and the object he contemplates is fraught with such dramatic importance that it requires his entire attention. The speaker is completely absorbed by the spectacle he views (and creates); and, as we have seen in the "Ode to Pity," the speaker is actually absorbed *into* the object of his contemplation ("In Dreams of Passion melt away, / Allow'd with Thee to dwell"). This theme of absorption, as Michael Fried has shown, is central to much French painting in this period, but we can see it at work in the poetry of the time as well.[26] Fried argues that the audience, neglected and thereby "neutralized" by the painter, is consequently able to enter the artist's scene in a manner precluded by the normal frame or barrier of conventional paintings (in which the painter's figures eye us directly). Drawn into the painting, the viewer is implicitly absorbed into the contemplative world he beholds. Fried's analysis appears to have particular relevance to Collins's strategy, for the personification that we and the speaker behold are actually qualities that we, like the speaker, either share or have lost. Collins implicitly invites us to join his search for these emotional forces, to absorb these qualities into our own lives.

But if this psychological reintegration is to be successful, the speaker must first enact it within himself. The suggestion that the poet and the personified object exchange roles indicates the process by which this absorption becomes possible. The poet is the grammatical subject of his poem (the "I" of the "Ode to Pity," for example), but the thematic subject is an abstract quality that, once bodied forth by the poet, becomes an object of such admiration that the speaker quickly "subjects" himself to its force. The poet and the personification, in other words, are both subject and object, and in their eventual exchange of roles lies the dramatic recognition (Aristotle's *anagnorisis*) that makes their ultimate fusion possible.[27] The speaker's recognition of the nature of this quality leads to his identification with it and to his ultimate desire to have his spirit newly infused. We have seen this identification at work in the "Ode to Fear" ("Like Thee I start, like Thee disorder'd fly"), and this infusion invoked in the "Ode to Simplicity" ("To my admiring Youth, / Thy sober Aid and native Charms infuse!").[28]

The emotion, as we have seen, must be externalized and analyzed before it can once again be absorbed. In the "Ode to Pity," for example, the speaker first calls forth the spirit of pity (in general) and thus the capacity for pity in himself. In invoking pity as a goddess, however, he places himself in a subordinate position: if he is to receive Pity, she must take pity on him. He must also be worthy of her visitation, and this he hopes to demonstrate by creating works infused with an appropriate emotion and by erecting a habitation for her (in his own mind). The works he will write, build, or paint, moreover, will evoke pity in those who view them. Thus by isolating, understanding, and refining this emotional quality in himself, the poet will be able to elicit it, and make it more fully comprehensible, in others. This psychological process resembles the external progress of the ode, but its most crucial moments exist in those scenes where the speaker equates himself with the object he invokes. Their relationship, Collins implies, is reciprocal: Pity is portrayed as a "relenting Maid," a goddess who causes us to relent and who must herself relent if she is to visit us. The speaker similarly aspires "In Dreams of Passion [to] melt away, / Allow'd with Thee to dwell"; he will melt into his own dreams, that is, if Pity herself will "melt" by allowing him to dwell with her. Here, as elsewhere, a coalescence of subject and object (or of dramatic functions) successfully allows the speaker to reintegrate this emotional quality into his own psyche.

Collins's personifications appear as both subject and object because they are conceived as reflexive figures. Thus Fear, when she first appears, is described as "appall'd" and "frantic," a goddess who is fearful of the horrid train of monsters that follows her. But later in the ode Collins reveals that Fear herself is fearsome: he will "know" her by listening to his throbbing heart; he will receive inspiration from her "with'ring Pow'r." Still later he addresses her as a "Dark Pow'r":

> And lest thou meet my blasted View,
> Hold each strange Tale devoutly true;
> Ne'er be I found, by Thee o'eraw'd,
> In that thrice-hallow'd Eve abroad.

> (ll. 56-59)

This reflexiveness reaches its height in "The Passions," where Fear is shown to be afraid even of "the Sound himself had made." Like several of the other characters in Collins's musical ode (Joy and Chearfulness in particular) he is both an emotion's cause and its recipient. Collins, of course, draws on an allegorical convention in presenting both "sides" of his personified characters. Sidney, in one of his sonnets, closely foreshadows Collins's portrait of Fear: "A Satyre once did runne away for dread, / With sound of horne, which he him selfe did blow, / Fearing and feared thus from himselfe he fled, / Deeming strange evill in that he did not know."[29] And Spenser, in his depiction of the House of Pride, emphasizes similar characteristics in the seven deadly sins: Gluttony gorges himself and paradoxically starves himself to death; Envy preys on others although "inwardly he chawed his owne maw"

(*Faerie Queene* I.iv.30). Like his predecessors, Collins is able to represent the broad range of our emotional responses in the complexity (and reflexivity) of his central figures.

Personification lends Collins's poetry its unity and structure, its pictorial suggestiveness, and its linguistic complexity. It also lies at the heart of the psychological drama in the *Odes*, providing the grounds for discovering the nature of emotional or moral qualities and establishing a framework of dramatic confrontation in which these qualities are ultimately absorbed or infused. In building his odes around a personified figure, Collins clearly hit on a new principle of growth for his work, but, as Earl Wasserman has shown, his personification should not be thought of as simply a poetical device. Personification "is not merely a poetic symbol through which an idea is perceptible, nor a rhetorical language translatable into an idea. Were it only that, one might justifiably object that the physical imagery is too scanty to clothe thought, that it restricts while thought expands." The image actually *is* the abstraction, "for abstract ideas and their attendant values cannot otherwise be given linguistic form."[30] Wasserman carefully examines eighteenth-century aesthetic theory to document the epistemological validity of personification, a process writers considered "semantically as close an approximation as possible to the human understanding of an abstraction." Externalizing moral abstractions, moreover, "is not merely rhetorical in purpose, but is assumed to follow logically from the natural kinship of the physical and moral worlds."[31] The principal charm of personification, Hugh Blair wrote, is "that it introduces us into society with all nature, and interests us, even in inanimate objects, by forming a connexion between them and us, through that sensibility which it ascribes to them."[32] Blair and other contemporary theorists describe a phenomenon of discovery and identification that we have already seen at work in Collins's odes: personification provides our way of knowing, and stresses our natural kinship with the qualities it bodies forth.

But even as we strive to claim our natural kinship with these qualities, we must remember that they are often portrayed as shadowy and indeterminate forces. Collins manipulates many of the most striking features of his odes—the cloudy imagery of the "Ode to Fear," the pervasive ambiguity and obscurity of the "Ode on the Poetical Character," and (as we shall see) the subtle blendings in those poems that focus on the particulars of nature—to create a characteristic indeterminacy of language and idea. What we witness in his poetry, especially at those moments of confrontation and transcendence, is a fundamental revaluation of that which is hidden, dark, and difficult, and of the imagery by which the obscure is represented.

Burke was to pay particular attention to the value of obscurity in the second part of his treatise on the sublime: "To make any thing very terrible," he states, "obscurity seems in general to be necessary. When we know the full extent of any danger, when we can accustom our eyes to it, a great deal of the apprehension vanishes."[33] Burke consequently offers an interesting interpretation of the cloudy shapes and shadowy forms in which Collins cloaks his personified emotions. "It is one thing to make an idea clear," Burke writes, "and another to make it *affecting* to the imagination"; and in his analysis of passages in *Paradise Lost*, passages with which Collins was certainly familiar, Burke argues that "The mind is hurried out of itself, by a croud of great and confused images; which affect because they are crouded and confused. For separate them, and you lose much of the greatness, and join them, and you infallibly lose the clearness."[34] Similarly, in his commentary on a passage in the book of Job, Burke states that the sublimity we experience there is "principally due to the terrible uncertainty of the thing described."[35] These remarks provide ample justification for the mechanics of what we might call the "emotional" or "psychological" sublime. Just how profound a change has taken place can be gauged by comparing Burke's statements with Johnson's pronouncements on language in the *Idler*, the *Adventurer*, and his "Life of Cowley," where obscurity is thought to counteract "the first end of writing," and where there is little appreciation of inherent ambiguity, unresolved paradox, or deep-lying irony of meaning.[36]

In his own poetry Collins begins to develop an imagery and sense of the transcendent moment that are later associated with other cloudy scenes of confrontation and insight, near the Simplon Pass or on the sides of Snowden. But he also, and perhaps more significantly, suggests the importance of shadowy truths that are still to be grasped even if they lack the coherence and determinacy of visions presented with such assurance in *The Seasons* and *An Essay on Man*. This has been disparaged as the "cloudy Sublime,"[37] but, as we have already seen, Mrs. Barbauld understood that the very elusiveness of Collins's sublimity invested it with its characteristic power: "In his endeavours to embody the fleeting forms of mind, and clothe them with correspondent imagery, he is not unfrequently obscure; but even when obscure, the reader who possesses congenial feelings is not ill pleased to find his faculties put upon the stretch in the search of those sublime ideas which are apt, from their shadowy nature, to elude the grasp of the mind."[38] In his "Life of Collins" Johnson concluded that, if his friend's efforts "sometimes caused harshness and obscurity, they likewise produced in happier moments sublimity and splendour."[39] I would suggest, on the other hand, that it is precisely Collins's difficulty and obscurity that produces much of the sublimity and splendor we do find in his work.

III. The Scheme of the *Odes*

Ever since H. W. Garrod published the first major study of Collins in 1928, critics have argued whether or not the poet arranged his twelve odes in a coherent pattern or scheme. Garrod provoked the debate by stating that Collins's volume was "badly printed, very badly punctuated, and, in respect of its contents, ill arranged."[40] Garrod contended that the "Ode to Peace" was misplaced, that it belonged among the patriotic odes that form the central section of the volume (a section whose continuity is interrupted by the "Ode to Evening"). This distinction between the patriotic odes and the other poems in the volume has been refined by later critics, but their conclusions do not differ dramatically from Garrod's. One reader emphasizes Collins's interest in "the nature of the True Poet" and argues that each ode "is descriptive of one of the qualities or circumstances essential to the attainment" of the poet's stature; but he nevertheless divides the odes into three distinct groups (psychological, political, and natural), despite the difficulties in justifying this third category, which includes only the "Ode to Evening."[41] Ricardo Quintana also divides the odes into three groups: the first four and last two poems in the collection, he argues, are preoccupied with the different "kinds" of poetry (tragic, pastoral, moral, musical), whereas the five central odes are primarily patriotic; the "Ode to Evening" thus serves as a link between these two groups.[42] This last point, however, is particularly tenuous: some of the patriotic odes also suggest an elegiac or pastoral mood, but not all of them; some of the aesthetic odes are concerned with patriotism —and some with pastoralism—but not all of them. Quintana and others are on firmer ground when they analyze Collins's experimentation with different meters and with different poetical forms.[43]

These variations in form and meter actually suggest a principle of diversity and modulation rather than a strict thematic arrangement in Collins's collection, and I would argue that this emphasis on variety captures the spirit of the *Odes*. Collins specified in his title that his poems were based on "Several Descriptive and Allegoric Subjects." As we have seen, the descriptive and allegorical elements in the odes are tightly entwined, but the qualifying "several" in Collins's title indicates both "many" and "various" poetical subjects. Johnson defined "several" in this context as "Different; distinct; unlike one another," and it was this use of the word that Collins was surely familiar with in

the titles of Milton's *Poems, &c. upon Several Occasions* (1673) and
Akenside's *Odes on Several Subjects*. Warton similarly entitled his volume *Odes on Various Subjects*, and his poems, like Akenside's, cover a
broad range of topics. We sense this diversity of subject (as well as
meter and form) throughout Collins's volume. The titles of two odes
announce their specific occasions—the "Ode, to a Lady," and "Ode,
Written in the beginning of the Year 1746"—and the other three political poems are also closely tied to public events. Collins may have
entertained hopes of seeing "The Passions" performed on the stage,
but this ode, however, like the other "aesthetic" poems and the "Ode
to Evening," is an independent work, unconnected with any specific
event in the poet's life or the nation's history.

We might therefore ask if there is any single thematic concern that
binds these twelve odes together. As I have suggested, I believe that
one central concern is implied by the very nature of Collins's poetic
method and structure: the poet's predominant use of personification
—within each kind of ode—provides a consistent emphasis on the qualities that shape our emotional and moral life. This focus on what Collins
and his contemporaries called the "passions" can most easily be seen
in the odes to Pity and Fear, which merge these emotions with the
tragic forms that gave them expression, and in the volume's final ode,
entitled "The Passions," which is a poem for and about music and an
analysis of the entire spectrum of human emotional responses. But
even in the odes devoted to qualities that appear to lie outside our
emotional life (political mercy, peace, liberty, evening), Collins suggests a thematic connection by giving these qualities human form and
by portraying their influence on sensitive individuals.

Pope supplied a conventional but powerful definition of the passions
in *An Essay on Man*:

> Passions, like Elements, tho' born to fight,
> Yet, mix'd and soften'd, in his work unite:
> These 'tis enough to temper and employ;
> But what composes Man, can Man destroy?
> Suffice that Reason keep to Nature's road,
> Subject, compound them, follow her and God.
> Love, Hope, and Joy, fair pleasure's smiling train,
> Hate, Fear, and Grief, the family of pain;
> These mix'd with art, and to due bounds confin'd,
> Make and maintain the balance of the mind:
> The lights and shades, whose well accorded strife
> Gives all the strength and colour of our life.
>
> (II.111-22)

Although Collins was to explore the passions in a very different manner, his central concerns are nicely captured in Pope's couplets. The
simile of Pope's first line is more tightly constructed in an earlier passage in the poem:

> But ALL subsists by elemental strife;
> And Passions are the elements of Life.
> The gen'ral ORDER, since the whole began,
> Is kept in Nature, and is kept in Man.
>
> (I.169-72)

The passions are the basic components of our life; they must be ordered, and to be ordered they must first be understood. The burden
of ordering the passions falls upon man, who must reconcile the war-
ring factions of his soul. Pope suggests, in language that reminds us of
the "Ode on the Poetical Character," that both God and man must
function as artistic creators. His analogy is drawn from painting, and
his emphasis (as in Collins's "Ode to Evening") is placed on "composure" and "composition." Man is composed of diverse elements; he
must restrain and order these passions if he is to compose himself; and
in "composing" himself he is, in effect, making an artistic composition
of his life. Like Collins, Pope cannot invoke "pleasure's smiling train"
or "the family of pain" without providing an artistic context (a suggestion of the means by which these emotions are expressed) or without associating the formation of character with the creation of artistic
compositions. For Pope, as for Collins, the exploration of emotion
almost always involves an invocation of those artful forms that capture
and express "the strength and colour of our life."

Pope's analysis of the passions in *An Essay on Man* anticipates
Collins's extended examination of human emotion in several intriguing
ways, but we must not minimize the differences between these two
approaches. According to Pope, "Two Principles in human nature
reign; / Self-love, to urge, and Reason, to restrain" (II.53-54). The
passions represent the "Modes of Self-love," and Pope proceeds to
demonstrate the manner in which reason restrains these impulses: "On
life's vast ocean diversely we sail, / Reason the card, but Passion is the
Gale" (II.107-08). Reason provides the chart that allows us to adhere
to "Nature's road," a nautical metaphor that reinforces Pope's emphasis in these lines on limitations, boundaries, union, balance, and
confinement. Reason, in short, restrains us from giving full vent to the
gale within us.

Collins, significantly, makes no such distinction between reason and
the passions, and it should not surprise us that he mentions reason only

once in the entire collection of odes (and then contemptuously).[44] Collins is interested not in defining the limitations that keep the passions on a straight course but in exploring these emotional qualities in all of their richness, diversity, and volatility. One of Collins's greatest achievements, as we have seen, lies in his ability to cross the thresholds that connect our waking, daylight world with the shadowy realm (the "unreal Scene") that lies within.[45] Ernst Cassirer, in his summary of the French philosopher Vauvenargues's work, published in 1746, could also be describing Collins's explorations that year in his slim volume of *Odes*: "The true nature of man does not lie in reason, but in the passions. The Stoic demand for control of the passions by reason is and always will be a mere dream. Reason is not the dominating force in man; reason is comparable only to the hand that tells the time on the face of a clock. The mechanism that moves this hand lies within; the motivating force and ultimate cause of knowledge lie in those primary and original impulses which we continually receive from another, a completely irrational realm."[46]

I do not wish to introduce a new Procrustean bed that will merely replace those I have discarded. It should be clear that my argument makes better sense of some poems than it does of others; there is a difference, for instance, between the odes addressed to a specific human emotion (the "Ode to Fear" or "The Passions") and those, like the "Ode to Liberty" and the "Ode to Peace," that invoke broader abstractions, even when those qualities are given a human context and a human guise. I do wish, however, to reemphasize the essentially psychological nature of Collins's several odes and their common technique of personification, both of which cut across the boundaries earlier critics have erected. All of the odes are concerned with human qualities or aspirations, even when they are addressed to political or poetical abstractions. Collins's early readers in fact made no clear distinction between the patriotic poems and the odes that take art itself for their subject. Their preoccupation was with Collins's use of personification (his ability to paint in verse) and his focus on the various scenes of human life. The patriotic odes were simply considered part of the poet's central concern. As Langhorne put it in his edition, Collins "chose such subjects for his lyric essays as were most favourable for the indulgence of description and allegory; where he could exercise his powers in moral and personal painting; where he could exert his invention in conferring attributes on images or objects already new known, and described, by a determinate number of characteristics; where he might give an uncommon eclat to his figures, by placing them in happier attitudes, or in more advantageous lights, and introduce new forms from the moral and intellectual world into the society of impersonated beings."[47]

IV. The Patriotic Odes

Collins's wide-ranging exploration of the human passions provides an appropriate context for his otherwise puzzling emphasis on political or warlike subjects. These patriotic odes have often proved disappointing to modern readers, and there is, undeniably, a disparity between the conventional diction and attitudes of many of these poems and the intensity, rich texture, and high polish of the odes devoted to poetical subjects. But the similarities between these two general groups of poems should also be clear: the patriotic odes furnish dramatic situations in which we may glimpse these emotional qualities unleashed. This strategy, of course, Collins also follows in the so-called "aesthetic" odes. Each character in "The Passions" must demonstrate his musical skill in an "Ecstatic Trial"; in the "Ode to Fear" Collins celebrates Aeschylus' prowess both as a poet and as a warrior:

> Yet He the Bard who first invok'd thy Name,
>> Disdain'd in *Marathon* its Pow'r to feel:
> For not alone he nurs'd the Poet's flame,
>> But reach'd from Virtue's Hand the Patriot's Steel.

(ll. 30-33)

In his discussion of the passions, Pope stressed the inherent warfare between elements that were "born to fight," and even suggested that their eventual composure could be accomplished only through "well accorded strife." Collins also senses that the emotions must be seen in action, even warlike action, if they are to be understood. The external struggles in his odes, in other words, are not unlike the struggles within. We can observe this quite clearly in the "Ode to Mercy," where the struggle of emotion in the human breast is directly related to the nation's struggle to disarm the figure of war. In the "Ode, to a Lady," moreover, Fancy is "to Herself unkind," and Collins suggests that this is true of many of our emotional (and patriotic) impulses.[48] Throughout the odes we find an insistence on the sacrifice of human endeavor, whether it is offered up to liberty's shrine or to poetry's.

The value of human sacrifice in Collins's patriotic odes, however, has been seriously challenged by Patricia Meyer Spacks in her ironic reading of the "Ode, Written in the beginning of the Year 1746," a poem usually considered Collins's simplest and most moving.[49]

How sleep the Brave, who sink to Rest,
By all their Country's Wishes blest!
When *Spring*, with dewy Fingers cold,
Returns to deck their hallow'd Mold,
She there shall dress a sweeter Sod,
Than *Fancy*'s Feet have ever trod.

By Fairy Hands their Knell is rung,
By Forms unseen their Dirge is sung;
There *Honour* comes, a Pilgrim grey,
To bless the Turf that wraps their Clay,
And *Freedom* shall a-while repair,
To dwell a weeping Hermit there!

Spacks asks us to consider what kind of wishes the nation bestows on its dead: the nation may wish them peace (which they ironically have), or escape from the evils of their society (which they also have), or "more bitter still, the country may actually wish the deaths of men so idealistically motivated." Why are there only imaginary, and not real, personages at their grave, and why does Collins emphasize its physical attributes? Spacks argues that Spring offers the dead only an irrelevant and ironic prettification of "the ugly reality of mold which is, however hallowed, nothing but mold." Why is Honor a "Pilgrim grey" and Freedom a "weeping Hermit"? Do Honor and Freedom reside only with the dead? Spacks contends that the poem, "far from glorifying the dead, insists rather on their lack of significance." These deaths should not blind the nation to the facts of social corruption, nor make the survivors unaware that honor and freedom are not automatically associated with England.

I have recounted Spacks's argument at some length because her close attention to the text is provocative and because her conclusions, if accepted, would force us to view Collins's other political poems in an entirely different light. I do not believe, however, that these conclusions accurately reflect either the tone of the poem or the political and poetical context in which Collins placed this ode. Spacks begins her discussion by arguing backwards from the troublesome personifications of the final lines; a careful sequential reading of the poem, on the other hand, removes many of the complexities that nourish an ironic interpretation. The opening word of the poem, we should notice, introduces an exclamation and not a question. The speaker's reaction is not one of ironic, questioning detachment, but one of wonder. The brave do indeed sink to rest rather than rise in glory in these lines, but the rhyme of Collins's couplet implies that their "Rest" is "blest!"

What, however, is the nature of "their Country's Wishes"? Surely these wishes do not differ from what any nation desires its fallen heroes to enjoy: the satisfaction of knowing that their sacrifice has not been in vain, that their deaths have had some share in the preservation of those values—liberty, freedom, eventual peace—that society prizes. The importance of cultural preservation is a theme that we have traced back as far as the *Oriental Eclogues* and the epistle to Hanmer, and it is a form of consolation, of course, enjoyed not by the dead but by the living. Collins's emphasis here, as in the "Ode, to a Lady," is fixed on the human reaction to death, be it a general lament or an individual response.

But if this is true, why then does Collins appear to stress the physical aspects of their grave? Spacks is certainly astute in noticing how fully this poem is concerned with "the fact of ending," but the nature of that ending does not necessarily warrant an ironic view of the soldiers' sacrifice. The poem's title supplies a temporal context that should not be ignored: Collins celebrates those soldiers who fell "in the beginning of the Year 1746." It is therefore not surprising that Spring will later appear with her "dewy Fingers cold": the first touch of spring (as Robert Frost's poem "Spring Pools" delicately demonstrates) *is* cold. "Cold" and "Mold" are indeed coupled in Collins's rhyme, but the mold is nonetheless "hallow'd," a sign that the nation's wishes have in fact "blest" this common grave. Their hallowed mold, moreover, is subsequently described as a "sweeter Sod, / Than *Fancy*'s Feet have ever trod," and sweetness is, throughout the odes, one of Collins's highest forms of praise. Their sod is sweeter than Fancy's, moreover, because reality outstrips even imagination here. This, finally, is Collins's greatest acknowledgment of the power of death; as in the "Ode, to a Lady," death intrudes on us in its sweetness or its horror more forcefully than does imagination's power.

The second stanza of Collins's brief ode introduces the two figures who pay tribute to the fallen soldiers. An ironic interpretation depends heavily on the poem's replacement of actual mourners by these two imaginary personages, but I believe that such a reading ignores the general nature of Collins's lament. The men he celebrates are simply called "the Brave"; the personification of abstract qualities (Honor and Freedom) is therefore appropriate to the form of this communal elegy. Similarly, in the "Ode, to a Lady," Collins appropriately balances the particular death of Captain Ross with the homage of a single hind and the grief of a single lady. Honor is a pilgrim here not because he can only be found abroad but because his function leads him on a continual journey to pay tribute to those who die honorably or fight in an honorable cause. He does not reside exclusively with the dead, but he honors them in their turn; he comes to honor "the shrine which gives him his being."[50] Similarly, Freedom appears wherever her battles are fought; she sheds tears of tribute and penance for those who fall while defending their country's liberty. Freedom demands a constant sacrifice; her battles are never over; she will repair at this particular shrine only "a-while."

The contemporary political context also refutes an ironic reading of this poem. Collins's deliberate dating of the ode suggests an occasion following the battle between the English army and the Scottish rebels at Falkirk on 17 January 1746. The battle of Falkirk (like that at Preston Pans in September of the preceding year) was a setback for the English troops in Scotland. The Young Pretender's victory gave the English a serious scare. Dodsley's *Museum* (to which Collins would contribute his "Ode, to a Lady") recorded that when "the News of this Battle reached *London*, it made it necessary to provide for the immediate Extinction of so dangerous a Flame."[51] The Duke of Cumberland himself took charge of the English forces, and the rebellion was crushed April 16 at the bloody battle of Culloden. Such a background—specifically invoked in Collins's title—provides another compelling reason for us to consider the speaker's tribute to be deeply felt. The intrusion of war into the life of a nation is serious enough, but the perils of civil war are even greater. In the related "Ode to Mercy," which finally urges sympathy for the Scottish rebels, Collins powerfully depicts the threat posed by the Pretender or by the Satanic discord of war itself (foreign or civil): "The *Fiend of Nature* join'd his Yoke, / And rush'd in Wrath to make our Isle his Prey" (ll. 15-16). Similarly, in the lengthy "Ode to Liberty," Collins explicitly states that Freedom, following her precarious progress through Europe, has finally made England her home. But even here, of course, she must be continually nourished; and in the close of this ode, as in the following "Ode to Peace," Collins calls for the return of both external and internal concord.

Collins's invocation of these qualities, however, reveals the dangers that continued to vex English liberty during the summer and autumn in which he wrote these three additional odes. The trial of several prominent Scottish noblemen for high treason in July of 1746 provoked a debate that tore the nation in two.[52] In the "Ode to Mercy" Collins asks his goddess to acknowledge his nation's tribute to her: "Thou, Thou shalt rule our Queen, and share our Monarch's Throne!" By influencing the queen, he argues, Mercy will share the English throne and thereby rule her divided subjects. Collins hopes that the entire nation (including the king) will be swayed by mercy, but the poet himself performs the actual invocation. In a similar manner, Collins concludes the "Ode to Peace" by wedding Peace with Honor, and he closes his "Ode to Liberty" by welcoming "Blithe *Concord's* social Form" back to England's shores: "Thou, Lady, Thou shalt rule the West!"

In each of these odes we hear the hopeful voice of the poet as well as his difficulty in writing patriotic verse. His own art, he counsels in the "Ode, to a Lady," has certain limitations; its "pictur'd Glories" cannot always displace the distressful scenes of death. Nor, perhaps, can modern art successfully invoke that national spirit so essential to Collins's classical models. In the "Ode to Liberty" in particular—a poem that has several interesting affinities with the "Ode on the Poetical Character"—Collins suggests the burden of fulfilling the patriotic functions of the poet:

> Who shall awake the *Spartan* Fife,
> And call in solemn Sounds to Life,
> The Youths . . . .
> . . . .
> What New *Alcæus*, Fancy-blest,
> Shall sing the Sword, in Myrtles drest,
>   At *Wisdom's* Shrine a-while its Flame concealing,
> (What Place so fit to seal a Deed renown'd?).
>
> (ll. 1-3, 7-10)

The very existence of the poem answers these questions; Collins himself will attempt to fulfill this role, even though he senses the difficulties of his task. The modern poet must somehow emulate the ancient poet's powers. His singing must bring the youths "in solemn Sounds to Life," an undertaking that approximates God's animating force in the "Ode on the Poetical Character": "He, who call'd with Thought to Birth / Yon tented Sky, this laughing Earth" (ll. 25-26). The poet, too, must be "Fancy-blest," fired both by imagination and by Freedom's awesome flame.

And yet, even if he is blessed with these divine attributes, the modern bard will encounter serious difficulties as he interprets "Time's backward Rolls" and attempts to locate Liberty's shrine:

> Whether the fiery-tressed *Dane*,
> Or *Roman's* self o'erturn'd the Fane,
> Or in what Heav'n-left Age it fell,
> 'Twere hard for modern Song to tell.
>
> (ll. 97-100)

But the shrine, Collins tells us, has not been overturned: "The beauteous *Model* still remains" (l. 106). And in this significant departure from the "Ode on the Poetical Character" (where Heaven and Fancy "o'erturn'd th' inspiring Bow'rs") we begin to sense the comparative weakness of the odes addressed to Mercy, Liberty, and Peace. Their tone is more hopeful than realistic; their communal goals—which include the poet's aspirations—are envisioned with appropriate anxiety but realized with too much ease. "How may the Poet now unfold, / What never Tongue or Numbers told?" he asks, and yet the following passage quickly limns this ancient shrine, which blends Grecian grace with Gothic splendor. It is difficult to believe that Collins's confidence is actually justified here.[53] In the central stanzas of the "Ode to Liberty," his desire to fulfill his patriotic obligations seems to have drawn him into an uncharacteristic celebration of his own poetic powers. His political odes, like those devoted to poetry itself, are most convincing when they convey an awareness of their limitations.

5

Collins's Elusive Nature

Looking back on his friend's work in 1763, Johnson pointed out that Collins "employed his mind chiefly upon works of fiction, and subjects of fancy; and, by indulging some peculiar habits of thought, was eminently delighted with those flights of imagination which pass the bounds of nature, and to which the mind is reconciled only by a passive acquiescence in popular traditions."[1] Our tendency today is to emphasize the unconscious rather than the supernatural in Collins's work and, in so doing, to take the poet at his word when, in poems like the "Ode to Fear," he summons forth the insubstantial shapes that inhabit the shadowy realms beyond this waking world. And yet if most critics agree that our interest in Collins's poetry lies primarily in his flights beyond "the bounds of nature," there has been a surprising neglect of the forces that prompted Collins's departure. Why did "nature," recently celebrated in her varying forms by Pope and Thomson, suddenly become a troubled issue for the poets who followed in their wake?

The answer appears to lie in Collins's insistence that the particulars of external nature—so firmly tied to cohesive and general abstractions in Thomson and Pope—are themselves as shadowy, as fluctuating, and as ill-defined as the subjective world that lies within. Nature, in Collins's eyes at least, seems to have lost much of its unity and coherence; it strikes us as a restless phenomenon, transient and fleeting. In his elegy on an unknown female painter, for example, he attempts to capture the distinctive atmosphere of "Mid night's hour":

> The Moon with dewy lustre bright
>   Her Mild Æthereal radiance gave
> On Paly Cloisters gleam'd her light
>   Or trembled o'er th' unresting wave
> · · · · · · · · · · · · · · · · · · ·
> Long o'er the Spires and Glimmring Tow'rs
>   The whispring Flood, and silv'ry sky
> As One whom Musing Grief devours
>   She glanc'd by turns her silent Eye!

(Fragment 7, ll. 1-4, 9-12)

Collins's diction in this fragment is heavily indebted to both Thomson and Pope, but his depiction of a scene in intermittent light and in shadowy reflections clearly anticipates the suggestive technique of the odes, both those that explore psychological states and those that examine the appearances of nature.

Closely associated with this elusive quality in nature is the difficulty the artist faces in evoking or capturing these forces in his canvas, poem, or song. Thomson had already raised this problem in *The Seasons*:

> But who can paint
> Like Nature? Can imagination boast,
> Amid its gay creation, hues like hers?
> Or can it mix them with that matchless skill,
> And lose them in each other, as appears
> In every bud that blows? If fancy then
> Unequal fails beneath the pleasing task,
> Ah, what shall language do?

("Spring," ll. 468-75)

But even if Thomson cannot rival Nature in her artistry, he is nonetheless able to present an essentially coherent view of this world. He may describe nature as "this complex, stupendous scheme of things," but it is a unified scheme in which "to every purer eye / The informing Author in his works appears" (ll. 858-60). But matters are not this simple—or at least not this clear—in Collins's poetry: if we find it difficult to observe nature in the first place, we shall find it more difficult to re-create it, to give it imaginative life. Collins is painfully aware of this dilemma; he realizes that even poetry's sister arts (painting in particular) must suffer these limitations. But his poems nevertheless suggest that an ever-changing nature can be captured or endowed with coherence only by the artist himself, limited as his powers may be. And thus he often approaches nature with other artful representations, usually drawn from the visual arts, clearly in view.

We can begin to see this approach in Collins's eighth fragment, which quickly bears us from the "sounding street" and "echoing squares" of the city to a series of landscapes, each representing a separate time of the day:

> Some times when Morning oer [the] Plain
>   Her radiant Mantle throws
> I'll mark the Clouds where sweet Lorrain
>   His orient Colours chose
>
> Or when the Sun at Noon tide climbs
>   I'll hide me from his view
> By such green Plats and chearfull Limes
>   As   Rysdael drew
> . . . .
> But when Soft Evning o'er the Plain
>   Her gleamy Mantle throws
> I'll mark the Clouds whence sweet Lorraine
>   His   Colours chose.
>
>   (ll. 25-32, 41-44)

In this preliminary draft of an ode, we can clearly see Collins's continual struggle to find the appropriate adjectives for these evasive effects. His principal mode in these fragments is pictorial: he suggests a suitable image, and then acknowledges the source of his visual debt. I find this strategy of considerable interest, for it indicates that here, as well as in "The Manners" and the "Ode to Evening," Collins's approach to nature is significantly conditioned by the representations of visual art. In another stanza of the fragment, Collins states that he will stand on some bare and wild heath with more delight "Than He who sees with wondering air / The Works of Rosa's hand" (ll. 35-36). This boast is overturned, however, in the passage that immediately follows: when Collins is positioned within a rocky cavern or tawny dell he will "seem to see the Wizzard Shapes / That from his Pencill fell." Salvator Rosa's interpretation of this natural scene is never far from Collins's mind; even when his enjoyment of nature is most intense, he will gauge that enjoyment by the comparative pleasures of art.

A comparison of "The Manners" and the "Ode to Evening" may at first seem an unusual pairing, but both of these poems, like the preparatory fragments, depict a volatile nature and the stabilizing influence of art. Art, in this context, is both necessary and difficult. Can the delicate effects of light in a landscape, for instance, be adequately evoked or preserved by the artist? Collins praises Claude for just this achievement, and his references to these morning and evening scenes indicate that he was familiar with Roger de Piles's estimate in *The Art of Painting*: Claude was interested in discovering "the causes of the diversity of the same view or prospect, explaining why it appeared sometimes after one fashion, and sometimes after another, with respect to colours, instancing in the morning dews and evening vapours."[2] But there are some effects, especially when night has fallen, that not even Claude could capture:

> All Tints that ever Picture us'd
>   Are lifeless dull and mean
> To paint her dewy Light diffus'd
>
> What Art can paint the modest ray
>   So sober chaste and cool
> As round yon Cliffs it seems to play
> Or skirts yon glimmring Pool?
>
>   (Fragment 8, ll. 53-60; 56 is blank)

And in the final stanza of this fragment Collins admits that poetry, too, is inadequate to this task: no poet can successfully render night's "tender gleam" even though "he chuse the softest words / That e'er were sigh'd in air." It is thus with a sense of the elusiveness of nature that Collins turned once again to these problems in two of his most important odes.

I. "The Manners. An Ode."

"The Manners" is a curious poem that has largely been neglected or dismissed by Collins's readers. Its ostensible subject is conventional enough, but not far beneath the surface of the ode lie several intriguing implications about "the bounds of nature" and the function of art. In dating and commenting on the poem, scholars have usually followed the lead of Collins's first editor, John Langhorne: "From the subject and sentiments of this ode, it seems not improbable that the author wrote it about the time when he left the University [*c.* early 1744]; when weary with the pursuit of academical studies, he no longer confined himself to the search of theoretical knowledge, but commenced the *scholar of humanity*, to study nature in her works, and man in society."[3] There is good reason to believe, however, that "The Manners" is contemporaneous with the major odes of 1745-46, and that it does not simply depict Collins's freedom of spirit as he joyfully bids farewell to an Oxford education.[4] The poem continues to provide an interesting commentary on Collins's work, but this is less the poet's perspective on his own career as a "literary adventurer" than it is a perspective—an "argument of images"—supplied in definition of nature "as she lives around."

The disenchantment with philosophy with which the poem opens is in fact closely allied to the cleavage between the world of empirical reality, on the one hand, and abstract reasoning on the other:

> Farewell, for clearer Ken design'd,
> The dim-discover'd Tracts of Mind:
> Truths which, from Action's Paths retir'd,
> My silent Search in vain requir'd!
> No more my Sail that Deep explores,
> No more I search those magic Shores,
> What Regions part the World of Soul,
> Or whence thy Streams, *Opinion*, roll.

> (ll. 1-8)

Collins does not deny that philosophy presents great potential. The philosopher is portrayed as an explorer in search of magic shores; his pursuit, moreover, draws him to the inner reaches of discovery: "that Deep," the "Tracts of Mind." But these deeps are often treacherous, as Locke had pointed out in his disparaging remarks on those who first contemplate the objects of understanding rather than the mind itself. Too often we allow our thoughts to wander

> into the vast Ocean of *Being*, as if all that boundless Extent, were the natural, and undoubted Possession of our Understandings, wherein there was nothing exempt from its Decisions, or that escaped its Comprehension. Thus Men, extending their Enquiries beyond their Capacities, and letting their Thoughts wander into those depths, where they can find no sure Footing; 'tis no Wonder, that they raise Questions, and multiply Disputes, which never coming to any clear Resolution, are proper only to continue and increase their Doubts, and to confirm them at last in perfect Scepticism.

Locke therefore asks us to discover the horizon that "sets the Bounds between the enlightned and dark Parts of Things."[5]

Collins adopts this motif of exploration and imagery of sight, but he nevertheless gives speculative philosophy a wide berth. His farewell to the theoretical science is for "clearer Ken" designed. The tracts of mind are actually only dimly discovered (presumably by philosopher and neophyte alike). The poet's search has been a vain one, and Collins's description of it leads us to believe that it could hardly have been otherwise: it is a "silent Search" in pursuit of truths that are from "Action's Paths retir'd." We may also doubt the "magic" of foreign shores that reveals only the origin of Opinion or the separation of soul from the material world. This separation is only too easily seen in philosophy's own works, as Collins's source in "Il Penseroso" makes clear: "What Worlds, or what vast Regions hold / The immortal mind that hath forsook / Her mansion in this fleshly nook" (ll. 90-92). The very separation of philosophy's truths from the tangible world leads Collins to invoke "the Spear and Shield" on his behalf as he contemplates battling the "Wizzard *Passions*" and "Giant *Follies*" who inhabit "such Fairy Field."

This spirit of gentle deflation, which plays upon the contrast of light and darkness, continues in the following stanza. The Athenian portico where philosophers gathered is "seen, / Arch'd with th' enlivening Olive's Green." But "*Science*," although "prank'd in tissued Vest" and richly attired by Reason, Pride, and Fancy, is come only "To wed with *Doubt* in *Plato*'s Shade." It is thus appropriate that the poet-youth of the third stanza be described in terms of his clarity of vision:

> Youth of the quick uncheated Sight,
> Thy Walks, *Observance*, more invite!
> O Thou, who lov'st that ampler Range,
> Where Life's wide Prospects round thee change,
> And with her mingling Sons ally'd,
> Throw'st the prattling Page aside:
> To me in Converse sweet impart,
> To read in Man the native Heart,
> To learn, where Science sure is found,
> From Nature as she lives around.
>
> (ll. 19-28)

Observation replaces philosophy; the quick, uncheated sight of an ampler range, of life's wide prospects, replaces Plato's shade; and the "*Science*" of line 15, showily arrayed, is replaced by "Science sure," to be found in Nature. The poet asks Observance to throw the "prattling Page" of philosophy aside as he now reads his lesson in mankind. The explorer of the first stanza is finally rewarded with an appropriate prospect and an attainable goal. The deeps and dangers of philosophy are forsaken for surer knowledge, available closer at hand.

This conventional argument is complicated, however, in the following lines, which provide an intriguing focus for the entire ode:

> And gazing oft her Mirror true,
> By turns each shifting Image view!
>
> (ll. 29-30)

Collins, having established man and nature "as she lives around" as the objects of observation, now modifies this image by gazing not at nature but into her "Mirror true." But nature's "Mirror true" must accurately reflect nature herself; why then introduce the image of the mirror in order to focus the powers of observation? Collins seems to be playing on the double conception of the mirror in the eighteenth century. Johnson was to define it in his *Dictionary* in two ways: as a "looking-glass; any thing which exhibits representations of objects by reflection"; and as a "pattern; for that on which the eye ought to be fixed; an exemplar; an archetype." This second definition not only describes Collins's use of the mirror, but uncannily supplements the very language of the ode. For the youth of quick, uncheated sight, nature is the model, the pattern, the exemplar on which the eye ought to be fixed.

But although this definition of the mirror supports the grand archetype of nature that Collins invokes in the poem, it does not fully suit the poet who will "By turns each shifting Image view." Collins draws on the sense of mirror as looking-glass as well. The image of shifting perspectives is in fact closely tied to his earlier description of Observance's "wide Prospects" that "round thee change." The poet's vision here is kaleidoscopic, and his description of the landscape's prospects reflects the early eighteenth-century interest in the images of the camera obscura.[6] The object on which the eye ought to be fixed is both nature as a general model and the artificial reflection of the original. As Addison claimed in his essays on "the pleasures of the imagination," the camera obscura presented "the prettiest Landskip I ever saw, . . . drawn on the Walls of a dark Room, which stood opposite on one side to a navigable River, and on the other to a Park. The Experiment is very common in Opticks. Here you might discover the Waves and Fluctuations of the Water in strong and proper Colours, with the Picture of a Ship entering at one end, and sailing by Degrees through the whole Piece. On another there appeared the Green Shadows of Trees, waving to and fro with the Wind, and Herds of Deer among them in Miniature, leaping about upon the Wall."[7] Addison ascribed the image's pleasantness not only to its novelty but to its ability, unlike other pictures, to give "the Motion of the Things it represents" as well as their shape and color. If, as Addison argued, "we may be sure that artificial Works receive a greater Advantage from their Resemblance of such as are natural," so too we find that "the Products of Nature rise in Value, according as they more or less resemble those of Art."

Thus Collins presents the changing images of the looking-glass as a complement to the workings of Observance and the objects of nature that she reveals directly to the poet's eye. And, interestingly, it is only when the artifice of the mirror is introduced into the poem that the carefully controlled distance between subject ("Thou") and object ("me") finally collapses. Appearances to the contrary (as they often are in Collins's syntax), the subject throughout lines 19–34 is not the youth but Observance (or her "Walks"). It is Observance who is addressed as a deity in these lines; Observance, in fact, not only imparts knowledge "in Converse sweet" with the poet, but actually is the agent who throws aside "the prattling Page" of philosophy. In direct confrontation with nature as she lives around, the poet assumes a passive, withdrawn pose: the objects appear to move around him, not he amidst the variety of nature's works.

Just as important is the variation Collins makes on his source for these lines in Pope's conclusion to *An Essay on Man*:

> urged by thee, I turn'd the tuneful art
> From sounds to things, from fancy to the heart;
> For Wit's false mirror held up Nature's light.

(IV.391–93)

Although Collins's argument is similar to Pope's—both concentrate on the world of things and the human heart—wit's distortions have disappeared (to be replaced, presumably, by philosophy's), while the mirror, now in its double sense, has been transferred to nature itself. Nature's mirror is not only the source of light (a model on which knowledge, understanding, "Science" is based), but the complementary reflection of light as well.

The image of the mirror, however, is only a prefiguration of artful reflection in the poem. The lines that follow (and, indeed, the rest of the ode) introduce the important role art will play in understanding the manners. The poet will view each shifting image in nature's mirror

> Till meddling *Art's* officious Lore,
> Reverse the Lessons taught before,
> Alluring from a safer Rule,
> To dream in her enchanted School.

(ll. 31-34)

At first glance this description seems to lie uncomfortably close to the work of philosophy: both provide "officious Lore," and art's enchantment echoes philosophy's "magic Shores" and "Fairy Field." But Collins's apparent criticism of art can also be read as a gesture of affection: art simply allures us from the safer instruction of nature towards "the understanding of human manners through art, by the agency of Fancy."[8] Meddling art has, in fact, already introduced its officious lore in the reflections of nature's looking glass.

The manners, moreover, are not mentioned until Collins turns to art proper in the poem's fourth stanza:

> Retiring hence to thoughtful Cell,
> As *Fancy* breathes her potent Spell,
> Not vain she finds the charmful Task,
> In Pageant quaint, in motley Mask,
> Behold before her musing Eyes,
> The countless *Manners* round her rise.
>
> (ll. 37-42)

Collins's focus is again on vision, but now at a further remove. As Art retires like a hermit to her "thoughtful Cell," she, by aid of Fancy, raises new objects before our eyes through the contrivances of her art.[9] The countless manners rise in pageant and masque, to be observed by Contempt as she "applies her Glass" (another mirror-image in the ode). The promise of magic in the poem is finally fulfilled, but it is the magic of art's charmful spells, not the exotic shores to which philosophy may perhaps lead us. Similarly, as we now dream in Art's "enchanted School," the personified manners of pageant and masque afford a sharp contrast to Science's disappointing train in the second stanza. Our observation of the masque, meanwhile, is reinforced by the different roles Art plays. She is not only the subject of the stanza (and also its chief agent), but the primary spectator as well. We are asked to "Behold" while "before her musing Eyes, / The countless *Manners* round her rise." It is Art who watches as Contempt applies her glass, and it is she too who "views" Humor in his robe of "wild contending Hues." As spectators we view both Art's presentations and Art herself (as conjuror and beholder) much as we viewed Nature in her double aspect in the previous stanza. Our perspective is at a remove, but even within this enlarged prospect, Art (in her role as stage-manager) is better able to focus our eyes on the objects of her magic.

An even more telling distinction, however, lies in the contrast Collins draws between Plato's shade (at the close of his satire on philosophy) and the description of Wit at the conclusion of Art's dreamlike spectacle:

> Me too amidst thy Band admit,
> There where the young-eyed healthful *Wit*,
> (Whose Jewels in his crisped Hair
> Are plac'd each other's Beams to share,
> Whom no Delights from Thee divide).
>
> (ll. 53-57)

The poet asks admittance to Humor's band primarily because of the allurements of Wit, who in turn is patterned after the poet himself. The "young-eyed healthful *Wit*" clearly echoes the "Youth of the quick uncheated Sight," and the false mirror he bore in Pope's poem is now fashioned into the greater instruments of light in his hair. One of Collins's early editors, Benjamin Strutt, claimed that "The image of Wit is truly characterized. The mingled lustre of jewelry in his head-dress well describes the playful brilliancy of those ideas which receive advantages from proximity to each other."[10] What is important in our reading is that Collins concludes his description of art's enchantments with his brightest vision of light in the poem. Collins apparently based his description on a passage in Corbyn Morris's treatise on wit, a passage echoed not only in the ode but in Johnson's definition of the mirror as well: "It is then adorn'd with the Charms of *Propriety*, *Clearness* and *Illustration*; It dispels the Darkness around an Object, and presents it distinctly and perfectly to our View; chearing us with its *Lustre*, and at the same time informing us with its *Light*."[11]

It is no great leap, then, as has sometimes been thought, for Collins to introduce the prose romance in the penultimate stanza. Prose fiction, after all, most clearly shares with drama the powers of characterization that Collins ascribes to the manners. The progression is from one form of art to another, from the visions of Fancy in the enchanted cave to the fictional enchantments of the Milesian tales, Boccaccio, Cervantes, and Le Sage. What distinguishes the prose romances, however, is their ability to instruct the reader in the art of living. Thus Boccaccio is praised for all he "taught the *Tuscan* Maids, / In chang'd *Italia*'s modern Shades" (another benighted realm); and Cervantes is distinguished for having "Refin'd a Nation's Lust of Fame." The art of fiction, as theorists would soon make clear, lay in its ability to hold up the mirror to nature, to present vibrant characterizations—like Le Sage's Blanche, the "sad *Sicilian* Maid"—and yet the mirror of this art is only the final reflector introduced in Collins's ode.[12] Art, in a general sense, is the primary mirror-image of the poem. We progress from reflection without light (philosophy) to the direct light of nature, from which (by the agency of Nature's mirror true) we turn to reflections of that light in art itself—as mirror, as masque, as novel.

The mirror is first introduced, in fact, in Collins's own battle with philosophy:

> If e'er I round such Fairy Field,
> Some Pow'r impart the Spear and Shield,
> At which the Wizzard *Passions* fly,
> By which the Giant *Follies* die!
>
> (ll. 9-12)

Lonsdale has suggested that Collins is referring to the Spenserian formula of "Spear and Shield" used to describe the function and power of knighthood, and that Collins is perhaps alluding specifically to Britomart's sword and Prince Arthur's magic shield (jewel-encrusted like Wit's crisped hair) in the *Faerie Queene*. What is equally probable is that Collins is thinking of the spear and shield that enabled Perseus to slay Medusa in Ovid's *Metamorphoses*: "On all sides through the fields and along the ways he saw the forms of men and beasts changed into stone by one look at Medusa's face. But he himself had looked upon the image of that dread face reflected from the bright bronze shield his left hand bore; and while deep sleep held fast both the snakes and her who wore them, he smote her head clean from her neck" (IV.779-85).[13] Collins invokes the spear and shield as appropriate weaponry for warding off the dangers that inhabit the "Fairy Field" in much the same way Shelley will in his characterization of Keats:

> Why didst thou leave the trodden paths of men
> Too soon, and with weak hands though mighty heart
> Dare the unpastured dragon in his den?
> Defenceless as thou wert, oh, where was then
> Wisdom the mirrored shield, or scorn the spear?
>
> ("Adonais," ll. 236-40)

In "The Manners" Collins draws upon the agency of the mirrored shield in order, like Perseus, to protect himself. But it is reality itself as well as philosophy's deeps that he characteristically views by reflected vision. Just as the mirror carries us past the dragons of philosophical study, so it provides us with the focus—actually the medium—for exploring nature herself. And nature, just as we encounter her in the third stanza of the poem, is in fact altered to a mirrorlike presence, both the source of understanding and the means by which we grasp it. Despite Langhorne's claim that Collins's intention in the ode was "to study nature in her works, and man in society," the real works in the poem are works of art, and man is viewed not in society but in the "social Science" that Heaven has blessed (ll. 35-36). And despite Collins's conventional conclusion, in which he vows to rove the "Scene-full World" with "Nature boon," art remains the true mediator of reality; the most likely scenes of contemplation are those within the artful works that the poem celebrates: masque, personified pageantry, and prose romance.

Marjorie Hope Nicolson has argued that a study of optics leads to questions of epistemology, and thus the implications of Collins's argument are particularly intriguing.[14] Although the poem appears to value the direct observation of nature as she lives around, finding in it a clearer ken than murky philosophy's, there is nevertheless reason to believe that reality itself, though it does not possess the Gorgon's metamorphic powers, may best be glimpsed through the reflectors of art. But why this necessity to capture—and perhaps transform—the reality celebrated in the ode? The argument of Collins's imagery is that beneath the generalized form that his personification has bestowed on reality lies a quicksilver world of flux and variety that must be momentarily frozen to be observed. This sense of an ever-changing nature is found both in Collins's description of nature ("Prospects round thee change," "each shifting Image view") and in his portrait of art's quaint pageantry. The figures pass in a "motley" masque; the manners are "ever varying"; Humor appears in a robe of "wild contending Hues"; and Wit's jewels are "plac'd each other's Beams to share."

Thus beneath the generalized surface of reality that we call nature lies a world of vivid particulars always capable of modifying our hasty or imperfect view, and this potential clash between particular and general is inherent in Collins's conception of the "Manners." Johnson defined them as our "General way of life; morals; habits," but it is clear that Collins also invokes them in the specific context of artistic representation. The "Manners" suggest both a general way of life and the individual characteristics by which men are differentiated from one another; they are, as Dryden put it, "those inclinations, whether natural or acquired, which move and carry us to actions, good, bad, or indifferent, in a play; or which incline the persons to such or such actions."[15] This potential clash, moreover, is also inherent in the double nature of mirror as looking-glass and archetype: "In its first meaning 'mirror' stands for the rendition of particular nature and is associated with the ancient notion of *enargeia*—that is, *evidentia*, force, vigor, strength, vividness, efficacy, palpability. . . . In its second meaning 'mirror' points to a generalized rendition of archetypal nature or to some kind of artistic idealization of the actual."[16] But even in the generalized and artful rendition of nature that Collins attempts in his poem, the force and vigor of the particulars (and their constant capability for change) remind us of how slippery the world of reality remains. The argument of Collins's ode is not that the poet has exhausted nature but that, in realizing its elusiveness, he can no longer celebrate it in a traditional way. Gone is the unified vision of Thomson's *Seasons*, in which nature (the "varied God") proved to be a cohesive, ordered, and explicable phenomenon.

The significance of Collins's "The Manners" lies in the fresh perspective it provides us on the poet's conception of nature. In spite of their traditional associations, natural elements may remain essentially elusive forces that will withstand our attempts to pin them down. The poet must now either celebrate nature in appropriate fashion, fully aware of its complexities, or accept the invitation to delve beneath its seductive surfaces. In "The Manners," just as our observation of an "objective," external nature is celebrated, so our ability to perceive that world in all its shapes and colors is seriously questioned, and our reliance on the reflections of art intricately established.

II. The "Ode to Evening"

Collins's task in the "Ode to Evening" is all the more difficult when we view it in the context of "The Manners." Collins's most celebrated ode is an attempt to evoke, to describe, and (more difficult still) to capture nature in one of her most attractive and elusive aspects. The very nature of the "shifting Image" of evening addressed here—not as volatile as in "The Manners," but nonetheless transitory, shadowy, almost evanescent—dictates the subtle blendings of a poem that manages, eventually, to endow evening with a more permanent form. Creating permanence where permanence is not naturally found is a difficult task, but difficult too is the poet's original intention of fashioning a music or song that will, by soothing the nymph of evening, enable the poet to suggest her transient state. The poem continues to intrigue its readers even if it does not always satisfy them. Part of the difficulty lies in the poem's tripartite structure, which quietly resembles the formal divisions of many of the other odes.[17] This structure is essential to the argument of the "Ode to Evening" because it emphasizes the developments in Collins's attitude toward both the nature he portrays and the art responsible for his portrayal.

The opening twenty lines of the ode focus on two concurrent processes: the slow-footed arrival of evening, and her simultaneous tutelage of the poet as he prepares to depict her approach in verse. These early passages represent a probationary period for him; he must attune his own music to the sounds of nature surrounding him, and consequently much of the natural description in these lines is closely associated with the sources and elements of his art. The opening lines introduce the aural insistence of this entire section:

> If ought of Oaten Stop, or Pastoral Song,
> May hope, chaste *Eve*, to sooth thy modest Ear,
>> Like thy own solemn Springs,
>> Thy Springs, and dying Gales.

> (ll. 1-4)

The ode's first line anticipates Blake's "Introduction" to his *Songs of Innocence*, in which a child on a cloud enjoins the speaker to pipe, sing, and ultimately write his rural song "In a book that all may read." In Collins's ode, the simple choice of instrumental music or vocal song also suggests an artistic process that will finally end in the poem we read. But these first lines are necessarily hesitant; Collins wonders whether anything he creates will soothe chaste Evening's modest ear. The predominant "o" and "p" sounds of the first two lines (especially in the 1746 version) contribute to this continual movement towards closure.[18]

This hesitancy and tendency towards closure are soon overpowered, however, by the flowing blank verse and by a visual and aural imagery that begins to suggest the delicate blending that is characteristic of the poem.[19] Collins's emphasis throughout this section is on the gentler aspects of nature. The revision of "brawling" to "solemn" springs enhances this softened mode and also points to the quasi-religious element in Evening. These are "solemn" springs in the sense that they are sacred, and they therefore serve as an appropriate source of inspiration for the aspiring poet. The repetition of "Springs" and the introduction of the "dying Gales," moreover, provide a soothing break in the poem and establish a general pattern of accretion and slow (almost sideways) development. As in the "Ode on the Poetical Character," few of the lines actually contribute directly to the development of Collins's argument. If any of my pastoral arts may hope to sooth you (1-2), Collins muses, then teach me to write in a manner (15-16) that will suit your own mood (18). But the remaining lines are obviously essential to the argument as well, even when they merely reintroduce the personified figure that Collins addresses. In the fifth line, for instance, Evening is invoked as a "*Nymph* reserv'd," a description that conveys not only her chastity (which we have already encountered), but also her caution and hesitancy. Evening, in other words, steals upon the landscape only gradually; she reveals herself to us only little by little.

The following lines therefore suggest the shadowy environment to which she returns:

> O *Nymph* reserv'd, while now the bright-hair'd Sun
> Sits in yon western Tent, whose cloudy Skirts,
>> With Brede ethereal wove,
>> O'erhang his wavy Bed:
> Now Air is hush'd, save where the weak-ey'd Bat,
> With short shrill Shriek flits by on leathern Wing,
>> Or where the Beetle winds
>> His small but sullen Horn,

> As oft he rises 'midst the twilight Path,
> Against the Pilgrim born in heedless Hum.
>
> (ll. 5-14)

This is predominantly a sheltered landscape. Even the "bright-hair'd" sun appears to our view as a veiled character, his radiance diminished by the cloudy tent in which he sits. The image of the western tent allows us to gauge the sun's progress (and thus Evening's as well), and also introduces the pervasive interweaving of elements and effects.[20] The tent's cloudy skirts are woven into an ethereal "Brede" or braid, usually associated with the prismatic coloring of the rainbow and not unlike Claude's attempts to capture the differing effects of light at various times of the day. Collins's image of the sun as it hangs suspended above its "wavy Bed" is borrowed from Milton's hymn "On the Morning of Christ's Nativity": "So when the Sun in bed, / Curtain'd with cloudy red, / Pillows his chin upon an Orient wave" (ll. 229-31). But in Collins's ode, the sun has not quite been put to rest; he sits hovering above the waters, a suspended figure whose predicament suggests our own suspension at this point in the poem.

The following lines also open with a temporal indication ("Now Air is hush'd"), but they also convey a sense that time has been arrested. There is little motion here—either in the landscape or in the argument of the poem—save for the single shriek of the flitting bat or the sullen sound of the solitary beetle who pours his breath through his diminuitive horn. The figures are introduced only to accentuate the essential stillness of the scene. The only direction we receive is a notoriously ambiguous one: the beetle rises " 'midst the twilight Path, / Against the Pilgrim born in heedless Hum," but we are uncertain whether it is the insect or the traveler who is borne along by his indifferent music (or, for that matter, whether he is "borne" or "born" in heedless hum).[21]

The concluding lines of this first section also stress a continued present tense, but there is a sense of temporal and thematic resolution here as well:

> Now teach me, *Maid* compos'd,
> To breathe some soften'd Strain,
> Whose Numbers stealing thro' thy darkning Vale,
> May not unseemly with its Stillness suit,
> As musing slow, I hail
> Thy genial lov'd Return!
>
> (ll. 15-20)

The speaker of the poem remains Evening's pupil, but there is already a change in their relationship. She is no longer a *"Nymph* reserv'd" but a *"Maid* compos'd." The ambiguity of this later description (which we have already noticed in *An Essay on Man*) lies at the heart of Collins's poem. The primary evocation here is of Evening's composure; she is calm and dignified, a model for her aspiring admirer. Her influence, moreover, instills these qualities in others. But Collins invokes her in the capacity of Muse as well: he asks not only that she calm him, but that she also inspire his composition. She must, in effect, compose the composer, and she will in turn be the subject of his composition. Collins's pun reminds us that the natural details of Evening's landscape also suggest the poem's literary terrain. The poet who hopes "To breathe some soften'd Strain" will see his numbers "stealing thro' thy darkning Vale" in their attempt to re-create the subtle processes of nature. He must learn a poetic process to capture a natural one. His aspiring strain, furthermore, is yet another term in a series of images devoted to breath and inspiration: oaten stop, dying gales, hushed air, the bat's shrill shriek, the beetle "winding" his sullen horn, and the pilgrim's heedless hum.

We might ask, however, why Collins waits so long to emphasize this important association between the landscape evoked and the means of evocation. The answer appears to lie in the nature of this probationary period. The poem opens with an association between a pastoral scene and a pastoral mode, but the uncertainty and hesitancy here must be dispelled in the practical lessons that follow. When the poet once again addresses his tutor, he does so with an increased confidence in his ability to invoke her. Before, she was reserved, half concealed; now she appears "composed," both calm and fully revealed. Her tutelage of the poet, in other words, has been successful: his soothing voice and growing artistry have both "composed" her. Like the other major personifications in Collins's odes, Evening is a reciprocal figure, both instilling and receiving the effects of her influence. She is consequently a "genial" presence, not only because she is cheering and enlivening (the primary meanings of the term), but also because she is generative and inspiring. Her "lov'd Return" brings with it a fecundity in nature and in the poet's own genial spirits.[22]

Only when the poet has passed through this probationary stage does his poem literally blossom as he dares to introduce Evening in the company of her traditional machinery:

> For when thy folding Star arising shews
> His paly Circlet, at his warning Lamp
> The fragrant *Hours*, and *Elves*

Who slept in Flow'rs the Day,
And many a *Nymph* who wreaths her Brows with Sedge,
And sheds the fresh'ning Dew, and lovelier still,
The *Pensive Pleasures* sweet
Prepare thy shadowy Car.

(ll. 21-28)

In the first section of the ode, Evening appeared primarily as a personified figure—womanly but virginal—in an appropriately simple and
natural setting. In the poem's second movement, however, she first
appears, if only briefly, as a fully mythological character (or, more
precisely, as an allegorical Vesper well suited to this mythological
"Car" and these traditional attendants).[23] These lines represent the
poet's attempt to clothe his elusive figure in classical and native superstitions. His strategy is one of association: we yoke Evening with those
creatures drawn from native folklore and—through a tissue of allusion—
with the numerous literary and pictorial sources that sustain them.
These lines allow Collins to broaden his portrait, but his depiction of
Evening (or of her "shadowy Car") is still far from determinate. The
concluding lines of this central section once again emphasize the am-
biguities and subtleties of this evening scene:

Then lead, calm *Vot'ress*, where some sheety Lake
Cheers the lone Heath, or some time-hallow'd Pile,
Or up-land Fallows grey
Reflect it's last cool Gleam.
But when chill blustring Winds, or driving Rain,
Forbid my willing Feet, be mine the Hut,
That from the Mountain's Side,
Views Wilds, and swelling Floods,
And Hamlets brown, and dim-discover'd Spires,
And hears their simple Bell, and marks o'er all
Thy dewy Fingers draw
The gradual dusky Veil.

(ll. 29-40)

As numerous commentators have pointed out, Collins's revision from
Evening's "religious Gleams" to "it's last cool Gleam" (where "it"
most probably refers to "some sheety Lake") produces a more attenu-
ated and less direct effect. Lighting, after all, is crucial to the force
Evening has on us; here we find that the lone heath is cheered by the
reflected light of the lake. When we actually reach the time-hallowed
pile and upland fallows, we find that these too are illuminated by a

"last cool Gleam" that belongs not to the sun (or to the shadowy car) but to a secondary source in the sheety lake.[24] What we witness, in fact, is a reflection of a reflection, made possible by the stillness of the fallows and by a glassy lake that differs sharply from the sun's tented and "wavy" bed. Nature here, as in "The Manners," is viewed through reflected light.

But this picturesque scene, kindred to the romantic canvases of Claude and Salvator Rosa, cannot last. Evening will lead the poet through a variety of landscapes and moods, all safely observed from a hut on the mountain's side. This is an extraordinary passage, one that sustains elements of the picturesque while also admitting the threatening particulars of the sublime. What may strike us as most intriguing, however, is the nature of the prospect here: the hut, not the poet himself, "Views Wilds, and swelling Floods, / And Hamlets brown, and dim-discover'd Spires." Sherwin views this unusual displacement as "a radical elision of the perceiving subject, which is the most revealing instance of the ode's practice of eroding the outlines of discrete, localized entities."[25] This is surely true, and accords well with the poet's intention of blending his own song with those of Evening. In a sense, they are now equals in his view; he addresses her not as a teacher but as a *"Vot'ress,"* a fellow suppliant on a similar pilgrimage. But we should also notice how closely this passage resembles the episodes in "The Manners" in which shifting images and prospects whirl around a strangely passive central consciousness. Observance and Art, who act as stage-managers and conjurers in "The Manners," have their equivalents here in the manipulative Evening whose dewy fingers draw "The gradual dusky Veil" across this theatrical scene. And here, as in the other ode, an inherently elusive nature will ultimately be transfixed by the properties of art.

The carefully dissipated vision at the close of these lines is therefore replaced by a different perspective in the final section of the ode:

> While *Spring* shall pour his Show'rs, as oft he wont,
> And bathe thy breathing Tresses, meekest *Eve!*
>> While *Summer* loves to sport,
>> Beneath thy ling'ring Light:
> While sallow *Autumn* fills thy Lap with Leaves,
> Or *Winter* yelling thro' the troublous Air,
>> Affrights thy shrinking Train,
>> And rudely rends thy Robes.
> So long, sure-found beneath the Sylvan Shed,
> Shall *Fancy*, *Friendship*, *Science*, rose-lip'd *Health*,

Thy gentlest Influence own,
And hymn thy fav'rite Name!

(ll. 41-52)

These lines are a radical departure from the opening passages of the poem, but they are consistent with Collins's attempt to capture Evening's fleeting qualities and give them more permanent form. We sense a certainty here that the earlier sections of the poem could not sustain; Evening's "gentlest Influence" will be acknowledged by this quartet of personified figures so long as each of the seasons continues to carry us through the varying stages of the year. And this interval is, of course, eternal, a perpetual renewal of Evening's power with the close of every day. This enduring vision, moreover, involves no narrowing of Collins's canvas: we shall continue to glimpse Evening both in her "ling'ring Light" and surrounded by the "troublous Air" that rudely rends her robes. The period of evening—so intimately tied to the transitory, so strictly confined by the eclipsing day and night it separates—is depicted here in the context of time both temporarily arrested and perpetually renewed.[26]

Part of this renewal is derived from the human qualities that owe their vitality in part, at least, to Evening's gentle force. These closing personifications have been questioned by Collins's most sympathetic critics, but they seem to stress once again the mutual dependence of man and nature. They are linked by the ambiguous image of the sylvan shed, which may be either a natural structure or a man-made building, and beneath which either these human attributes or Evening herself may be "sure-found." The ambiguity is carefully controlled. The image of the shed echoes the cloudy tent and rural hut of the previous sections; all are canopied shelters that suggest the benign influence of Evening. And here, more clearly than in the earlier images, we glimpse the reciprocal relationship between the human and natural elements of the scene as they mingle in a structure that belongs to both of them.

This description of the sylvan shed is also, we might claim, a description of the poetical structure Collins himself has created, and his too is a dependent work. Nature, or at least that portion of her that appears in the aspect of Evening, gradually reveals herself to him; in return for this disrobing, he clothes her in a language of permanence. Each has a shielding influence upon the other: she gently smooths the rough edges of nature and provides him with a sheltered view; he attempts to lengthen her shadowy reign and preserve her (in his verse) from the ravages of time. They are thus reciprocal figures, but they are not identical.[27] They nourish each other, and their spirits must be finely attuned, but Evening is not the only poetic source to which the poet can turn. Nor, as some critics have argued, does the poem's conclusion necessarily foreshadow the ominous darkness that closes the "Ode on the Poetical Character" and the elegy on Thomson.[28] Night never falls in this poem; the atmosphere of half-concealment contains revelations of its own: Evening's shadowy shapes provide the characteristic means for coalescence and insight. And in the suspended motions of the ode we glimpse the most direct anticipation of Keats's "Ode to Autumn": we enter the poem just as evening arrives and conclude our passage just before she leaves. We leave her, as we do autumn, knowing that she will fade; but we also grasp the conditions that will keep her fresh before us, in the cycle of the seasons and in the forms and language of art. In terms of Frye's famous distinction, we might say that the "Ode to Evening" is a poem-as-process that gradually evolves into a poem-as-product.[29] Those who cannot finally accept the ode in its entirety are largely responding to the consciously contrived artifact that the poem eventually becomes. But this impulse to capture and preserve, to remold these natural qualities through the contrivances of art, is as important a characteristic of Collins's work as is his attempt to demonstrate the elusiveness of nature.

6

Words for Music

Collins's readers have long acknowledged that the poet awarded "The Passions" pride of place in his collection of odes, but few have asked why this should be so. As we have seen, Collins appears to have placed this musical ode last because of the important ways in which it summarizes—and synthesizes—the modes and themes of the preceding poems. But a much simpler and equally compelling reason for the placement of the ode lies in Collins's interest in music, of which Gilbert White reported the poet to be "passionately fond."[1] Collins's letter to John Gilbert Cooper concludes with an animated description of London's musical life; his only other surviving letter thanks the composer William Hayes for setting "The Passions" to music and promises both a better copy of the ode and another poem on the music of the Grecian theater. Nearly a third of Collins's poems open with a musical motif or with a description of musical effects. In addition to the formal ode on "The Passions," Collins also drafted a verse-epistle to the musical theorist James Harris (Fragment 3) and a later fragment that he simply entitled "Recitative Accompanied." "The Passions" was performed at the Oxford Encaenia of 1750; in 1760, a year after his death, the ode was sung at Gloucester by Frasi and Beard, the two Handelian singers whom the poet mentions in his letter to Cooper.[2] Because music held such a pervasive influence over Collins and his work, the musical odes merit the same kind of serious attention that has already been paid to his interest in the visual arts.

135

I. The Background of "The Passions"

In composing an ode for music, Collins had a particularly rich background on which to draw. The poet could look to contemporary musical practice—with which he was quite familiar—as well as to the literary tradition of the *encomium musicae*, especially the great odes Dryden wrote for the celebration of St. Cecilia's day in 1687 and 1697. But the St. Cecilia odes themselves were fairly late attempts to incorporate musical ideas into poetic form. Much English poetry of the sixteenth and seventeenth centuries reflected the Renaissance's interest in ideas about the nature of music—*musica speculativa*—and about music's effects on men who heard, praised, and practiced it.

The starting point for most thinking about music is the nature of harmony. As John Hollander has shown in *The Untuning of the Sky*, modern conceptions of harmony involve a subtle but important change from ancient theory and practice.[3] The Greek notion of harmony is based on proportion; Pythagorean and Platonic theory held that harmony was derived from the relative ratios between quantities. In its simplest sense, this meant that musical harmony consisted of the blending of separate musical notes, not simultaneously (as in a chord) but consecutively (as in a melody). Essential to the Greek view of harmony is the notion of "scale," which was viewed almost in the architectural sense of "proportion." Thus harmony, in both a concrete and abstract sense, meant a "just disposition of the relative role of parts in a whole."[4] These conceptions of scale and proportion, moreover, were also applied to more complex relationships among the elements of the human soul and in the ordering of the cosmos.

These metaphors were later (and quite easily) converted into Christian analogies about the nature of heavenly music and the music of the individual soul. And, just as the conception of harmony was broadened, so in actual practice the perception of harmony changed to include the simultaneous blending of (often discordant) notes that led to polyphony and sweetness of sound. The idea of *harmonia mundi* was at the heart of this traditional conception of music; but, as the title of Hollander's study suggests, this great metaphor for the way the universe worked became a questionable (if highly useful) fiction in the seventeenth century. Poetical speculation about the nature of music turned from theories of a well-tuned cosmos (*musica mundana*) to the actual practice of those who tuned (and untuned) their instruments.

As belief in universal harmony waned, interest in the power and effects of music increased among Renaissance humanists. *Musica mundana* was replaced by *musica humana*, the moral power of music to arouse men's emotions and to control the different states of the soul. These two influential conceptions of music, equally old, were not necessarily antagonistic; but in the Renaissance the emphasis changed from the power of heavenly harmony (manifested in music) to the power of music itself. George Sandys's remarks on musical effects in his commentary on Ovid's *Metamorphoses* (1632) indicate how the repudiation of spherical harmony could be linked with an emphasis on human psychology:

> Yet musick in it selfe most strangely works upon our humane affections. Not in that the Soule (according to the opinion of the *Platonists*) consisting of harmony, & rapt with the sphearicall musick before it descended from Heaven to inhabit the body, affects it with the like desire . . . but because the Spirits which agitate in the heart, receave a warbling and dancing aire into the bosome, and are made one with the same where with they have an affinity; whose motions lead the rest of the Spirits dispersed through the body, raising or suppressing the instrumental parts according to the measures of the musick; sometimes inflaming: and againe composing the affections: the sense of hearing stricking the Spirits more immediately, then the rest of the sences.[5]

Statements like Sandys's did not mean, however, that the conception of heavenly harmony completely disappeared; poems in praise of *harmonia mundi* continued to be written throughout the seventeenth century.

Dryden's "A Song for St. Cecilia's Day, 1687" demonstrates how these two conceptions of music could be blended within one poetic utterance. The structure of the ode, and especially the transitions in the first two stanzas, suggest the tension between these two traditional views of music. The poem opens with an invocation of *musica mundana*:

> From Harmony, from heav'nly Harmony
>   This universal Frame began.
>   When Nature underneath a heap
>   Of jarring Atomes lay,
>   And cou'd not heave her Head,
>   The tuneful Voice was heard from high,
>   Arise ye more than dead.

                                                   (ll. 1-7)

In Dryden's creation myth, chaos represents a form of imprisonment from which Nature is freed by the ordering power of harmony. Dryden is specific about what kind of harmony this is; the repeated phrase of the opening line represents a specific emphasis (*heavenly* harmony) as well as an extended repeat for Draghi's musical setting. The structure of the universe, the universal "Frame," takes its name both from architecture and from the "scale" of well-proportioned harmony in Greek music. (So, too, the harmonious frame of the first stanza, repeated in the last, represents Dryden's own dramatic frame in the ode.) Universal order is drawn from harmonious music, but music itself is really only an accompaniment to the creator's words here; "tuneful" itself, the creator's voice also tunes and orders the great frame of nature:

> Then cold, and hot, and moist, and dry,
> In order to their stations leap,
>   And MUSICK'S pow'r obey.
> From Harmony, from heav'nly Harmony
>   This universal Frame began:
>   From Harmony to Harmony
> Through all the compass of the Notes it ran,
> The Diapason closing full in Man.

(ll. 8-15)

We should sense both an important transition here and a significant change of prepositions in the movement from l. 11 ("From Harmony, from heav'nly Harmony") to l. 13 ("From Harmony to Harmony"): "What is meant now is a melody, an interval, or more probably a chord, instead of the abstract sense of harmony as order in the original and repeated lines."[6] In other words, the final movement of the first stanza emphasizes not the tenets of *musica mundana* but the beauty and power of music itself, which closes here "full in Man." Dryden then turns in the following stanza to the power of music to affect the emotions of men, beginning with a tribute to *musica humana*: "What Passion cannot MUSICK raise and quell!" Each of the subsequent stanzas in the ode describes the success of an individual musical instrument in drawing forth human emotion: anger and courage, love and pity, jealousy and despair, and the peace and power of religion. Universal harmony enters only in the concluding "Grand Chorus"; in Dryden's later ode for music, "Alexander's Feast," it barely enters at all.

Dryden's interest in representing the passions is an important landmark in English thinking about music, one that was to influence Pope a generation later and Collins and Gray later still. And, like his successors, Dryden was able to draw not only on early English poetry devoted to musical expression but to a standard musical iconography as well. Particular instruments were thought to educe and express specific emotions, and certain musical odes (Lydian, Dorian, Phrygian, and so forth) were believed to express those emotions best. Closely associated with this collaboration between the poetic and the musical was a corresponding emphasis on the pictorial expression of emotion; each expressive stanza of Dryden's ode, for example, includes not only an appropriate instrument and emotion (and an appropriate musical mode and metrical equivalent) but a typical "scene" as well. The painter Poussin, who became an influential spokesman for the relationship between musical forms and pictorial style, proposed a marriage between classical musical modes and modern styles in painting: "Our wise ancient Greeks, inventors of all beautiful things, found several Modes by means of which they produced marvellous effects. . . . I hope, before another year is out, to paint a subject in this Phrygian Mode. The subject of frightful wars lends itself to this manner."[7] André Félibien (to whom Collins was to allude in two of his fragments) pointed out that Poussin was able to control the elements of his art—colors, for instance—as if they were tones in music.[8] Another French academician, Charles LeBrun, published an influential handbook in which sketches of different characters (each representing an emotional state) were accompanied by an interpretative text.[9] Thus, by the early eighteenth century, poets, painters, and musicians were able to draw on a firmly established tradition of how the passions were to be portrayed. And these formalized conceptions of character had an influence in other fields as well: it was only a step from the portrayal of emotions in poetry and painting to their representation in the theater, and at least one great actor (Thomas Betterton) was famous for his ability to delineate these passions on the stage.[10]

This interest in tracing *musica humana* back to its classical sources led to an important conclusion among late seventeenth-century writers: the music of ancient times, especially Greek music, was thought to be superior to the debased melodies of the present day. No modern musician (or poet) could be said to have the powers traditionally ascribed to Orpheus or Amphion. In his essay "Of Musick" (1697), Jeremy Collier weighed the possible causes for this artistic decline:

> That the Musick of the Antients could command further than the Modern, is past Dispute. Whether they were Masters of a greater Compass of *Notes*, or knew the Secret of varying them more artificially: Whether they adjusted the Intervals of Silence more exactly, had their hands or their voices farther improved, or their Instruments better contrived: Whether they had a deeper Insight into the Philosophy of Nature, and understood the *Laws* of the *Union* of the Soul and Body more thoroughly; and from thence were enabled to touch the Passions, strengthen the *Sense*, or prepare the *Medium* with greater advantage: Whether they excell'd us in all, or in many of these ways,

> Is not so Clear. However this is certain, That our Improvements of this kind are little better than an Ale-house-Crowds, with respect to theirs.[11]

Other surveyors of contemporary music often established harmony and polyphony as their focus of criticism. John Wallis, who was asked by the Royal Society to investigate the claims made for the powers of ancient music, reported that "When *Musick* arrived to great Perfection, it was applied to particular Designs of exciting this or that particular Affection, Passion, or Temper of Mind; the *Tunes* and *Measures* being suitably adapted to such Designs. But such Designs seem almost quite neglected in our *present Musick*. The chief Design now, in our most accomplished Musick, being to please the Ear; when by a sweet Mixture of different *Parts* and *Voices*, with *Cadencies* and *Concord* inter-mixed, a grateful sound is produced, which only the judicious *Musician* can discern and distinguish."[12] Commentators like Wallis soon began to argue that instrumental music was unintelligible, that pure sound was "empty." Charles Gildon summarized the standard view in *The Complete Art of Poetry in Six Parts* (1718):

> The Greeks, quite contrary to the moderns, were a people too rational and of too fine and just a taste, to encourage or even relish any musical performance, that consisted meerly of sound, since that could afford little or no entertainment to the mind, or at all engage the understanding, without which they never thought any diversion worthy their attention. They gave Amphion and Orpheus charming voices, and words divinely inspir'd to produce the wonders they tell us of their lyres, which serv'd only to accompany their vocal performance.[13]

Musical sound, Gildon and others concluded, was produced at the expense of sense; the most effective music, they argued, represented a blending of music and poetry.

But a more radical proposal, stressing not only the marriage of music and poetry but also that which is musical *in* poetry, had already been suggested by Dryden. In his preface to *Albion and Albanius* (1685), Dryden stated that the principle of musical poetry lay in "the choice of Words; and by this choice I do not here mean Elegancy of expression, but propriety of sound to be varyed according to the Nature of the Subject. Perhaps a time may come, when I may treat of this more largely, out of some Observations which I have made from *Homer* and *Virgil*, who amongst all the Poets, only understood the Art of Numbers, and of that which was properly call'd *Rhythmus* by the Ancients."[14] D. T. Mace has shown in his study of the doctrine of *rhythmus* that Dryden was indebted to Isaac Vossius's *De poematum cantu et viribus rhythmi* (1673) for his conviction that rhythm was the basis for the astonishing effects of the ancient musicians.[15] Only through a reformed rhythm could modern poets attain the powers of their ancient models; Dryden's own success in the expressive stanzas of his "Ode for St. Cecilia's Day" is produced by careful rhythmic variations. The modern *encomium musicae* was to have its own music; Vossius even believed that contemporary poetry could duplicate ancient effects if it observed the rhythmical proportions of the classical feet. Vossius's conception of rhythm was also related to the art of painting the passions: "Is not rhythm the most palpable, physically the most immediately comprehensible of all musical elements, the one most naturally susceptible of being moulded into a *representation* of emotion, into an *image* which, like bodily movement, paints the inner and hidden passions of the soul?"[16]

Vossius's preference for rhythm rather than harmony or polyphonic counterpoint, for the word rather than the sound, was especially significant for the practicing poet. Music, in seventeenth-century English poetry, had become a metaphor for poetry itself; the poet was now instructed to fuse the properties of both arts. In many ways Dryden's ode for St. Cecilia became a touchstone for the various debates over the powers of the sister arts, and these tensions can be felt even in our own critical approaches to the ode. Hollander, whose subject is harmony, stresses the artful construction of the opening and closing stanzas of the poem; Mace, whose subject is rhythm, almost dismisses these stanzas. Dryden himself seems finally to have been dissatisfied with the ode, and in its successor ten years later he not only emphasized the portrayal of the passions but also added a more thorough (and fool-proof) structure on which the composer could base his setting. To be successful the *encomium musicae* had to meet rather rigid requirements, and Dryden's poems soon became models for the formal ode for music.[17] These were often rather Procrustean standards, of course, and it is not surprising that Dryden's successors produced odes easily as mediocre as his predecessors' for the annual St. Cecilia's day performances. Such rigidity also produced parody, and the stream of comical "cantatas" from Addison, Swift, Bonnell Thornton, and others was aimed as much at the musical ode as it was at Italian opera, long thought to be the epitome of senseless sound.

Collins's first poem with a musical subject, written two generations after Dryden's, is a fragmentary verse-epistle addressed to James ("Hermes") Harris, a theorist best known for his later work in linguistics.[18] Harris apparently caught Collins's attention in 1744 when he published his *Three Treatises*, which contains a commentary on art in general, on the sister arts of music, painting, and poetry, and on

happiness.[19] In the second treatise Harris focuses on the properties of
these three arts, showing how, in their different aspects, they either
resemble or differ from each other. Harris's commentary on music is
based on the conception of *musica humana*: "There are various *Affec-*
tions, which may be raised by the Power of *Music*. There are Sounds
to make us *chearful*, or *sad*; *martial*, or *tender*; and so of almost every
other Affection, which we feel."[20] This is traditional theory, as we
have seen, but Harris qualifies his remarks by examining the basis of
musical effects. He argues for a *"reciprocal Operation"* between our
affections and our ideas; each is able to raise the other. In making this
distinction, Harris associates music solely with the arousal of emotion,
and poetry primarily with the "images" of our understanding. Music
and poetry can therefore be combined as allies; if music precedes poetic declamation, it will not only soften the audience (thus making it
responsive to the poet's art), but may also, through its various musical
effects, anticipate the poet's ideas "in their several Imaginations."

Harris consequently views music as an expressive and not an imitative art. Music raises the affections, to which our ideas may correspond. Harris's ideal is therefore an amiable union of "GOOD POETRY
. . . JUSTLY SET TO MUSIC." These two arts "can never be so powerful *singly*, as when they are *properly united*": poetry needs the energy
of music, music the lasting images of poetry. But poetry itself must
"ever have the *Precedence*" because of its utility and dignity.[21] This
last remark is important, for it may appear at first glance that Harris
reserves undue praise for music. It is true that Harris does not emphasize the expressive powers of poetry (as Vossius and Dryden had done),
but his insistence on the primacy of the word is entirely consistent
with the proponents of *rhythmus*. Poetry is sensible; it appeals to the
understanding. Music, on the other hand, makes its appeal only to our
emotions, and therefore lacks both the utility and dignity of its sister
art. But Harris is able to praise both poetry and music by showing that
they are able to reinforce each other precisely *because* they differ. His
preference for an amiable union between the two arts therefore represents a convenient justification of the ode for music. But Harris's
conclusions would seem to endorse other artistic unions as well, and
it is not surprising that his examples are often drawn from opera seria,
especially those of Handel, "from whom this Treatise has borrowed
such eminent Examples, to justify its Assertions in what it has offer'd
concerning Music."[22]

Collins's epistle to Harris is both enthusiastic and (initially) surprising. The poem opens with an address to music:

> These would I sing—O Art for ever dear
> Whose Charms so oft have caught my raptur'd Ear
> O teach me Thou, if my unpolish'd lays
> Are all too rude to speak thy gentle praise
> O teach me softer sounds of sweeter kind.
>
> (ll. 1-5)

Even in this early poem we find the poet in a characteristic pose: addressing a personified deity, he prays for assistance in performing his celebratory rites even as he practices them. The "Charms" belong both to the idealized woman he beholds and to ancient music's affective powers. Music, as a woman, paradoxically ravishes the poet's ear; but the appeal of the invocation is to music's softer powers. Like the speaker of the "Ode to Evening," the poet here asks to be taught composure so that he may better frame his composition. Collins's emphasis, like Harris's, is on *musica humana*.

But in the following lines we are granted a glimpse of an unexpected contention between the other sister arts:

> Then let the Muse and Picture Each contend
> This plan her Tale, and that her Colours blend
> With me tho' both their kindred charms combine
> No Pow'r shall emulate or equal thine!
>
> (ll. 7-10; 6 is blank)

Collins surprisingly disregards Harris's vision of a harmonious union of music and poetry so that he may praise music above its kindred arts. Collins's reasoning is not entirely clear here, but subsequent passages in the fragment suggest that the attraction of music lies primarily in the vitality of its effects. After ceremoniously addressing Harris as the "Son of Harmony," Collins envisions a tableau in which he is introduced by the theorist into the company of Philosophy, there to become the "meanest of her votive train." Harris will teach the poet why his soul obeys music's "pow'rfull Art":

> Why at her bidding or by strange surprise
> Or wak'd by fond degrees my Passions rise
> How well-form'd Reed's my sure Attention gain
> And what the Lyre's well-measur'd strings contain.
>
> (ll. 23-26)

Music provides Collins with a traditional and effective metaphor for displaying human emotions. Poetry, of course, also essays this task; Harris had argued that poetry was especially adapted to all subjects framed so as "to lay open the *internal Constitution of Man*, and give us an Insight into *Characters*, *Manners*, *Passions*, and *Sentiments*."[23] Collins's distortion of Harris's conclusions surely signifies his enthusiastic discovery of a related mode by which to develop his allegorical visions, but poetry itself is not entirely neglected in the fragment:

> The Mighty Masters too unprais'd so long
> Shall not be lost, if Thou assist my Song
> They who with Pindars in one Age bestow'd
> Cloath'd the sweet words which in their numbers flowd
> And Rome's and Adria's Sons—if Thou but strive
> To guard their Names, shall in my Verse survive.
>
> (ll. 27-32)

The "Mighty Masters" are the Greek musicians who set the works of Pindar and his colleagues to music. Collins salutes the poets and musicians together, while also emphasizing the musical elements in the poet's sweet words and flowing numbers. Collins evokes an ancient culture in which music and poetry are as well formed and well measured as Music's reed and lyre. The restoration of a golden age of song (in its double sense) is the final burden of Collins's first poem on music and provides the controlling frame for his ode on "The Passions" as well.

II. A Reading of "The Passions"

The opening of Collins's ode for music is closely modeled on the second stanza of Dryden's "Song for St. Cecilia's Day." In Dryden's poem, Jubal's "Brethren" are awed by the "Celestial Sound" of the corded shell; in Collins's ode, the passions themselves are swayed by the divine lessons of music:

> When Music, Heav'nly Maid, was young,
> While yet in early *Greece* she sung,
> The Passions oft to hear her Shell,
> Throng'd around her magic Cell,
> Exulting, trembling, raging, fainting,
> Possest beyond the Muse's Painting;
> By turns they felt the glowing Mind,
> Disturb'd, delighted, rais'd, refin'd.
>
> (ll. 1-8)

The time of this allegorical action lies somewhere between the creation of the world in "A Song for St. Cecilia's Day" and the Hellenistic setting of "Alexander's Feast." Music is pictured in her "magic Cell," a setting that suggests both her religious nature (she is a "Heav'nly Maid," "Sphere-descended") and her artistic powers. Like the seductive Art of "The Manners," Music produces similar enchantments within her magic cave; and although she does not, like Art, stage-manage the ensuing action of the poem, she is in fact the source of the pageant that now unfolds before our eyes. Collins disrupts the dominant iambic tetrameter of the opening stanza to emphasize the transforming power of music over the emotions in ll. 5-6; here the altered rhythm of the trochees begins to reveal the extent of Music's influence. "Exulting, trembling, raging, fainting," the Passions are soon "Possess beyond the Muse's Painting." Music is seen, as in the epistle to Harris, to convey a power exceeding the limitations of pictorial art. As each Passion is touched by the "glowing Mind" of Music, it becomes "Disturb'd, delighted, rais'd, refin'd." Hagstrum has argued that Collins's lines in this poem are too often "filled with lists of words in unsubordinated relationship,"[24] but here the progression in meaning is fairly clear and is supported poetically by alliteration and by the natural rise of the rhythm (an iambic meter that has succeeded the concluding trochees of the previous lines). Music's power first disturbs, then delights; delight leads in turn to a raised sensibility that issues in the refined purity of these separate emotional states.

But if these passions are purified to a point of emotional distinctness, they are also heightened to a pitch approaching the mad scenes in "Alexander's Feast":

> Till once, 'tis said, when all were fir'd,
> Fill'd with Fury, rapt, inspir'd,
> From the supporting Myrtles round,
> They snatch'd her Instruments of Sound,
> And as they oft had heard a-part
> Sweet Lessons of her forceful Art,
> Each, for Madness rul'd the Hour,
> Would prove his own expressive Pow'r.
>
> (ll. 9-16)

The characteristic "once, 'tis said" heralds the beginning of Collins's own myth, a legend not unlike that of the "Ode on the Poetical Character." The various Passions, inspired by Music, are eventually moved to "snatch" the "Instruments of Sound" from her; each passion, formerly tutored by Music, will now attempt to "prove" its own power and express its own voice with an appropriate musical instrument. This action appears to be a natural consequence of Music's influence, but there is also a sustained violence in Collins's lines, for he paints a scene of rapture that borders on violation. Just as the Passions are carried away ("rapt, inspir'd") by the power of music, so they in turn carry away her instruments, intent on proving themselves in a trial of strength similar to the tourney of the "Poetical Character." The submerged element of rape (in the baroque sense of a rapturous penetration by the power of music)[25] is reinforced by the sensuousness of Collins's heated imagery: music's "glowing Mind," as well as "fir'd" emotions that are "Fill'd with Fury, rapt, inspir'd."

The first emotion to place itself on "Ecstatic Trial" (l. 80) is appropriately Fear, a suitable contender in a scene of emotional "Madness." Collins demonstrates, however, how Fear's brisk entrance soon concludes in the hesitancy of fearful emotion:

> First *Fear* his Hand, its Skill to try,
> Amid the Chords bewilder'd laid,
> And back recoil'd he knew not why,
> Ev'n at the Sound himself had made.

(ll. 17-20)

Collins's portrayal of Fear is consistent with his full-length description in the earlier ode. The allegorical figure is both fear-inspiring and fearful, a double conception skillfully developed in the musical tableau. Fear is afraid of himself, afraid "Ev'n at the Sound himself had made"; but this sound also defines fear, for the "expressive Pow'r" of each passionate performance expresses the nature of that emotion. Fear chooses to play upon Music's lyre, a traditional emblem of harmony and concord.[26] But Fear can only lay a "bewilder'd" hand amid the strings, and Collins's description creates not only a concrete image of Fear's hesitant musicianship but a metaphorical depiction of an emotional state that lies between ("amid") the melodious chords of the lyre. Collins's pun on "Chords" is both traditional and effective, and the further association between the cords of the lyre and the cords of the heart reinforces the poet's conception of this fearful figure. So too does Collins's manipulation of language and syntax. The stanza begins briskly and ends tamely. The description of a recoiling figure of Fear in the third and fourth lines of the stanza is supported both by the indirection of the syntax and by the metrical emphasis on the reflexive words ("And báck," "recóil'd," "himsélf"). The linguistic suppleness of this passage suggests that to speak of meter and syntax is to talk as well about the nature of the personified emotion. Collins seems to have been able to put the advice and example of Vossius and Dryden to good use.

But this first stanza devoted to the passions also points to an important change in emphasis from Collins's models. "An Ode for St.

Cecilia's Day" opens with the (musical) creation of the universe and ends with the last trump, but embedded within this universal sequence are examples drawn from human as well as sacred history (Jubal, Cecilia).[27] The passions themselves are treated only in the central stanzas of the poem, and then only indirectly. In the third stanza, for example, the primary emotions are anger and martial courage, but these passions are actually subordinated to the musical expression of the instruments:

> The TRUMPETS loud Clangor
> Excites us to Arms
> With shrill Notes of Anger
> And mortal Alarms.
> The double double double beat
> Of the thundring DRUM
> Cryes, heark the Foes come;
> Charge, Charge, 'tis too late to retreat.

In the following stanza the principal emotion is introduced through one appropriate instrument and then subsumed by yet another:

> The soft complaining FLUTE
> In dying Notes discovers
> The Woes of hopeless Lovers,
> Whose Dirge is whisper'd by the warbling LUTE.

And in the next stanza the "Sharp VIOLINS" that express the major passions of jealousy and desperation actually become the unhappy suitors of a "fair, disdainful Dame." Dryden's characteristic focus in the poem is on the instruments of sound; the various instruments produce and represent different emotional states that really have no independent reality of their own. Similarly, in "Alexander's Feast," the master-musician plays upon the king and his companions by singing a variety of songs; the emotions that are raised and quelled are strictly confined by the narrative framework of the poem.

Collins's strategy in "The Passions" is an intriguing reversal of Dryden's. Collins confronts the passions directly; the actual musical instruments provide appropriate expression for the emotions, but the passions appear as full-fledged allegorical figures before the instruments are introduced.[28] The opening of the poem is fully as direct as the affective stanzas that follow. Gone is Dryden's grand framework of creation, or the discovery of the organ, or the triumphs of Alexander; we are simply introduced to Music where she lives. And Music herself is envisioned as a fully allegorical character, not a traditional figure like

Orpheus, Cecilia, Timotheus, or even God. This reversal is obviously crucial to Collins's transformation of the *encomium musicae*. As we have seen, Collins was attracted to music because of its ability to evoke and represent the passions; and thus the *encomium musicae*, in his hands, is employed less to praise the powers of music than to explore the nature of the passions. Collins's interest in *musica humana* is even more human than was Dryden's. In this final poem in his volume, Collins's focus is directly on those psychological states examined—or at least momentarily evoked—in the preceding eleven odes.

Each of the following stanzas is devoted to a single emotion. Fear is followed by Anger, whose brutal musicianship succeeds the bewildered hesitancy of his predecessor:

> Next *Anger* rush'd, his Eyes on fire,
>   In Lightnings own'd his secret Stings,
> In one rude Clash he struck the Lyre,
>   And swept with hurried Hand the Strings.

                                        (ll. 21-24)

The sweep of Collins's lines suggests the impetuosity of the player. The heat of the introductory tableau is now fused in Anger's traditionally fiery eyes, associated here with an internal lightning that strikes with "secret Stings" as Anger plays the lyre. Fear and Anger play upon the same instrument, but with a different touch: Anger now violently strikes the lyre with a lightning-like "Clash." In the next stanza, Despair, playing the same instrument, produces "Low sullen Sounds" in "woful Measures," and Collins emphasizes the transition in musical effect by beginning the second line with a spondee. Despair, moreover, vacillates between emotional states; the "mingled Air" he plays represents his own mingled emotions, which are then embodied in the following line: " 'Twas sad by Fits, by Starts 'twas wild." Collins playfully toys with the idiomatic "fits and starts" and "fits of despair" while fashioning a syntactical reversal in the line that suits the sudden shift in feeling.

Music's lyre is soon taken up by Hope in an extended passage that contrasts sharply with the preceding stanzas:

> But Thou, O *Hope*, with Eyes so fair,
>   What was thy delightful Measure?
> Still it whisper'd promis'd Pleasure,
>   And bad the lovely Scenes at distance hail!
> Still would Her Touch the Strain prolong,
>   And from the Rocks, the Woods, the Vale,
> She call'd on Echo still thro' all the Song;

> And where Her sweetest Theme She chose,
> A soft responsive Voice was heard at ev'ry Close,
> And *Hope* enchanted smil'd, and wav'd Her golden Hair.
>
> (ll. 29-38)

The "delightful Measure" and fair scenes evoked by Hope come as a welcome relief after the dismal cadences of Fear, Anger, and Despair. Collins's emphasis falls on the sweetness and softness of the sounds Hope produces: her melodic touch on the lyre now animates a vocal accompaniment as Echo joins in the song; her sympathetic vibration ("soft responsive Voice") serving as a traditional image of concord and harmony.[29] Hope's "sweetest Theme" is double-edged: Collins suggests that our greatest expectations are consonant with musical motifs that are "well-tuned." And Hope, significantly, is the first personified figure to enjoy the Orphic powers of enchantment over the imagined landscape of the poem.

Hope's pleasures, however, are only promised, and Collins's technique in this passage poetically reinforces a sense of continuation. We are offered hope of "promis'd Pleasure" at some future time; like Hope, we must hail her lovely scenes only at a distance (a spatial perspective that is stressed by the addition of an extra metrical foot). The dominant musical and emotional motif of the passage is embodied in the repeated "still" (ll. 31, 33, 35), which suggests both the whispers of Hope and our continued expectations. Hope's song is appropriately continued by Echo, who is introduced in another line that has swollen from four to five iambic feet. Collins rounds out his description of Hope's prolonged song by drastically varying the rhyme scheme of the stanza as well: most of the rhymes are closely paired in this passage, but the concluding "fair" of the initial line is skillfully allowed to dangle until it is finally matched by "Hair" as the stanza closes.

Collins's lines on Hope demonstrate perhaps his greatest success in experimenting with rhyme, meter, musical motif, and allegorical construction. Only a sudden transition can jar us from the comforts of Hope's harmonious song, and Collins accomplishes this with the intrusion of Revenge, the first figure to discard the well-tuned lyre:

> And longer had She sung,—but with a Frown,
> *Revenge* impatient rose,
> He threw his blood-stain'd Sword in Thunder down,
> And with a with'ring Look,
> The War-denouncing Trumpet took,
> And blew a Blast so loud and dread,
> Were ne'er Prophetic Sounds so full of Woe.

> And ever and anon he beat
> The doubling Drum with furious Heat;
> And tho' sometimes each dreary Pause between,
> Dejected *Pity* at his Side,
> Her Soul-subduing Voice applied,
> Yet still He kept his wild unalter'd Mien,
> While each strain'd Ball of Sight seem'd bursting from his Head.
>
> (ll. 39-52)

Hope's smile is replaced by Revenge's frown, just as the harmonious "Close" of her song is usurped by the rhyming "rose" of line 40. Revenge, a survivor of Collins's "patriotic" odes, matches the lightning of Anger with the thunder of his sword. He chooses to play the prophetic trumpet, but his song announces only war. And yet he is a skillful player: Collins suggests the unique power of his music ("Were ne'er Prophetic Sounds so full of Woe") in one of the two lines in the poem that has no corresponding rhyme. Revenge also beats the "doubling Drum" in a passage largely derived from Dryden's portrayal of Anger in "A Song for St. Cecilia's Day." But Collins qualifies this traditional scene by introducing a frustrated duet between Revenge and the "Soul-subduing Voice" of Pity. For the first time we witness a battle between the forces that raise and quell the emotions; but, just as there is no place for pity in our vindictive actions, so Collins's figure here sustains his frightful song and keeps his "unalter'd Mien." The violence of Revenge's music is aptly conveyed in the final line: Revenge's musical "strains" are suggested only in each "strain'd Ball of Sight"; his "bursts" on the trumpet are visualized in eyes that "seem'd bursting from his Head."

The contending elements within Jealousy, however, end in an emotional and musical stalemate:

> Thy Numbers, *Jealousy*, to nought were fix'd,
> Sad Proof of thy distressful State,
> Of diff'ring Themes the veering Song was mix'd,
> And now it courted *Love*, now raving call'd on *Hate*.
>
> (ll. 53-56)

Jealousy is the only figure in the poem denied an instrument of musical expression; caught between Love and Hate, Jealousy cannot fix his veering song to any steady theme. Nor can he fix the "Numbers" of his song, a point Collins expresses in the stanza by varying the length of the two sets of rhymed lines and then extending the final line by yet another foot.

The restless agitation of Jealousy is succeeded by the slower measures of Melancholy, retired to "her wild sequester'd Seat." Melancholy pours her pensive soul through "the mellow *Horn*" in notes that are "by Distance made more sweet," a suitable musical expression for the emotional distance that sets the melancholic figure apart. Melancholy's song is joined by the echoing answer of the stream:

> And dashing soft from Rocks around,
> Bubbling Runnels join'd the Sound;
> Thro' Glades and Glooms the mingled Measure stole,
> Or o'er some haunted Stream with fond Delay,
> Round an holy Calm diffusing,
> Love of Peace, and lonely Musing,
> In hollow Murmurs died away.
>
> (ll. 62-68)

The "mingled Measure" of her song refers not to a contention between emotions or musical modes but to the sympathetic concord of nature. But it is the fate of Melancholy's song to be dissipated as soon as it swells: the "fond Delay" of the song (emphasized in extended lines) is soon contracted in the shorter lines that close the stanza. Melancholy "diffuses" her plaintive song, which dies away "In hollow Murmurs." Collins envisions Melancholy as a figure whose performance on the mellow horn symbolizes an emptying out of her soul, as a musician who finally loses even the notes of her song.

Chearfulness appears as a vibrant successor to the enervated Melancholy:

> But O how alter'd was its sprightlier Tone!
> When *Chearfulness*, a Nymph of healthiest Hue,
> Her Bow a-cross her Shoulder flung,
> Her Buskins gem'd with Morning Dew,
> Blew an inspiring Air, that Dale and Thicket rung,
> The Hunter's Call to *Faun* and *Dryad* known!
>
> (ll. 69-74)

Chearfulness, like Melancholy, is an inhabitant of the wilderness; but, cast as a Diana-like figure, she is also surrounded by fauns, dryads, satyrs, and sylvan boys. Her turn at the horn produces an inspiriting air that summons forth the figures of Exercise and Sport. These characters are followed in the next stanza by Joy, a lively figure whose "Ecstatic Trial" reminds us of how far we have strayed from the original tableau of the poem. Chearfulness and Melancholy have led us to their own territory, a world of "sequester'd Seats" or "Alleys green."

With the arrival of Joy, however, these fancied landscapes momentarily disappear or are, at most, submerged in the image of Joy's "viny Crown."

Joy first addresses the "lively Pipe," but "soon he saw the brisk awak'ning Viol, / Whose sweet entrancing Voice he lov'd the best." Joy's choice of the viol returns us to a traditional stringed instrument of reason, but this instrument—like the lyre—possesses liberating powers. In lines reminiscent of Warton's ode "To Fancy," Collins suggests a musical voice for Joy that paradoxically wakes us into a trance. The concluding lines in this stanza reveal the vision Joy has framed:

> They would have thought who heard the Strain,
> They saw in *Tempe*'s Vale her native Maids,
> Amidst the festal sounding Shades,
> To some unwearied Minstrel dancing,
> While as his flying Fingers kiss'd the Strings,
> LOVE fram'd with *Mirth*, a gay fantastic Round,
> Loose were Her Tresses seen, her Zone unbound,
> And HE amidst his frolic Play,
> As if he would the charming Air repay,
> Shook thousand Odours from his dewy Wings.
>
> (ll. 85-94)

Joy's exalted vision takes us away from the trial-by-music of the opening lines, but it also provides a Grecian landscape closely resembling the pastoral world of sphere-descended Music. Tempe had recently been celebrated by Akenside as the "haunt belov'd of sylvan powers, / Of nymphs and fauns; where in the golden age / They play'd in secret on the shady brink / With ancient Pan."[30] Collins depicts a timeless moment in which perpetual dance is inspired by unwearied musicians. This is a world of direct and innocent sensuality, where Love and Mirth together pursue their frolic play, where the five senses combine to create a moment worth regaining.

This restoration of a golden age of art is Collins's ultimate theme:

> O *Music*, Sphere-descended Maid,
> Friend of Pleasure, *Wisdom's* Aid,
> Why, Goddess, why to us deny'd?
> Lay'st Thou thy antient Lyre aside?
> As in that lov'd *Athenian* Bow'r,
> You learn'd an all-commanding Pow'r,
> Thy mimic Soul, O Nymph endear'd,
> Can well recall what then it heard.
>
> (ll. 95-102)

The lyre now serves as synecdoche for music, music for art. Collins's vision is remarkably close to that of the "Ode on the Poetical Character": powers that would enable us to rival ancient achievements are now "to us deny'd." Collins asks Music to "Arise as in that elder Time," concluding his ode with a formal exhortation:

> 'Tis said, and I believe the Tale,
> Thy humblest *Reed* could more prevail,
> Had more of Strength, diviner Rage,
> Than all which charms this laggard Age,
> Ev'n all at once together found,
> *Cæcilia*'s mingled World of Sound —
> O bid our vain Endeavors cease,
> Revive the just Designs of *Greece*,
> Return in all thy simple State!
> Confirm the Tales Her Sons relate!
>
> (ll. 109-18)

Cecilia's entrance is an ambiguous one; music itself (and perhaps the *encomium musicae* dedicated to her) has become a charmless jumble. Collins prays for the return of musical simplicity, energy, design, sublimity, and ultimate divinity, and of a world like that praised by Greece's poetical sons. In his own concluding lines, Collins attempts to capture the design and energy of the art he wishes to restore. The close of the ode marks a return to Greece, a return to the opening setting of the poem, and a return to the regularity of the opening rhythms and rhymes as well. Only now can we see how the two structural elements of the poem—the balanced mythological frame and the enclosed descriptions of the passions—are related. The simple and direct setting, in which the poet calls for a return to traditional forms of artistic expression, functions as the appropriate frame for direct allegorical representations of emotion that are examined as closely as possible. The elemental passions are best explored in a poetry or music that itself embodies an elemental simplicity.

Collins's attack on the artificiality of contemporary music in "The Passions" has its counterpart in the "Ode on the Poetical Character," but this final poem also serves as a close companion to "The Manners," in which Collins suggests that we turn from an exploration of external nature to an examination of the world within. "The Passions" is in fact an attempt to summarize the psychological representations of an entire volume of odes, and to synthesize their various artistic modes. And here, as in his general arrangement of the *Odes*, he represents the different passions in a variety of rhymes and meters.[31] Like Dryden,

Collins intended to express the very music he advocated; and like Dryden he attempted to shape a musical ode in each "of the senses suggested by that compound: an ode set to, about, purporting to resemble, and even substituting for music. More than that, it implicitly stipulates for its own age and for successive ones as well what music is, and how it should be considered."[32] If we broaden Hollander's conclusion to include poetry as well, we shall have begun to unravel Collins's accomplishment in the *Odes*.

III. The Revival of the Musical Ode

In spite of its merits as a concluding poem in his volume of odes, "The Passions" apparently later struck Collins as a not entirely satisfactory ode for music. In a letter to the composer William Hayes, who had recently set the poem to music for the Oxford Encaenia of 1750, Collins described both an improved version of the ode and a new poem on a similar subject:

> Mr Blackstone of Winchester some time since inform'd Me of the Honour You had done me at Oxford last Summer for which I return You my sincere thanks. I have another more perfect Copy of the Ode, which, had I known your obliging design, *I would* have communicated to You. Inform me by a Line, If You should think one of my better Judgment acceptable; In such Case I could send you one written on a Nobler Subject, and which, tho' I have been persuaded to bring it forth in London, I think more calculated for an Audience in the University. The Subject is the Music of the Græcian Theatre, in which I have, I hope, Naturally introduc'd the Various Characters with which the Chorus was concern'd, as Oedipus, Medæa, Electra, Orestes &c &c The Composition too is probably more correct, as I have chosen the ancient Tragedies for my Models, and onely copied the most affecting Passages in Them.[33]

A revised version of "The Passions" has never been found (it may never have been written), and apparently Collins's ambitious poem on the Grecian theater was neither finished nor performed. It is nevertheless important that we notice Collins's interest in contemporary music at this time, and that we realize that Collins was now envisioning his work with an actual musical performance in mind. William Hayes, Professor of Music at Oxford, was a substantial figure in the musical world, and Collins also knew the Winchester composer Jasper Clarke and the Vauxhall organist John Worgan (Collins goes on to mention both of these men in his letter to Hayes). But even though Collins is resolute in the letter, it would have been characteristic of him, as

Lonsdale has suggested, to describe an ambitious poem as finished when it had only been conceived or just begun.

Among the fragments at Trinity College, Oxford, however, is a poem almost certainly associated with this projected ode on the music of the Grecian theater. Without Collins's letter to Hayes we would have difficulty in making sense of the fragment (and even in determining whether or not the poem is indeed fragmentary); but Collins's description of his projected ode suggests that Fragment 11 may represent a starting point for this ambitious poem. The fragment is best quoted in full:

> Recitative Accompanied.
>
> When Glorious Ptolomy by Merit rais'd
>   Successive sate on Ægypt's radiant Throne
> Bright Ptolomy, on whom, while Athens gaz'd
>   She almost wish'd the Monarch once Her own
> Then Virtue own'd one Royal Heart;
>   For loathing war, humanely wise
> For All the Sacred Sons of Art
>   He bad the Dome of Science rise.
> The Muses knew the festal day
>   And call'd by Pow'r Obsequant came
> With all their Lyres and Chaplets gay
>   To give the Fabric its immortal Name
>   High oer the rest in Golden Pride
>   The Monarch sate, and at his side
>   His Fav'rite Bards—His Græcian Quire
>   Who while the Roofs responsive Rung
>   To many a Fife and many a tinkling Lyre
> Amid the Shouting Tribes in sweet succession Sung.

Though short, this fragment is immensely suggestive. It seems clear that the poem, whatever its relation to the larger ode on Greek music may be, is carefully modeled on Dryden's "Alexander's Feast," which opens with a similar setting:

> 'Twas at the Royal Feast, for *Persia* won,
>   By *Philip's* Warlike Son:
>   Aloft in awful State
>   The God-like Heroe sate
>   On his Imperial Throne.

This parallel is especially intriguing when we consider Dryden's own dissatisfaction with his first musical "Song for St. Cecilia's Day," and his attempts in its successor to create a historical frame for his description of the passions and to provide his own clear markings of where the musical repeats and choruses should fall. Collins headed his lines with the musical notation "Recitative Accompanied," and then began to fashion a tableau that was also centered on an ancient monarch.

Collins's Ptolomy, however, differs sharply from "*Philip*'s Warlike Son." Ptolomy Philadelphus (308-246 B.C.) was "rais'd" to the throne by his father, Ptolomy Soter, even though he was not the eldest son; he ruled with his father, and then succeeded him. Collins stresses Philadelphus' patronage of the arts, especially his establishment of the famous Museum in Alexandria.[34] Philadelphus in fact counted Callimachus and Theocritus among his friends, and Alexandria was occasionally compared to the court of Pope Leo X (Leo was the projected hero of Collins's *History of the Revival of Learning*). Ptolomy's Alexandria is pictured as a center of Hellenistic culture, a site from which (as Athens enviously "gaz'd" at its ruler) the monuments of Greek art could be preserved and surveyed.[35]

In his *General History of Music*, Charles Burney was to sketch the important influence Egypt exercised on Greek music; but Collins's focus on the Alexandrian period suggests that he was more interested in the later perspective Egypt provided on Greece. This emphasis may in turn indicate how Collins's fragment was meant to serve as an opening to a major ode on the music of the Grecian theater: the central characters of the three great tragedians would have their principal passions reenacted in the central sections of the ode as each of the Grecian choirs successively sang their songs. This argument, although not conclusive, is nevertheless consistent both with the evidence of the letter and fragment and with the structure of Collins's earlier ode for music. Collins, moreover, seems to have found his source for the historical setting in the *Deipnosophistae* of Athenaeus, his quarry earlier for the Athenian references in the "Ode to Liberty." Athenaeus' speaker describes the great Bacchic Festival staged by Philadelphus in Alexandria in which large choral groups were featured: "There were other carts besides, which carried images of kings and of gods as well, many of them. After them marched a choral band of six hundred men; among them three hundred harp-players performed together, carrying harps gilded all over, and wearing gold crowns" (V.201 f). The opulence and extravagance of Ptolomaic Alexandria are perhaps oddly suited to the simplicity and dignity Collins traditionally stresses in Greek music, but the court of Philadelphus nevertheless represented a culture in which the achievements of Greek drama and music continued to be celebrated.

The importance of Greek drama in Collins's work has already been stressed; here, in his later work, we see the poet also emphasizing the relationship between ancient drama and music. Greek odes were meant to be sung; Greek tragedy was a structured balance between dramatic recitation and choral chanting. Eighteenth-century commentators on music were eager to point out the interdependence of music and poetry in ancient drama; they were also eager to point out music's subservient role in that relationship. Much of this commentary was occasioned by contemporary dissatisfaction with Italian opera: although it had undeniable roots in Greek tragedy, it was thought to have broken sadly from its source. The music was inappropriately dominant; recitative action was too often ludicrous; and the libretto, after all, was not even in English.[36]

The continuing eighteenth-century debate over opera and music in general was closely tied to the even older "battle" of the ancients and moderns. Writers like Sir William Temple, who championed ancient learning and ancient poetry, considered music another art lost in the modern wilderness: "'Tis agreed by the Learned that the Science of Musick, so admired of the Ancients, is wholly lost in the World, and that what we have now is made up out of certain Notes that fell into the fancy or observation of a poor *Fryar* in chanting his Mattins."[37] But the arguments of Temple, Wotton, and Bentley did not bring the debate over music to an easy close. As we have already seen, James Harris was still determined to define the distinct qualities of the different arts—and their relative importance—in his *Three Treatises* of 1744. Harris's preference for a union of the arts (in which poetry nevertheless remained dominant) helped determine the terms of a debate that was to stretch from Charles Avison's *Essay on Musical Expression* (1752) to Burney's impressive *General History* (1776–89). The mid-century debate over the nature and function of music is an intriguing skirmish, but also a confusing one. The terminology of the various writers is not consistent, nor are their perspectives. Lawrence Lipking has cogently summarized the problems: "No consensus existed on even the most fundamental questions: whether instrumental music without the support of words and voices could be said to be music at all, whether literal imitation of natural sounds was a beauty or a blemish, whether large scale musical forms contradicted the emotional nature of music, whether music itself was basically a speculative or a practical art."[38]

One document in this controversy is of considerable assistance, however, in clarifying Collins's position in his poems and in speculating on how the poems themselves are related to contemporary musical practice. Dr. John Brown published *A Dissertation on the Rise, Union, and Power, Progressions, Separations, and Corruptions, of Poetry and Music* in 1763, and, as his imposing title suggests, he views the corruption of these sister arts as a consequence of their separation. Brown's method is a blend of history, psychology, and anthropology. He attempts to re-create the world of the ancient Greeks by examining the state of the American Indian. Like Collins, he emphasizes the simplicity of ancient music; like Vossius, whom he often invokes, he stresses the importance of rhythm in music and poetry: "In the *early* Periods (in which *Music* boasted its *greatest Power*) the ruling Character of the *Melody* was that of *Simplicity*; and that it derived a chief Part of its *Force* from its mere *Rythm* or *Measure*."[39] Brown's discussion of music is also closely tied to two elements that are important to Collins: the origin and nature of Greek theater, and the larger issue of the degeneration of liberty and the political state.

In Brown's view, the revival of learning in the Renaissance brought with it a knowledge of the important literary forms of Greece and Rome that was restricted to scholars, "the *sequestered Few*, who were swallowed up by a literary Application, often ignorant of the Powers of Music, and little acquainted with Society and Mankind."[40] This separation between poetry and music is so great that "even *Tragedy* and *Ode*, whose End is to shake the Soul with Terror, Pity, or Joy, by a *theatrical Exhibition*, and the *Powers* of *Music*;—even these, in many Instances and in different Periods, were *divorced* from their *Assistant Arts*, and became the *languid Amusement* of the *Closet*." Modern writers have digested the external form and poetic ornaments of these genres, but not their animating principles. The consequences, Brown argues, are tragedies that cannot be acted and odes that cannot be sung. This false taste in ode writing has become so firmly established that now "an *Ode* of the *true* Character is stiled (by Way of Distinction) *An Ode for Music*."[41] And music has suffered in its turn: "As the Separation of the Poet's from the Musician's Art produced an *improper Poetry*; so the Separation of the Musician's from the Poet's Character was productive of improper and *unaffecting Music*: For the Composer, in his Turn, intent only on *shining*, commonly wanders into unmeaning Division, and adopts either a delicate and refined, or a merely popular Music, to the Neglect of true musical Expression."[42]

Brown attempts to substantiate these general conclusions by examining the operas and oratorios of Handel, in which he finds this characteristic separation between poetical inspiration and corresponding musical expression. But the fault is not entirely Handel's; because he was the first to introduce the oratorio in England, he necessarily succumbed to the "Degradation" of employing writers who were "*Versifiers*" rather than poets.[43] The effects of this unhealthy collaboration can be seen both in the structure of the work and in the nature of the musical accompaniment: "Although no Man ever possessed greater Powers of musical Expression; yet, when the Writer gave him sometimes little, and sometimes nothing to express, the main Foundation of his Art failed him" (a situation akin to the painter who must by colors alone give life to a dead and unmeaning design). Too often the general composition of the oratorio is "unconnected, weak, and unaffecting"; the works lack contrast and succession of pathetic songs and choruses; the elements stand single, whereas "in a well-conducted Poem, the Effect of every *succeeding* Song or Choir would be heightened by the Power of the *preceding*." Brown's terms stress the essential union between poetry and music that he desires: musical works are described as poems; carefully constructed poems are "well-conducted." Only occasionally is this union actually achieved: *Messiah* is an exception because it is essentially undramatic; *L'Allegro ed Il Penseroso*, fine as it is, is still "merely *descriptive*, and in no Degree pathetic."[44]

Brown is not so naive as to believe that the poet and composer can once again be united in one person. Instead he offers practical advice on how the various literary forms might be fused and subsequently set to music. Neither the epic nor the tragic poem can again be united with music; the ode, "or *hymnal* Species," may hold out some hope, but the inherent simplicity of the form has found little favor among contemporary writers. Brown therefore proposes an artistic union that "may properly be styled the *Narrative* or *Epic Ode*" in which "the Action [is] to be simple and impassioned; the *Poem*, the *Music*, and *Performance*, if well conducted, will be attended with such a Degree of *Nature* and *Probability*, as will give the Alliance of Poetry and Music their highest Power and Pathos. The intermixed Narrations must be short and animated: The Songs and Choirs various and expressive; and being frequently interrupted by the brief Recitals, may by these Means be inspirited far beyond the simple and continued Ode, which from its unbroken Length often degenerates into Languour."[45] The proposal is ambitious, but not novel: "Of this *narrative or Epic Ode*, we have two fine Examples in our Language, written by POPE and DRYDEN." But even these odes are not without their blemishes. Pope's "Ode for Musick" is not entirely unified in its subject, and "Alexander's Feast" is imperfect "in the *moral End*." Nor are the structural breaks always clear: "The *Narrative* Part is not always sufficiently *distinguished* from the *Song*. They run into each other in such a Manner, that the musical Composer must often find himself embarassed, whether to accompany with Recitative, or a more compleat Melody."[46] But the properties and powers of the extended ode are nevertheless clearly suited to the potential reunion of poetry and song. The poet may draw his subject from either sacred or *"ethnical"* history; in each case the epic ode, if skillfully written, composed, and performed, will provide our surest link with the harmonious unions of the ancient bards.

Although Brown does not cite Collins as one of his examples (Collins's reputation really stems from the collected editions of his works issued in 1763 and 1765), the argument of Brown's *Dissertation* provides an articulate commentary on Collins's unfulfilled attempts to revive the musical ode. Collins's projected ode on the music of the Grecian theater—even more than "The Passions"—reveals his own endeavors to produce a poem close to Brown's *"ethnical"* epic ode. And the nature of the one musical fragment we do have—the "Recitative Accompanied"—suggests that Collins, like Brown, believed that the successful lyric poet must have a firm sense of how his own literary work would be musically structured.

IV. The Musical Structure of Poetry

Like most musical elements in the seventeenth and eighteenth centuries, "recitative" had a variety of possible meanings. In its simplest function, recitative was meant "to match in song the rhythm of the spoken word,"[47] a function not unlike that envisioned in Vossius's doctrine of *rhythmus*. As a set piece, the operatic recitative was originally quite elevated; but often, by the mid-eighteenth century, it approached ordinary conversation. The basic *stile recitative*, imported with the Italian opera, involved a harpsichord accompaniment that was to throw the vocal line into strong relief, thus producing a measure of freedom for the singer. But this simple style was often paired with the *recitative stromentato* or *accompagnato*, which accommodated both more instrumental accompaniment and more freedom for gesture and movement by the singer. The accompanied recitative was normally used for expressive declamation and the establishment of dramatic tension.

Fragment 11 suggests that this is what Collins had in mind: a set piece of declamation, accompanied by several instruments, that was itself not entirely undramatic. The recitative would presumably be followed by a series of separate arias expressing the various passions (here personified by the characters of Greek tragedy). Although Collins did not indicate the musical structure of "The Passions" in his text, it is clear that this earlier ode is structured in much the same way: the central passages of the poem, each focused on a separate, personified passion, function as arias designed to show off the emotional (and virtuoso) powers of the singers; the opening stanza, akin to declamatory recitation, sets the dramatic scene of the piece; and the final stanza, perhaps also recitative, would eventually close in a concluding —and harmonizing—chorus.

This implicit structure became explicit in the later fragment, perhaps through the actual performance of "The Passions" at the Oxford Encaenia. Collins, whom we assume received a copy of the printed ode from Hayes, would have discovered that the composer had set his poem to music in roughly this manner. Hayes's composition opens with an overture (entirely instrumental), which is then followed by the recitative of the first stanza (Hayes heads the recitative "Accompaniment"). Each of the following stanzas is set as an "Air," probably an aria in style but perhaps also occasionally the arioso compromise between aria and recitative. The shorter arias follow each other directly, but some of the longer stanzas (Hope's, for instance) have an introductory recitative. The first part ends with Revenge's violent song, a complete da capo aria that is then repeated by the chorus. The second part opens with a "Symphony" (a short instrumental prelude) before proceeding by aria and recitative to the final "Chorus of Passions." There is much in Hayes's conclusion that would have displeased Collins, not least of all the substitution of an entirely new closing stanza by Oxford's Chancellor, the Earl of Litchfield. In Hayes's version, the examination of the passions dramatically breaks off near the end of "*Joy's* Ecstatic Trial." The final recitative indicates the shift in Hayes's emphasis:"——*But, ah!*—Madness *away!* / *Some goddess sure—— Hark! hark!* '*tis* Reason *sings.*"[48] And Hayes concludes the work in a full chorus of the various passions, all now praising the "*harmonious maid*" of music who quells the jarring elements (and emotions) of her song.

This is not what Collins intended in his own conclusion to the ode. Although the allegorical nature of "The Passions" implies that the contrasting emotions vie for dominance within the poem (and within us), Collins does not explicitly call for a harmonious union of these disparate elements in his conclusion. His focus instead is on the failure of contemporary music and poetry to provide the artistic structures that would enable us to examine and consequently understand the nature of our emotional life. It has been argued that the turbulent activity of the passions could not find credible expression in harmonious forms: "In representations of the passions equality, balance, consonance, all the objective characteristics of 'harmonious' form tended to be subordinated to 'irregular' representative forms whose justification was that they were analogues of the 'motions' of the affective life."[49] It would be incorrect to argue that Collins abandons equality, balance, and consonance in "The Passions," or to suggest that regularity had become a dead end in eighteenth-century art. The "just Designs" and "simple State" of Greece were, after all, elements of the artistic return Collins advocates in his own conclusion to the ode. But this argument nonetheless suggests a powerful rationale for the preoccupation of Collins and his contemporaries with the irregularity of Pindaric poetry. Collins did not intend to drown out the emotional vitality of his central stanzas in the concluding strains of a grand chorus of the passions, now praising, in one voice, the harmonizing power of reason. Collins's arias are an attempt to embody the (often unbalanced) nature of the emotions in poetry and song.

The implicit musical structure of "The Passions" and the explicitly titled "Recitative Accompanied" show how well Collins understood the compositional elements of contemporary opera, oratorio, and musical ode; they also prompt us to inquire in what other ways he attempted to reflect baroque music in his own poetry. Correspondences between the two arts are often difficult to draw, and the problem of actual influence must remain, at least in Collins's case, a vexed one. But central to both "The Passions" and contemporary music is the creation and resolution of dramatic tension through contrast and repetition. Contrast in baroque music was often achieved through the adaptation of the Greek modes, which were usually transposed to the various modern musical keys. Attempts to introduce the modes in the sister arts can be seen in the paintings of Poussin and in Charles LeBrun's treatise on the passions, as well as in much of the most influential poetry of the seventeenth century. In "L'Allegro" and "Il Penseroso," for instance, Milton not only derives his titles from musical terminology but also skillfully modulates the changing moods of the poems by relying on shifts in rhythm and mode.[50] In "A Song for St. Cecilia's Day," Dryden structures each stanza on the eight Greek modes that correspond to the notes of our octave scale.[51] Thus the description of Jubal and the corded shell, for example, is based on the solemnity and religious power of the Dorian mode, while Anger, in the third stanza, is molded in the warlike Phrygian mode.

Collins's invocation of the Lydian mode in his "Ode to Liberty" suggests that he was familiar with the literary adaptation of the ancient modes, and the nature of the affective passages in "The Passions" suggests that this was a practice that had not entirely died out by the middle of the eighteenth century. But Collins's reliance on the modes is not as explicit as Milton's, nor is his stanzaic structure as fully unified as Dryden's. We might argue that Collins's lines on Joy are essentially Lydian, and that those on Despair are Mixolydian, but no clear pattern appears to control the entire poem. Handel declared that he could not "see of what use the Greek Modes can be for modern music,"[52] and much the same could be said of their relevance to contemporary poetry. The influence of the Greek modes can best be seen in their expressive function in the description of the various passions and in the traditional alternation that provided the composer, painter, or poet with a dramatic focus. This influence can be gauged in the conventional "a-b-a" structure of the aria da capo, for instance, in which the material of the first movement is transposed and contrasted in the second movement, which is then succeeded by the traditional return of the close.[53] This alternation is also occasionally the structural basis of extended musical forms, as Manfred Bukofzer has pointed out in his analysis of Purcell's cantatas.[54] Charles Rosen has made even more sweeping claims for this structure in his analysis of the "linear" development of baroque music. The essential dramatic device in opera seria and oratorio, he argues, is juxtaposition rather than development. Rather than periodic phrasing, the baroque composer relies on sharp contrast between succeeding arias or in the alternation of single voice and chorus: "Handel can deploy two or more rhythmic blocks, and without making any attempt at transition between them, place them side by side with the most vigorous contrast, and then pile them one on top of another, all of this with a motor energy that has never been surpassed for excitement."[55] Rosen's description of Handel's method begins to suggest some of the effects and excitement that Collins's readers felt in "The Passions," thus making it a stock piece of declamation later in the century.

This kind of dramatic development can be seen in the sudden transitions of Handel's shorter vocal works (such as the cantata "Lucrezia") as well as in the skillful modulations of the oratorios, especially *Saul*. Of particular relevance to Collins's method in his musical ode, however, is Handel's adaptation of "L'Allegro" and "Il Penseroso" in 1740. Joseph Warton pointed out that these companion poems, although "now universally known" (in 1756), "lay in a sort of obscurity, the private enjoyment of a few curious readers, till they were set to admirable music by Mr. Handel."[56] Collins's debt to these two poems has long been stressed: the odes to Pity and Fear are clearly structured on Milton's pattern, as Collins insists in the two invitations that conclude the poems; even more important is the allegorical mode that Milton's poems established with their alternating psychological emphases. Handel's restructuring of Milton's poems in *L'Allegro ed il Penseroso* shares obvious affinities with Collins's ode. Handel, with the assistance of his librettist, Charles Jennens, created a new work in three parts: the first two sections comprise arias and recitatives drawn from Milton's poems; the final part, entitled *Il Moderato*, is an entirely fresh work, a moderate and rational compromise or synthesis of the opposing forces in the earlier sections (a resolution not unlike the epode of classical drama or, for that matter, William Hayes's conclusion to "The Passions"). Jennens, to his credit, devised this last section as a part detachable from the rest of the work; and Handel, in later performances, dropped *Il Moderato* and wrote additional arias for the first two parts.

L'Allegro ed il Penseroso, in its ultimate form, is a beautifully balanced work, but the balance is not derived from a simple separation of the two modes. Jennens successfully attempted to reflect the Miltonic connections between the joyful and pensive elements of the poems by combining both modes in each section. Thus the opening recitative aria of the "Allegro" voice is directly followed by a corresponding recitative and aria belonging to "Il Penseroso." The dramatic tension of the poem stems from the sharp contrast of forces that are seen as both opposing and complementary. The opening songs are particularly effective: "The two characters begin by singing the other's music, as though they know, at heart, that the one is inseparable from the other."[57] The two sections of Handel's ode are nominally headed *L'Allegro* and *Il Penseroso*, but both voices appear in each part and each concluding chorus achieves its own resolution. As in Collins's late fragment, many of the recitatives are accompanied (and thus suitable to expressive development and gesture); many of the arias, on the other hand, are for unaccompanied solo. Handel's emphasis throughout the composition is on a musical variety and inventiveness that will reflect the alternations of the emotional states. The work as a whole, although still not well known, has been called Handel's most adventurous and exploratory composition.[58]

Although it is quite possible that Collins heard Handel's work in performance at London or Oxford, our interest in *L'Allegro ed il Penseroso* lies not so much in any actual influence it may have had on Collins's poetry as in their mutual striving toward a satisfactory form for expressing the passions.[59] The striking alternation of Milton's two voices, now re-created in musical form, also represents the essential structure of Collins's ode. Despair succeeds Anger and Hope succeeds Despair (as they play upon the same lyre) in much the same way that

Handel's description of the lark is followed by a passage devoted to the nightingale. This dramatic structure is dictated, in turn, by the principle of modulation that controls our emotional responses. LeBrun illustrated this point by ordering his own discussion of the passions according to the ways in which they were related to each other, and his sequence closely resembles those fashioned by Milton, Handel, and Collins: "Hatred proceeds from Jealousy"; Hope, which lies between Fear and Certainty, leads either to Despair or Fear; "Anger is sometimes succeeded either by Rage or Despair."[60] In Collins's ode, as in Handel's composition, the juxtaposition of contrary emotions shows each off to its best advantage (poetically, pictorially, musically), and also reflects those sudden changes in temperament that characterize our fluctuating emotions. The vitality of the baroque contrasts in Handel's ode pleased even the prickly John Brown. Charles Burney, moreover, drew on the ode to refute the claims of Brown and Vossius: "*Mirth, admit me of thy crew,* by Handel, as well as several popular songs by Dr. Arne, Mr. Jackson, and others, are sufficiently conformable to poetical numbers and *Rhythm,* to satisfy the greatest admirers of ancient simplicity, or even such as love poetry better than music."[61] Handel's dramatic method is also Collins's; and thus in some, at least, of the most imaginative and characteristic music of his contemporaries, the poet could have found elements of the ancient simplicity, force, and design that he intended to re-create in his own work.

7

Last Poems

It is entirely possible that Collins wrote as many as ten of his twelve *Odes on Several Descriptive and Allegoric Subjects* during the year in which they were published. It is likely, moreover, that he wrote most of these poems—including the "Ode on the Poetical Character," the "Ode to Evening," and "The Passions"—during the six-month period following his meeting in May with Joseph Warton. Judged by any standards, this is a period of intense activity and considerable accomplishment. As we have already seen, John Ragsdale remembered Collins as being frenetically—and rather playfully—at work in London during this productive year:

> To raise a present subsistence he set about writing his *Odes*, and having a general invitation to my house, he frequently passed whole days there, which he employed in writing them, and as frequently burning what he had written, after reading them to me. Many of them which *pleased me*, I struggled to preserve, but without effect; for pretending he would alter them, he got them from me and thrust them into the fire.[1]

The years following the publication of the *Odes*, on the other hand, reveal a substantial decline in Collins's productivity. We can be fairly confident that Collins was responsible for the revisions that appeared in several of his odes when they were reprinted in Dodsley's *Collection* in 1748, and we also know that he devoted much of his attention to other literary projects at this time. But the poems dating from this period, the last creative passage in Collins's life, are occasional pieces,

166

each prompted by a particular event: the death of Thomson, the departure of John Home, or the performance of "The Passions" at the Oxford Encaenia. These last works—especially the elegy on Thomson and the "Ode to a Friend on his Return &c"—are among Collins's very finest poems; they display a complexity of structure and statement that we expect at the end of a poet's career. But, at the same time, these final poems suggest Collins's increasing awareness of the limitations inherent in the particular kind of poetry he had chosen to make his own.

I. A Tribute to Thomson

James Thomson died at Richmond on 27 August 1748. Collins, who had met Thomson as early as 1744 or 1745, settled in Richmond in 1747 and became a member of that circle of friends described by Thomson in *The Castle of Indolence*. His "Ode Occasion'd by the Death of Mr. Thomson," which appeared in June 1749, keeps the circumstances of their friendship steadily in view. The ode is almost a coterie poem, closely tied to a few people and to a specific location. The preliminary pages of the folio edition include not only appropriate mottoes from Virgil's *Eclogues* but the unusual addition, as well, of a formal dedication to George Lyttelton and an "Advertisement" informing his readers that "The Scene of the following Stanzas is suppos'd to lie on the *Thames* near *Richmond*."[2] George (later Lord) Lyttelton had been one of Thomson's greatest patrons and closest friends, and after the poet's death he was one of his executors. Collins's mention of the Thames near Richmond, an area rich in literary associations long before Thomson's time, reinforces our sense that this is a poem of place. The poem itself describes the Aeolian harp (which Thomson had helped reinvent), Ease and Health (characters borrowed from *The Castle of Indolence*), and the "whit'ning Spire" of Richmond Church; even Collins's adaptation of Thomson's boast in "A Hymn on the Seasons" emphasizes his familiarity with this congenial circle of friends and the works they left behind. As the second of the two mottoes points out, "Me, too, Daphnis loved."

But there is also an ambivalence in Collins's tribute to the man who was both his friend and a poet of extensive influence and fame. We have seen that Collins was an attentive critic of Thomson's revisions in *The Seasons*, that he later drew on these changes when he revised his own *Oriental Eclogues*, that Thomson's reworked images enabled him to lessen his early debt to Pope. But we have also seen how common images were put to sharply different use by Thomson and Collins, how antithetical (in fact) their poetical method and conception of nature actually were. The first motto, also selected from Virgil's fifth eclogue, introduces the terms of Collins's ambivalence: "These rites shall be thine for ever, both when we pay our yearly vows to the Nymphs, and when we traverse our fields."[3] Collins implies that his tribute will also last forever, but it is nevertheless an homage of duty as much as love, strictly bound to the natural world with which Thomson was so closely identified. The unusual and complex structure of Collins's ode sustains this central tension between a tribute to a close friend (who is to be remembered "for ever") and a perspective on that friend's cohesive and intelligible world (which fades from sight as the elegy closes).[4]

Like Collins's previous elegies, the ode on Thomson opens with a candid acknowledgment of the finality of death:

> In yonder Grave a DRUID lies
> Where slowly winds the stealing Wave!
> The *Year*'s best Sweets shall duteous rise
> To deck *it's* POET'S sylvan Grave!

But if these quiet lines insistently point to Thomson's death, they also suggest the manner in which his loss will be most appropriately mourned. Thomson is pictured as a druid—an ancient bard of the woods—whose celebration of nature during the varying seasons of the year is now reciprocated in nature's tribute to him.[5] The introductory tableau depicts the course of the year's "best Sweets" as they rise to deck the poet's grave, but this rising movement entails a corresponding demise as the sweets, the perfumed flowers of summer, undergo a similar death in honor of the man whose grave they deck. These opening lines imply that even in death Thomson will not be far removed from the natural elements he chose to praise in life.

Collins's own presence in the ode's first stanza is revealed by his view of "yonder" grave, surveyed from his perspective on the Thames. This distance is shortened slightly in the following stanza, as Collins focuses his attention on the banks of the river near Thomson's grave:

> In yon deep Bed of whisp'ring Reeds
> His airy Harp shall now be laid,
> That He, whose Heart in Sorrow bleeds
> May love thro' Life the soothing Shade.

> (ll. 5-8)

The "deep Bed" is momentarily ambiguous until we realize that it is a skillfully drawn transition between the grave and the river's banks.

The bed of whispering reeds is still viewed at a distance ("yon"); but it is also a median point between the grave and the elegiac spectator, and —more important—a communicative medium through which Thomson and his mourner are once again united. Collins decrees that this reedy bed shall house the Aeolian harp, the "natural" instrument whose music is produced as the wind sweeps over its strings. The image may seem fanciful but it is nonetheless effective: Thomson's own "music," long associated with nature, will now be returned to nature itself. Music functions as a mediator here, linking Thomson even more fully with the natural landscape into which he has been laid, and providing a vital memento—at once artistic and natural—for the friend "whose Heart in Sorrow bleeds." Collins will thus "love thro' Life the soothing Shade" for a variety of reasons: because this peaceful scene is hallowed by the spirit of his friend; because it is the source of airy music; because, as Collins's pun here and in the "Ode, to a Lady" suggests, the place itself has become one with the "Shade" who now inhabits it. By the end of the second stanza, both Thomson and his art have become completely submerged in the natural elements that gave them sustenance.

The following three stanzas introduce other mourners—maids and youths, Remembrance, Ease and Health—who view the grave and grassy banks from Collins's perspective on the river. The distance here is both spatial and temporal; our progression is not a simple one. These lines (like waves) produce a swell of emotion as they literally carry us closer to Thomson's grave, but their focus (as the introduction of Remembrance implies) remains on a future prospect from which we shall look back on Thomson's death. The repetition of the lines ("REMEMBRANCE oft shall haunt the Shore . . . And oft suspend the dashing Oar . . . And oft as EASE and HEALTH retire") promises substantial activity and energy, but there is also a considerable halt in motion as well (as the suspension of the "dashing Oar" suggests). The most dramatic progression in these lines lies in Collins's gradual development of his personifications. The third stanza opens with a glimpse of "Maids and Youths" who linger on the river in remembrance of Thomson, but the music these realistic mourners hear reaches them through "Pity's Ear" (if Thomson has become all sound, his mourners have become all ear). The process of diffusion that began in the opening lines has now become a part of the poem's pattern, and thus it is only a short step to the full-fledged personifications of Remembrance, Health, and Ease in the following lines.

Only in the sixth stanza, at the center of this eleven-stanza elegy and midpoint in his journey down the Thames, does Collins actually turn to the poet in his grave:

> But Thou, who own'st that Earthy Bed,
> Ah! what will ev'ry Dirge avail?
> Or Tears, which LOVE and PITY shed
> That mourn beneath the gliding Sail!
>
> (ll. 21-24)

The connection between Thomson's sylvan grave and the river's bank is now made explicit in the description of the "Earthy Bed," but this focus at the center of the poem cannot be held for long. Collins immediately acknowledges the limited effect of his lament; even in his deepest grief, weeping beneath the gliding sail, he is still cut off from the friend he mourns.

The frustrations of this admittedly restricted grief issue in a curse in the following stanza, but it is a curse with an appropriate source:

> Yet lives there one, whose heedless Eye
> Shall scorn thy pale Shrine glimm'ring near?
> With Him, Sweet Bard, may FANCY die,
> And JOY desert the blooming Year.
>
> (ll. 25-28)

These lines are essentially an adaptation of a passage in Thomson's "Hymn on the Seasons":

> For me, when I forget the darling theme,
> Whether the blossom blows, the summer-ray
> Russets the plain, inspiring autumn gleams,
> Or winter rises in the blackening east,
> Be my tongue mute, may fancy paint no more,
> And, dead to joy, forget my heart to beat!
>
> (ll. 94–99)

Like Thomson, Collins equates the cessation of joy in natural beauty with the simultaneous extinction of inspiration (fancy), but his version also entails a twist. Thomson's own demise is now wished upon his heedless visitor, who forsakes not only nature but Thomson's shrine as well; Thomson actually replaces nature in Collins's revision of the "Hymn."

The depiction of Thomson's pale shrine indicates that, even as the grave recedes behind us, it still remains "glimm'ring near." The concluding stanzas, however, waft us "from the green Hill's Side / Whose cold Turf hides the buried FRIEND!" (ll. 31-32). The Thames is addressed as a forlorn river, bereft not only of Thomson but of those "sedge-crown'd SISTERS" who were traditionally viewed as the inspiring

Muses of the stream. The Naiads have now deserted the Thames, and with their departure our very perception of the natural landscape begins to weaken:[6]

> And see, the Fairy Valleys fade,
> > Dun *Night* has veil'd the solemn View!
> —Yet once again, Dear parted SHADE
> > Meek NATURE'S CHILD again adieu!

(ll. 33-36)

Collins steals one last glimpse of his departed friend, but his final address to the retreating "SHADE" reinforces our sense that this sacred scene ("solemn View") is not so much protected from the sun as it is permanently lost in night. The veil drawn over this landscape is a sinister reminder of similar curtains in *The Dunciad* and in the "Ode on the Poetical Character." The natural resources of poetry appear to fade with Thomson's death.

The elegy closes, however, with hopeful vows. Thomson will be mourned in death by those "genial Meads" that blessed his life, providing artistic nourishment as well as simple joys. His tomb will be dressed by hinds and shepherd girls well-suited to his rural environment, and will move to tears those who valued the man and his work:

> Long, long, thy Stone and pointed Clay
> > Shall melt the musing BRITON'S Eyes,
> O! VALES, and WILD WOODS, shall HE say
> > In yonder Grave YOUR DRUID lies!

(ll. 41-44)

Our attention is directed once more to the actual grave, viewed once again at a distance that is both temporal and spatial. The ode's conclusion echoes its beginning, but there are two important differences here. The first lies in the transition from "a" druid in the opening stanza to "YOUR" druid at the poem's close.[7] The alteration provides a final demonstration of the general pattern of the ode: Thomson is placed firmly within the landscape he celebrated as Collins passes on his own protective role to nature itself ("VALES, and WILD WOODS"). The second development lies in a similar exchange of roles. Throughout the poem, Collins's voice has functioned as a central consciousness; even the introduction of abstract personifications has reinforced his point of view. He is the friend "whose Heart in Sorrow bleeds" in the second stanza; it is he who sheds tears of love and pity as he mourns beneath the gliding sail. We share his perspective, however, and ultimately claim it as our own in the final stanza. When Collins depicts the musing Briton, we realize that he is describing both himself and those readers who have been moved by his tribute. Collins, after all, has already spoken the line that is both an introduction and a conclusion to his poem; by finally placing that line in the mouth of a generalized figure—the musing Briton—he implies that the elegy he has delivered will be shared and repeated by others.

The circular structure that the final lines suggest is an appropriate tribute to a friend whose memory Collins hopes will be eternal. The closing stanza bears us back to the opening with renewed interest, and anticipates Coleridge's notion of the perfect form of the Romantic lyric (the serpent with its tail in its mouth). The elegy is Collins's own tribute to Thomson: itself circular, it suggests the poetical garland he lays at his grave, an homage closely resembling the dutiful sacrifice of the year's best sweets, the Thames's summer wreaths, and the sedgy crowns once sported by the departed nymphs. The structure of Collins's tribute may have been suggested by Spenser's *Prothalamion*, which, while necessarily varying from the elegy in certain ways, is also characterized by the symbolic weaving of circular forms.[8] Collins's poem shares with Spenser's its triumphal form, its tribute to a central figure introduced at midpoint in the poem. This is a strategy we have already encountered in *An Epistle: Addrest to Sir Thomas Hanmer* (with the introduction of Shakespeare) and in the "Ode on the Poetical Character" (with the entrance of Apollo). Here we find Collins bestowing an equal stature on his contemporary and friend.

There is another way, however, in which poets may emphasize the symbolism of the center.[9] The midpoint of a poem may be conceived as the center of a circle or as the halfway point in a linear progression, and Collins clearly has both structures in mind. The image of the circle provides a suitable structure for a tribute that is to last "for ever" (as the motto suggests), and that will find its deepest expression among the circle of friends that placed Thomson at its center. It is partly as a member of that coterie that Collins himself wishes to be remembered ("Me, too, Daphnis loved"); but perhaps of greater force in the elegy is the poetic structure that places Thomson at midpoint in the poem, a figure who is eagerly approached but ultimately left behind. Tillyard was the first to notice the double progression in the poem (of nightfall and of the boat on the Thames) as well as Collins's careful division of the ode into two groups of five stanzas each, separated from each other by the crucial central passage. The ode's development, he stated, "agrees exquisitely with the experience of approaching and leaving an attractive object."[10] Less attention, however, has been focused on what remains once we have left this attractive figure behind. The temporal structure of the circular pattern promises eternal homage and praise; the temporal structure of the linear pattern promises us evening, gloomy ("Dun") night, and the virtual extinction of the landscape into which Thomson has vanished. Collins's journey down the Thames literally carries him past Thomson, and past the natural scene that has become so closely identified with Thomson's poetic achievement.

The dark side of this linear progression is emphasized by Collins's use of chiasmus in the ode. Rhetorical chiasmus involves an inversion of the order of words or phrases that are repeated or referred to later in a sentence; in a broader context, chiasmus also embodies the inversion of ideas. The center of a poem or passage may serve as a turning point from which the enveloping lines or passages work forwards and then backwards.[11] In the linear structure of Collins's ode, the sixth stanza is literally and figuratively a decisive turning point in Collins's journey down the Thames. The fifth stanza, for instance, describes "The Friend" who, viewing "yon whit'ning Spire," will "'mid the varied Landscape weep"; the corresponding seventh stanza, however, envisions a figure with "heedless Eye" who will shed no tears as he glimpses Thomson's "pale Shrine glimm'ring near." The fourth stanza introduces father Thames dressed in summer wreaths, but in the eighth stanza Collins addresses the river as a "lorn STREAM, whose sullen Tide / No sedge-crown'd SISTERS now attend," and whose summer wreath has been replaced by the "cold Turf" that hides the buried friend.

Much the same pattern governs the entire poem, whose chiastic structure can be represented as a-b-c-d-e-f-g-f'-e'-d'-c'-b'-a'. In the third stanza, the maids and youths who linger in this rural scene are able to hear their "WOODLAND PILGRIM'S Knell" in the sounds of the transplanted Aeolian harp; in the corresponding stanza, however, the departure of the nymphs has brought an end to our enjoyment of nature's enchantments ("the Fairy Valleys fade"), and Collins must bid farewell to a friend who is perceived not as a pilgrim but as "Meek NATURE'S CHILD." The Aeolian harp in the bed of whispering reeds (in the second stanza) held out a promise that even with Thomson's death we might "love thro' Life the soothing Shade," but in the penultimate stanza this sequence is reversed: there the genial meads assigned to bless his life will simply mourn his early doom. The opening and closing stanzas, as we have seen, offer similar echoes and inversions. The linear structure of the elegy involves more than a mere tightening and relaxation of tension (as Tillyard believed). A more apt analogue might lie in a musical progression that, once it has reached its highest note, continues its passage in an altered mode.

This sense of diminishment is both structural and linguistic. With the exception of the muted personifications in the first stanza, the natural and human figures at the opening of the ode are relatively simple and concrete. Only in the third stanza does the personifying process begin, but the personifications themselves do not fully emerge until we have journeyed closer to Thomson's grave. The central stanzas of the poem (4-8), however, more than compensate for this initial simplicity. The area immediately surrounding Thomson's grave is populated—at one time or another—by Remembrance, Thames, Ease, Health, Love, Pity, Fancy, Joy, and the sedge-crowned Naiads. Only in the ninth stanza does this abstract and figurative language begin to evaporate, as quickly as it appeared. Dun Night, in veiling this solemn scene, also draws to a close the highly imaginative language of the poem; the "Fairy" landscape into which Thomson fades from sight is endowed with an allegorical and fanciful idiom that vanishes with the departed friend. The poem ends with the simple and diminished diction with which it began. Like Gray in the "Sonnet on the Death of Mr. Richard West," Collins makes use of two different kinds of language—one simple and concrete, the other luxuriant and more traditionally "poetic"—to express his distance from the friend he has lost. But whereas Gray associates this vibrant language with the world that exists outside his grief, Collins uses it to describe his friend's cohesive and unified world, which he has now sailed past.

At the close of "A Hymn on the Seasons" Thomson contemplates his own inevitable death:

> When even at last the solemn hour shall come,
> And wing my mystic flight to future worlds,
> I cheerful will obey; there, with new powers,
> Will rising wonders sing: I cannot go
> Where universal love not smiles around,
> Sustaining all yon orbs and all their sons;
> From seeming evil still educing good,
> And better thence again, and better still,
> In infinite progression. But I lose
> Myself in him, in light ineffable!
> Come then, expressive Silence, muse his praise.
>
> (ll. 108-18)

Thomson views his death as a certain rebirth. His mystic journey will refine him out of nature and his earthly imperfection; even as he is lost to nature, he will be absorbed into a god who is envisioned as "light ineffable." Collins, however, offers himself and his friend few of these traditional consolations. His elegy embodies a progression of a different kind: Thomson, like Wordsworth's Lucy, is refined *into* nature rather than out of it; the promise of light ineffable is replaced by a pervasive darkness; and the conventional vision of *The Seasons* (in which nature is viewed as a unified and intelligible phenomenon) vanishes from sight. Collins's elegy laments both the passing of a friend and his friend's way of perceiving the world.

II. An Epistle to Home

Collins's "Ode to a Friend on his Return &c" was written in the fall or winter following the publication of the elegy on the death of Thomson. Collins addressed the poem to the dramatist John Home, whose departure for his native Scotland was prompted by his failure to place his tragedy *Agis* on the London stage. Collins showed a copy of the ode to the Wartons when they visited Chichester in 1754, and Johnson records that they thought it "superior to his other works."[12] Much later Thomas Warton remembered with particular relish the "beautiful description of the Spectre of a Man drowned in the Night, or in the language of the old Scotch Superstitions—*seized by the angry Spirit of the Waters*, appearing to his wife *with pale blue cheek, &c.*"[13] Collins also presented a copy of the poem to Home, and it was this copy —both unfinished and defective (one quarto page had disappeared)— that was published in 1788 under the descriptive title "An Ode on the Popular Superstitions of the Highlands of Scotland, considered as the Subject of Poetry." The rediscovery of this manuscript in 1967 has revealed that this title is far more elaborate than the one Collins prefixed to the poem, but it nevertheless serves as an accurate summary of the fresh poetical subjects—and powers—to which Collins turned in the ode.[14]

But the poem's altered title and its posthumous publication appear, at the same time, to have discouraged any serious consideration of how this lengthy and unusual ode is related to the works that preceded it. In several ways, some more crucial than others, Collins's "Ode to a Friend" serves as a companion poem to the "Ode Occasion'd by the Death of Mr. Thomson." Both poems are addressed to friends departed or about to depart; both are addressed to poets whose poetic resources are substantially different from Collins's. Thomson and Home are poets whose sources of inspiration can be celebrated by Collins (even if he cannot wholly embrace them); both friends are also closely associated with literary circles that provided vital nourishment to him in the years 1748-50.

Like its predecessor, the ode to Home opens almost as a coterie poem. Collins pays tribute to his friendship with Home, and praises the "cordial Youth" (Thomas Barrow) who brought them together:

> H— Thou return'st from Thames, whose Naiads long
>   Have seen Thee ling'ring with a fond delay
>   Mid' those soft Friends, whose hearts some future day
> Shall melt perhaps to hear thy Tragic Song
> Go not unmindfull of that cordial Youth
>   Whose
> Together let us wish Him lasting truth
>   And Joy untainted with his destin'd Bride
> Go! nor regardless, while these Numbers boast
>   My short-liv'd bliss, forget my social Name
> But think far-off how on the Southern coast
>   I met thy Friendship with an equal Flame!
>
> (ll. 1-12)

Numerous echoes of the recently published elegy occur here and in the following three stanzas of the ode. In both poems Collins carefully measures the distance that separates him from his friends: Collins will imaginatively precede Home in his journey to Scotland, but he remains securely anchored on England's southern coast. Both odes are also poems of farewell that stipulate a transference of protection. At the close of the elegy, Collins relinquishes his care of Thomson to the vales and wild woods that have inspired his friend's work; the concluding lines of the "Ode to a Friend" reveal a similar wish for Home:

> Where'er he dwell, on Hill or lowly Muir
>   To Him I lose, your kind protection lend
> And touch'd with Love, like Mine, preserve my Absent Friend.
>
> (ll. 217-19)

In these closing lines, however, Collins invokes a natural environment that is sustained by supernatural traditions; the natural scene of these lines will not fade from view. The elegy, as we have seen, is a lament for a kind of poetry (and a kind of vision) that has been lost, whereas the ode addressed to Home is (at least vicariously) a celebration of a new visionary source that has yet to be fully tapped.

The artistic possibilities of this fresh material provide the focus of Collins's poem. Throughout the ode he emphasizes the power, variety, and scope of traditional folklore sustained by a romantic environment:

> Fresh to that soil thou turn'st, whose ev'ry Vale
> Shall prompt the Poet, and his Song demand;
> To Thee thy copious Subjects ne'er shall fail
> Thou need'st but take the Pencil to thy Hand
> And paint what all believe who own thy Genial Land.
>
> There must Thou wake perforce thy *Doric* Quill
> 'Tis Fancy's Land to which thou set'st thy Feet
> Where still, tis said, the Fairy People meet
> Beneath Each birken Shade, on mead or Hill.
>
> (ll. 13-21)

Collins's immediate theme is the effortlessness and inevitability of the writer's task. The poet will be prompted by "ev'ry Vale" in this fresh landscape; the seemingly inexhaustible subjects that demand his attention exclude the possibility of failure; Home needs only to lift his brush and paint what all believe. Collins's vision of this "Genial" land is both welcoming and inspiring: those who "own" the Highlands are in turn possessed by them, and Home's rustic quill will thus be waked "perforce" by the imaginative territory to which he sets his feet.[15]

Collins asks his friend to rediscover a region inhabited by "Fairy People" and ruled by "Fancy." Their native superstitions—"Strange lays whose pow'r had charm'd a Spenser's Ear"—have their origin in oral or "pre-literature"; they are traditional tales "Taught by the Father to his list'ning Son":

> At Ev'ry Pause, before thy Mind possest,
> Old Runic Bards shall seem to rise around
> With uncouth Lyres, in many-colour'd Vest,
> Their Matted Hair with boughs fantastic crown'd.
>
> (ll. 40-43)

The tableau Collins envisions bears a strong resemblance to Art's quaint pageant in "The Manners." The ancient bards appear to rise in masque-like fashion around the passive Home, whose mind is "possest" by these strange powers. The "many-colour'd Vest" and matted hair "with boughs fantastic crown'd" remind us of those central creative moments in Collins's earlier poems: the entrance of Humor in his "Robe of wild contending Hues" in "The Manners"; the appearance of Truth, "in sunny Vest array'd," in the "Ode on the Poetical Character"; and the description of Joy's ecstatic trial ("He with viny Crown advancing") in "The Passions." Collins argues that Home has the potential to adapt these powerful forces to his own poetry:

> 'Tis thine to Sing how framing hideous Spells
> In Skys lone Isle the Gifted Wizzard Seer
> Lodg'd in the Wintry cave with
> Or in the depth of Ust's dark forrests dwells.
>
> (ll. 53-56)

Simply by retelling these ancient tales the modern poet can, in effect, partake of their visionary power and share in their creative force.

The complementary alternative to the wizard seers is the more common occurrence of the "second sight." Home may choose instead to sing

> How They whose Sight such dreary dreams engross
> With their own Visions oft astonish'd droop
> When o'er the watry strath or quaggy Moss
> They see the gliding Ghosts unbodied troop
> ·
> For them the viewless Forms of Air obey
> Their bidding heed, and at their beck repair
> They know what Spirit brews the storm full day
> And heartless oft like moody Madness stare
> To see the Phantom train their secret work prepare!
>
> (ll. 57-60, 65-69)

The power of second sight is of particular interest because it is dangerous both to the viewer and the viewed. Those who have it are themselves enslaved by their dreary dreams, burdened by the supernatural knowledge they bear. Their sight produces a double image, combining the present and the future in an uneasy tension. This much Collins faithfully borrowed from his source in Martin's *Description of the Western Islands of Scotland*, but he also altered the passive nature of these seers, described by Martin as "generally illiterate, and well-meaning People, and altogether void of design."[16] In Collins's ode, the gift of second sight and mysterious knowledge ("They know what Spirit brews the storm full day") brings with it no show of mercy; these heartless characters share the "moody Madness" that rules the secret work of the phantom train.

Collins's version of the second sight clearly emphasizes a visionary power that controls the destinies of others even if it cannot forestall its own astonished response. How Collins intended to develop this theme is much less clear, largely because the following stanza and a half have not survived. When the Aldouri manuscript opens again, however, it is with the introduction of an equally harmful sprite and with an unrelaxed focus on the powers and limitations of sight. Although the story of the hapless swain caught up in the force of the kelpie's wrath is rather long, it is unusual enough to deserve quotation in full:

> What tho far off from some dark dell espied
>> His glimm'ring Mazes cheer th' excursive sight
> Yet turn ye Wandrers turn your steps aside
>> Nor chuse the Guidance of that faithless light!
> For watchfull lurking mid th' unrustling Reed
>> At those sad hours the wily Monster lies
> And listens oft to hear the passing Steed
>> And frequent round him rolls his sullen Eyes
> If Chance his Savage wrath may some weak wretch surprise.
>
> Ah luckless Swain, oer All Unblest indeed!
>> Whom late bewilder'd in the dank dark Fen
> Far from his Flocks and smoaking Hamlet then!
>> To what sad spot his
> On Him enrag'd the Fiend in Angry mood
>> Shall never look with Pity's kind concern
> But Instant Furious rouse the whelming Flood
> O'er it's drown'd Banks forbidding All return
> Or If He meditate his wish'd Escape
>> To some dim Hill that seems uprising near
> To his faint Eye the Grim and Griesly Shape
>> In all its Terrors clad shall wild appear.
> Mean time the Watry Surge shall round him rise
>> Pour'd sudden forth from evry swelling source
> What now remains but Tears and hopeless sighs?
>> His Fear-shook limbs have lost their Youthly force
> And down the waves He floats a Pale and breathless Corse.

                                              (ll. 95-120)

This extraordinary passage, placed at the heart of the poem, has long been admired by Collins's readers. Spacks cites it as the central confrontation of the ordinary and the supernatural, the supreme welding of the literal and the metaphoric: "The legend becomes an emotive objectification of the horror always potential immediately outside the bounds of normalcy, the terror that lies in wait for all."[17] This much is consistent, however, with the body of Collins's work, especially the "Ode to Fear." What I find particularly unusual, especially in Collins's last major poem, is his interest in the possibilities of an extended narrative.

Almost all of Collins's odes support the contention that mid-eighteenth-century poetry represents a dramatic shift from "action to image."[18] Collins's imagery does not suffer at the expense of action in the central passages of the "Ode to a Friend"; it simply plays a complementary role. The "weak wretch" who crosses the kelpie's path is initially led astray by glimmering mazes that cheer his excursive sight. The "faithless light" he glimpses, however, is that of the will-o-the-wisp or wild-fire, a deluding vision that draws him to the watchful monster who "frequent round him rolls his sullen Eyes." This water sprite, like the common folk who possess the second sight, "Shall never look with Pity's kind concern" on the luckless swain. The wily monster acts instead as a stage-manager, a malevolent Prospero, as he "Instant Furious" rouses "the whelming Flood / O'er it's drown'd Banks forbidding All return." Collins's syntax reinforces our sense of the kelpie's control over the forces of nature: instantly furious himself, he is also able to whip the whelming flood to a corresponding pitch of immediate fury.

Here and elsewhere Collins's unusual coalescence of action and image suggests the inescapable power of the water sprite's malignant design. The "unblest" traveler is literally caught up in the forces that surround him; everywhere he turns his "faint Eye" he will encounter "the Grim and Griesly" shapes of terror that have been artfully contrived by the wily conjuror. What he witnesses, in other words, is a series of terrifying images that shock him into a state of helplessness. There is little action on his part, nor on that of nature; the inexorable force of the passage lies in the supernatural workings of the kelpie. The swain is luckless, unblest, bewildered, faint, fear-shook, pale, and breathless; the kelpie, on the other hand, appears as a skillful wizard in his own deadly pageant. The play between secretive action and frozen image underscores the part played by fate, destiny, or inevitability throughout the poem (beginning, quite inauspiciously, with Collins's mention of Barrow's "destin'd bride"). The moment the swain meditates his wished escape to "some dim Hill that seems uprising near," that faint but hopeful image is replaced by an apparition "in all its Terrors clad." Caught between this threatening shape and the "Watry Surge," what remains for the unhappy Swain "but Tears and hopeless sighs?" The bewildered traveler is lost forever the moment he owns his strongest fears: "His Fear-shook limbs have lost their Youthly force / And down the waves He floats a Pale and breathless Corse."

The eventual death of the swain is as effortless as is his transformation into one of those "gliding Ghosts" perceived by the second sight.

Drawing upon the myth of Ceyx and Alcyone in Ovid's *Metamor-phoses,* Collins envisions the only kind of return the swain will ever make to the anxious wife he has left behind:[19]

> Alone if Night
> Her travell'd limbs in broken slumbers steep
> With Dropping Willows drest his mournfull Sprite
> Shall visit sad perhaps her silent Sleep
> Then He perhaps with moist and watry hand
> Shall fondly seem to press her shuddring cheek
> And with his blue swoln face before her stand
> And Shivring cold these piteous accents speak.
>
> (ll. 125-32)

His wife's "travell'd limbs" suggest both the travail of her anxieties and the fear-shook legs of her unfortunate traveler. But her husband has himself become a "mournfull Sprite," a supernatural being, hideous, frightening, unable to breach the gap between his new existence and the industrious, daily toils of his former life. Although he is not himself malevolent, his appearance nevertheless raises an involuntary response from her "shuddring cheek." The hapless swain and his wife are both tormented by supernatural forces that cannot be restrained by the human will.

"Scenes like these," depicting both the native terrors of the Highlands and the "primal Innocence" of St. Kilda, provide the native legends Home is called upon to "rehearse":

> In Scenes like these which daring to depart
> From sober Truth, are still to Nature true
> And call forth fresh delights to Fancy's view
> Th' Heroic Muse employ'd her Tasso's Art!
>
> (ll. 188-91)

The use of popular superstition by Tasso and Shakespeare provides Collins with an opportunity to celebrate his attraction to this kind of poem, to explain the extraordinary power it exerts on us (sophisticated though we may be). Collins illustrates his point by recalling a scene from *Jerusalem Delivered:*

> How have I trembled when at Tancred's stroke
> Its gushing Blood, the gaping Cypress pour'd
> When Each live Plant with Mortal accents spoke
> And the wild Blast up-heav'd the vanish'd Sword.
>
> (ll. 192-95)

Here, as in his own poem, Collins chooses to celebrate the supernatural transformation of nature, a metamorphosis whose truth is so compelling that it draws the sympathetic reader into its magical world:

> How have I trembled, when at Tancred's side
> Like him I stalkd and all his Passions felt
> Where Charmd by Ismen thro' the Forrest wide
> Barkd in Each Plant a talking Spirit dwelt!
>
> (ll. 192-95, first version)

The popular superstitions of the Highlands of Scotland represent a new storehouse of subjects and effects, a poetical quarry that rivals the resources Thomas Warton found in the old romances:

> such are their Terrible Graces of magic and enchantment, so magnificently marvellous are their fictions and fablings, that they contribute, in a wonderful degree, to rouse and invigorate all the powers of imagination; to store the fancy with those sublime and alarming images, which true poetry best delights to display.[20]

The poem's final stanza, however, once again evokes the inevitable distance that separates Collins from his friend and, ultimately, from poetic sources that are Home's rightful inheritance. The opening and closing stanzas, with their emphasis on Collins's "social Name," represent a conventional frame that places these copious subjects out of Collins's reach.[21] Collins envisions an actual visit to Home's native land in the final lines of the poem, but even here he is "by Fancy led," reenacting scenes celebrated by previous poets and borrowing heavily from their works.[22] Home returns to a native mythology that is properly his, but which Collins can only "at distance hail" (l. 207). But if this is Home's consolation (following his own disappointments), it is also—at least indirectly—Collins's as well. The entire structure of the ode is based on classical *praeterito*: just as the poem insists on a deprivation of poetical sources, so it paradoxically makes use of the very materials to which access is denied.[23] This is also the strategy of the "Ode on the Poetical Character," and like that poem, the "Ode to a Friend" ends in an apparent defeat that is, at the same time, a vicarious triumph. Here a revitalized nature once again provides enchanted ground for the undoubting mind; new regions, and new powers, are made accessible to the poet who by "indulging some peculiar habits of thought was eminently delighted with those flights of imagination which pass the bounds of nature."[24] Johnson's characterization was meant as a stricture, but these peculiar habits of thought also reveal the means by which Collins achieved at least one extended flight of the imagination.

8

Conclusion

At the close of his analysis of the "Ode to a Friend," Paul Sherwin offers a summary of Collins's career that has been voiced in similar fashion by several of Collins's readers: "Collins never comprehends, as do Milton and the Romantics, that his own personal history, in its totality, might serve as the starting point for a coherent body of poetry at once mythical and true."[1] This kind of complaint, which raises fundamental questions about Collins's achievement and about the relationship between his life and his work, certainly deserves a response from those who believe that Collins's poetry possesses a coherence, and a validity, of its own. We should begin by asking what critics like Sherwin mean by the phrase "personal history." Are we asked to consider Collins's character apart from his work (that private history which he chose, like Pope, to conceal or alter in his published poetry); or are we to consider his "literary character," a broadly conceived intellectual portrait—like Johnson's—that attempts to capture the essential similarities (or anomalies) between the man and his work? Sherwin speaks of Collins's "internal struggle" and "personal torment," but these terms remain as unprofitably ambiguous as "personal history." Conceptions of Collins's personal history drawn from his poetry alone are surely subject to serious qualifications, as we have already seen. The few facts we possess about Collins's life in the 1740s do not support the conclusion that the poetry written during these years was produced by the writer's sense of "personal torment" (at least not by those conventional torments—disappointed love, the loss of family or friends, severe illness, even madness—that we consider most basic). If we believe, however, that this torment derives primarily from literary anxiety, from Collins's sense of frustration and despair at the task of rivaling his predecessors' work, we must also realize that the manifestations of anxiety in his poetry are traditional tropes, frequently adopted by other poets. As Walter Jackson Bate concludes in his study of this issue, "the remorseless deepening of self-consciousness, before the rich and intimidating legacy of the past," is the greatest single problem faced by modern art.[2]

It would be most gratifying if we could replace the figure of "Poor Collins" with a more convincing portrait, one that would reconcile the man of flesh and blood with the character of his work; but this kind of critical synthesis—so successfully established for Johnson by Bate and for Pope by Maynard Mack—is not entirely possible for Collins.[3] There is not enough biographical evidence available for us to create a portrait of Collins apart from his work, but simply by stating the problem we are able to suggest one approach that may draw us nearer to Collins's elusive character. Perhaps the most interesting feature of the evidence we do have, spanning Collins's enrollment at Winchester College to his final days in Chichester, is the frequency with which the recorded episodes in his life are associated with his own poetical career or with his conception of the poet's life (both the idealized version of the "Ode on the Poetical Character" and the everyday existence of the "literary adventurer"). With the exception of some brief allusions to his travels, his business transactions, his short-lived attempt to win a curacy, and his eventual confinement in a mental institution, Collins's own letters and the accounts written about him are entirely devoted to his literary plans and aspirations. We may safely assume that the papers left at his death in 1759, which his sister Anne is reported to have burned, would have corroborated John Mulso's perception that his friend was "entirely an Author."

As we have seen, even Collins's earliest works were written in imitation of conventional literary forms and styles, and with the poet's traditional progress clearly in view. Winchester College provided its own traditions, and presumably Collins and his friend Joseph Warton were the two young students who erected a monument to Thomas Otway, also a Wykehamist, in the college's sixth chamber. By the time Collins reached Oxford, he was already an accomplished poet with considerable confidence in his own abilities. Gilbert White remarked that, because Collins "brought with him, for so the whole turn of his conversation discovered, too high an opinion of his school acquisitions, and a sovereign contempt for all academic studies and discipline, [so] he never looked with any complacency on his situation in the University, but was always complaining of the dulness of a college life."[4] White has also preserved our only glimpse of Collins's daily life at Magdalen:

> It happened one afternoon at a tea-visit, that several intelligent friends were assembled at his rooms to enjoy each other's conversation, when in comes a member of a certain college [James Hampton, later Collins's biographer], as remarkable at that time for his brutal disposition as for his good scholarship; who, though he met with a circle of the most peaceable people in the world, was determined to quarrel; and, though no man said a word, lifted up his foot and kicked the tea-table, and all its contents, to the other side of the room. Our poet, tho' of a warm temper, was so confounded at the unexpected downfall, and so astonished at the unmerited insult, that he took no notice of the aggressor, but getting up from his chair calmly, he began picking up the slices of bread and butter, and the fragments of his china, repeating very mildly, "Invenias etiam disjecti membra poetæ."[5]

Scattered fragments of the poet are all, in fact, that we shall find in most accounts of Collins's life. Collins apparently began his career as a "literary adventurer" before he left Oxford for London: it is there that he wrote the epistle to Hanmer (perhaps with university patronage in mind), and there that he probably made his transcription of Theodorus Prodromus' *Galeomyomachia*, "supposing it a relic of Aristophanes."[6] Projects such as these characterize his first two years in London. Johnson wrote that his friend arrived in town "with many projects in his head, and very little money in his pocket. He designed many works, but his great fault was irresolution, or the frequent calls of immediate necessity broke his schemes, and suffered him to pursue no settled purpose."[7] His one settled purpose, however, seems to have been his projected *History of the Revival of Learning*, for which he is said to have issued subscriptions in 1744. Mulso wrote to White that he saw "Collins in Town, he is entirely an Author, & hardly speaks out of Rule: I hope his Subscriptions go on well in Oxford."[8] But this grand historical project, even if begun (as Ragsdale says it was), was never finished, and Collins soon found himself in straitened circumstances. Mulso regaled White with a story of another tea-party that went awry:

> I can't help telling You, tho' 'tis a little uncharitable, that Collins appears in good cloaths & a wretched carcass, at all ye gay Places, tho' it was with ye utmost Difficulty that He scrap'd together 5 pound for Miss Bundy at whose Suit He was arrested & whom by his own confession He never intended to pay. I don't beleive He will tell ye Story in Verse, tho' some

circumstances of his taking would be burlesque enough. The Bailiff intro-
duc'd himself with 4 Gentlemen who came to drink Tea, & who all together
could raise but one Guinea. The ἀναγνώρισις (a word He is fond of) was
quite striking & ye catastrophe quite poetical & interesting.[9]

It is characteristic that Collins viewed his plight in literary terms, and
appropriate that he extricated himself from this scrape (or another one
similar to it) by promising to translate the work that gave "anagnorisis"
and "catastrophe" such widespread currency. Johnson writes that "by
degrees I gained his confidence; and one day was admitted to him
when he was immured by a bailiff that was prowling in the street. On
this occasion recourse was had to the booksellers, who, on the credit
of a translation of Aristotle's *Poeticks*, which he engaged to write with
a large commentary, advanced as much money as enabled him to escape into the country. He shewed me the guineas safe in his hand."[10]

Another anecdote from this period corroborates our portrait of an
unusual and amusing character who delighted in his pursuit of an un-
conventional life. Ragsdale recalled Collins's initial confrontation with
George Payne, who controlled the purse-strings of the Collins family
in London:

> he called on his cousin Payne, gaily dressed, and with a feather in his hat,
> at which his relation expressed surprize, and told him his appearance was
> by no means that of a young man who had not a single guinea he could call
> his own. This gave him great offence, but remembering his sole dependence
> for subsistence was in the power of Mr. Payne, he concealed his resentment,
> yet could not refrain speaking freely behind his back, and saying he thought
> him a d—n'd dull fellow; though indeed this was an epithet he was pleased
> to bestow on every one who did not think as he would have them.[11]

Ragsdale's friend appears here as a quasi-comical embodiment of the
"poetical character"; this is a title Collins clearly wished to claim, in
appearance at least, long before he could properly inherit it in verse.
Collins's dependence on the patronage of his cousin Payne and his
uncle, Colonel Martin, may occasionally have caused him to waver
from his goal, but eventually his friendship with the tobacconist
Hardham (who dissuaded him from the clergy) and with Joseph Warton
(whose example encouraged him to complete his odes) made a literary
life possible.

It was a career, at least after the publication of the *Odes* in 1746,
that was to be dedicated to other literary pursuits besides poetry: lives
for the *Biographia Britannica*, the founding of a new journal (to be
called *The Clarendon Review*), and continued work on *The History
of the Revival of Learning*.[12] Collins's letter of 1747, written to his

potential collaborator, John Gilbert Cooper, provides a sustained view of a fervid and undaunted mind, and the postscript to this letter attests to an abiding pleasure in the variety of the town. Later, in the years 1748–51, he exchanged the cultural life of London for renewed friendships with his literary colleagues in Richmond, Winchester, Chichester, and Oxford. His only other surviving letter, addressed to the composer Hayes in 1750, reveals that his interest in music, and in his own writing, remained firm. It is difficult to believe that anything less than severe illness, a "catastrophe" far heavier than the plights of his youth, could have brought this literary career to such an abrupt conclusion.

But we must realize at the same time that the period following the publication of the *Odes* was not a productive one for Collins. He often proposed literary projects, but proposals and subscriptions were all that he published. Each of the three poems that we can date from this period was, as we have already seen, prompted by a specific occasion. The ode on the music of the Grecian theater was never completed; the ode to Home was never published; the ode to Thomson contains ominous warnings of a diminished poetical sphere. Collins's "Ode to a Friend," which ostensibly celebrates fresh possibilities for the awakening poet, also establishes severe limitations for those who embrace this new poetical material. Collins is at one remove from his Scottish friend at the very beginning of the ode, but we must also ask whether Collins and Home are not both removed from "the Themes of simple sure Effect" (l. 33) that are said to add new conquests to the Muse's reign. The emotional quality of Collins's work is never quite this simple; the Scottish superstitions, like the romances before them, provide fresh subjects for Collins's poetry, but ultimately they are not substantial enough—and not native enough—to sustain more than one wistful poem.

The question of limitation and possible failure was apparently raised by Collins himself, at least if we can trust the compelling anecdote told by his old school-friend William Smith. Collins's dream is a remarkable one, well worth quoting once again:

> [Collins had been] observed one morning to be particularly depressed and melancholy. Being pressed to disclose the cause, he at last said it was in consequence of a dream: for this he was laughed at, but desired to tell what it was; he said, he dreamed that he was walking in the fields where there was a lofty tree; that he climbed it, and when he had nearly reached the top, a great branch, upon which he had got, failed with him, and let him fall to the ground. This account caused more ridicule; and he was asked how he could possibly be affected by this common consequence of a school-boy

adventure, when he did not pretend, even in imagination and sleep, to have received any hurt, he replied, that the Tree was the Tree of Poetry.[13]

An analyst might argue that Collins's dream is almost too good to be true, and it is surprising that his critics have not attempted to put it to use. The dream belongs to the schoolboy who is already publishing his poetry in the *Gentleman's Magazine*, and is remembered by the poet whose career has been prematurely shortened by illness. The anxiety and perils of literary attainment cannot be ignored: poetry is envisioned in the dream as a towering structure, one that must be explored and ultimately surmounted.

But poetry is also conceived in terms of a natural metaphor in Collins's dream, as a structure of organic growth, not unlike the re-created Eden of the "Ode on the Poetical Character" or the watery image Joseph Warton introduced in his claim that poetry should return to its *"natural channel."* In Collins's dream, his sudden fall to earth is not the inevitable result of his perilous climb, but the consequence of his trusting in one branch that "failed with him." Collins's "great branch," like Warton's natural channel, is an appropriate metaphor for the strengths and limitations of his own poetical achievement. Collins's is, for better and worse, a poetry of limitation. It would be difficult to think of another poet who has been so successful in emphasizing his own limitations, in suggesting poems that might be written and welcoming powers that might be felt. Collins's most impressive poems are often paradoxical or ambivalent, devoted either to the difficulties involved in achieving poetical success or to certain effects and materials that are considered to lie just beyond this poet's reach. But a poetry that celebrates its own limitations is ultimately constrained by them. I think we sense, especially in Collins's final poem, his own realization that there were certain boundaries beyond which his innovative approach could not be pushed.

If we are to search for a coherent body of poetry and a convincing personal history, perhaps we shall find them here: in the poet's self-conscious role as a literary innovator, in his examination of the poetical resources still available to him, and in his struggle to adapt the traditional forms and language of poetry. This final point deserves particular attention because it helps to explain how Collins's form of innovation differs from his contemporaries'. In an attempt to demonstrate the self-conscious character of mid- and late-eighteenth-century poetry, Bertrand Bronson has suggested that these writers were intensely aware that an age of mass publication had created an audience that was increasingly large and hence anonymous.[14] The private nature of lyric poetry had been seriously distorted, in other words, by the distance that had suddenly opened between the poet and his reader; poets consequently responded to this predicament by attempting—in a variety of ways—to alter their relationship with their audience. We may wish to qualify Bronson's argument by citing additional causes for this increased self-consciousness, but we cannot dismiss his central point: poetry after Pope often offered intriguing alterations of the poet's voice or of the poet's approach to his audience.[15] Both Gray and Cowper professed to write for a private circle of friends; Smart had recourse to a private idiom and visionary system; Chatterton and Macpherson both attempted to pass their poetry off as someone else's work (and as work from an age in which the poet enjoyed a more immediate relationship with his audience); Burns had a genuinely native language and folklore upon which he could continually draw. These distinctions, basic as they are, nevertheless emphasize the essentially traditional role Collins chose to assume in his life and in his work. Collins offered neither his poetry nor his "poetical character" under a different guise; the poet whose friend styled him "entirely an Author" was willing to make his mark within the great lyric tradition, even if this meant that his most successful poems would keep his own limitations firmly in view.

The burden of the past was also an inheritance of immense value for poets of the mid-eighteenth century (as, indeed, it has been for all writers), and we should remember that throughout his lifetime Collins intended to appraise the past in his grand *History of the Revival of Learning*. This historical project is of considerable interest, for in it Collins intended to trace the rich intellectual and literary traditions that were to make his own poetry possible. But his relationship to this legacy also produced an undeniable tension central to much of his most compelling work. Collins's ambivalence is accurately captured in two mottoes he suggested to John Gilbert Cooper for *The Clarendon Review*. One of these mottoes, Lucretius' address to Epicurus at the beginning of the third book of *De Rerum Natura*, reveals Collins's reverence towards those who preceded him: "O thou who first from so great a darkness wert able to raise aloft a light so clear, illumining the blessings of life, thee I follow." But he also suggested a quotation from the *Metamorphoses* in which Deucalion and Pyrrha, sole survivors of the deluge, survey the "deep silence" and "desolated lands" that are theirs alone. Deucalion's address to his wife invokes the excitement and perils of isolation, of originality, of the task of beginning anew, that Collins clearly felt as well: "Of all the lands which the rising and the setting sun behold, we two are the throng. The sea holds all the rest."[16] Collins's unusual candor may in turn explain why his own struggle with the past has been the focus of so much recent critical attention. The point is not necessarily that Collins experienced this burden more acutely than his contemporaries, but that he unflinchingly confronted it in a poetry that possessed its own coherence and its own distinctive voice.

Appendix: A Note on Modern Criticism and Scholarship

"Modern" criticism of Collins actually begins with those eighteenth-century readers who first sensed the originality and difficulty of his work. Collins's earliest editors—John Langhorne and Laetitia Barbauld—were quick to emphasize the freshness and even the presumptuous ambition of his poetry.[1] They were not afraid to praise his stylistic and formal difficulties, nor were they hesitant to begin the formidable task of elucidating the learned "obscurity" in which he often cloaked his poems. Samuel Johnson, Collins's most influential eighteenth-century commentator, could only fault his friend for what he believed to be deviations "in quest of mistaken beauties" and "flights of imagination which pass the bounds of nature"; but these were precisely the qualities that excited interest in Collins's poetry among critics of the following century—especially Hazlitt and Swinburne—and that continue to intrigue his readers today.

Swinburne's short essay on Collins, first published in 1880, is filled with rather extravagant praise for Collins's "purity of music" and "clarity of style," and for a poetic range that Swinburne finds to be both the narrowest and the highest among eighteenth-century poets.[2] Arnold praised Gray's poetry at the expense of Collins's, but Swinburne contended that Collins was the only poet of his age to possess the lyric impulse: "The Muse gave birth to Collins; she did but give suck to Gray." Of greater importance is Swinburne's emphasis on the pictorial nature of Collins's poetry. He calls Collins the "perfect painter of still life or starlit vision" and compares his work to the paintings of

191

Corot, Millais, and Courbet, citing the poet's "incomparable and in-fallible eye for landscape" and his "simple-seeming subtlety of tone." The visual qualities of Collins's poetry were subsequently ignored, however, until Jean H. Hagstrum's study appeared in 1958.

The first major study of Collins was published by H. W. Garrod in 1928.[3] Garrod continued the debate over the relative merits of Gray and Collins by examining the purity of their "verbal music," but his book is actually a careful refutation of Swinburne's exaggerated praise of Collins's work. We might characterize Garrod's study as a sympathetic depreciation; at the same time, the very minuteness with which Garrod examines Collins's poetry suggests the importance he placed on a figure "who is certainly not among the great poets of the world." This intensive (if often carping) analysis is one of Garrod's major contributions to modern scholarship; of similar importance is his brief consideration of Collins's relationship with the Wartons in the 1740s.

Garrod's attempt to depict the literary climate in which Collins wrote was soon amplified by A. S. P. Woodhouse in his pioneering essay on "Collins and the Creative Imagination: A Study in the Critical Background of his Odes (1746)."[4] Woodhouse convincingly demonstrated that Collins's finest work was but one important episode in the history of defining the properties of the "creative imagination," a conception of poetical power advanced most forcefully at the beginning of the century by Addison and ultimately embodied and celebrated at the century's close by Wordsworth and Coleridge. Glimpsed in this perspective, Collins's poetry (especially his "Ode on the Poetical Character") is shown to derive its originality—in a sense, its modernity—from its elaboration of the myths of creation and from its emphasis on the poet's power to imitate, however faintly, the life-giving spark of divine creativity. Like Joseph Warton, Collins valued the power of the imagination to transcend the actual and the immediate in order to create "its own romantic world of freer and intenser experience." Woodhouse traces the roots of this conception as far back as the early English Renaissance, and provides interesting examples from Collins's contemporaries. The virtue of Woodhouse's study, especially in comparison with Garrod's, is that for the first time we are able to see a coherent motif in Collins's work (one that Woodhouse later refined and sometimes modified in "The Poetry of Collins Reconsidered").[5] Both of these influential articles remain essential reading for anyone approaching Collins's poetry.

Edward G. Ainsworth's *Poor Collins*, which followed in 1937, is a less successful attempt to explore the contexts of Collins's work.[6] Encyclopedic in form, Ainsworth's book provides an occasionally helpful commentary on the poems, but it remains more of an edition *manqué* than a coherent critical study. Oliver F. Sigworth's *William Collins* (1965) is a more succinct introduction to Collins and eighteenth-century poetry, and it includes several spirited readings of the major odes.[7] Much of the most original work on Collins in the past thirty years, however, is to be found in works that do not focus on his poetry alone. Hagstrum explores Collins's interest in painting and the visual arts in *The Sister Arts*; Norman Maclean discusses several of Collins's poems in his lively history of the eighteenth-century ode; and Patricia Meyer Spacks offers the fullest analysis of the "popular superstitions" ode in *The Insistence of Horror* and *The Poetry of Vision*.[8] We still lack a study of the general cultural changes that influenced English poetry in the 1740s, but a series of important articles by John R. Sitter provides an interesting perspective on how Collins's odes reflect broad changes in the character and concerns of poetry during this crucial decade.[9]

The "Ode on the Poetical Character," singled out by Woodhouse as Collins's major statement on the creative imagination, remains a central text for critics concerned with the problem of poetic influence. Harold Bloom and Paul S. Sherwin are particularly interested in showing how closely Collins's "predicament" foreshadows the anxieties of Romantic poetry.[10] Read in this context, Collins's poems exemplify the plight of the poet who must both wrestle with and eventually absorb the work of previous writers—in Collins's case, Sophocles, Shakespeare, Spenser, and Milton—to fashion works that will ultimately distinguish his own contribution to English poetry. I have cautioned, however, that this focus on anxiety and influence is subject to two important qualifications: an analysis of poetic frustration, especially when it draws on biographical speculation, can easily distort the nature of Collins's poetry and its relation to contemporary literature; and the general tendency to see Collins and other poets "burdened" and in effect debilitated by the achievements of past writers may induce readers to ignore the creative opportunities that this dilemma also posed. Collins's confrontation with his "precursors" actually occasioned much of his most original work.

The psychological dimension inherent in a study of poetic influence and repression can also be found in two recent books that include major chapters on Collins's poetry. Thomas Weiskel and Paul H. Fry are both interested in the sexual dramas enacted within Collins's odes, and their provocative analyses open up several poems—especially the "Ode on the Poetical Character" and the "Ode to Fear"—to a psychoanalytical consideration of incest, sexual repression, and the primal scene.[11] Weiskel and Fry offer fresh and challenging readings of several poems, and their arguments, limited as they may be to a few odes, deserve careful scrutiny. Also of importance is their exploration of Collins's characteristic gestures and postures within his poetry. Weiskel, for instance, focuses on the relation between sublimation and sublimity, on Collins's choice of the "negative" sublime as a vehicle for human transcendence; Fry discusses Collins's sense of "calling" in the ode, the nature and limitations of his invocations. Both of these authors are demanding and sometimes convoluted, but their critical methodology is likely to stimulate similar approaches to Collins and his fellow eighteenth-century poets in the coming years.

There is at present no standard biography of Collins, although Mary Margaret Stewart has such a work in progress. The only full-length biography we now have, P. L. Carver's *The Life of a Poet*, is often unreliable, and there are only brief accounts of Collins's life in the opening chapters of the studies by Ainsworth and Sigworth.[12] Collins's readers do, however, have a variety of reliable editions from which to choose. Arthur Johnston's edition of the selected poems of Gray and Collins provides a useful commentary in its footnotes and in the short essays that precede the major poems.[13] Roger Lonsdale's edition of Gray and Collins in the "Oxford Standard Authors" series provides less annotation than Johnston's, but includes all of Collins's poems, including the Drafts and Fragments.[14] Lonsdale's edition of Gray, Collins, and Goldsmith in the "Longman's Annotated English Poets" series presents a modernized text, ample footnotes, and a full commentary.[15] The old-spelling text prepared by Richard Wendorf and Charles Ryskamp (in the "Oxford English Texts" series) comprises Collins's complete works, including his letters and Latin oration, and a discussion of his lost and unfinished poetry and literary projects.[16] This edition also offers the fullest editorial discussion of textual problems in Collins's poetry, but readers will continue to consult Lonsdale's annotated edition for his fine commentary and for his extensive quotation of poems to which Collins may have been alluding.

Notes

Abbreviations

All passages from Collins's poetry are quoted from Wendorf and Ryskamp; passages from Greek and Latin authors are quoted from the Loeb Classical Library. All books issued before 1900 are understood to have been published in London unless otherwise noted.

ECS	*Eighteenth-Century Studies*
ELH	*English Literary History*
GM	*Gentleman's Magazine*
JHI	*Journal of the History of Ideas*
MP	*Modern Philology*
NQ	*Notes and Queries*
PBSA	*Papers of the Bibliographical Society of America*
PMLA	*Publications of the Modern Language Association*
PQ	*Philological Quarterly*
RES	*Review of English Studies*
SEL	*Studies in English Literature 1500-1900*
SP	*Studies in Philology*
TLS	*Times Literary Supplement*

Collection	*A Collection of Poems by Several Hands.* Ed. Robert Dodsley. 6 vols. 1748-58.
Crider	Crider, John R. "Structure and Effect in Collins' Progress Poems." *SP*, 60 (1963), 57-72.
Dryden	*The Poems of John Dryden.* Ed. James Kinsley. 4 vols. Oxford: Clarendon Press, 1958.
Hagstrum	Hagstrum, Jean H. *The Sister Arts: The Tradition of Literary Pictorialism and English Poetry from Dryden to Gray.* Chicago: Univ. of Chicago Press, 1958.

Holt-White	*Letters to Gilbert White of Selborne from his intimate friend and contemporary the Rev. John Mulso*. Ed. Rashleigh Holt-White. London: Porter [1907].
Johnson	*The Yale Edition of the Works of Samuel Johnson*. Ed. E. L. McAdam, Jr. *et al.* 11 vols. New Haven: Yale Univ. Press, 1958- .
Johnston	Johnston, Arthur. "The Poetry of William Collins." *Proceedings of the British Academy*, 59 (1973), 321–40.
Langhorne	*The Poetical Works of Mr. William Collins*. Ed. John Langhorne. 1765 (rpt. 1771, 1776, 1781).
Lives	Johnson, Samuel. *Lives of the English Poets*. Ed. G. B. Hill. 3 vols. Oxford: Clarendon Press, 1905.
Lonsdale	*The Poems of Thomas Gray, William Collins and Oliver Goldsmith*. Ed. Roger Lonsdale. London: Longman, 1969.
Milton	*The Poetical Works of John Milton*. Ed. Helen Darbishire. 2 vols. Oxford: Clarendon Press, 1952–55.
Poetical Calendar	*Poetical Calendar*. Ed. Francis Fawkes and William Woty. 12 vols. (vols. XI–XII). 1763.
The Reaper	*The Reaper*, No. 26. *York Chronicle*, 16 Feb. 1797. Rpt. in Nathan Drake, *The Gleaner: A Series of Periodical Essays; Selected and Arranged from Scarce or Neglected Volumes* (1811), IV, 474–84. (Quotations are from the original.)
Sherwin	Sherwin, Paul S. *Precious Bane: Collins and the Miltonic Legacy*. Austin: Univ. of Texas Press, 1977.
Sigworth	Sigworth, Oliver F. *William Collins*. New York: Twayne, 1965.
Spacks	Spacks, Patricia Meyer. *The Poetry of Vision: Five Eighteenth-Century Poets*. Cambridge, Mass.: Harvard Univ. Press, 1967.
Spenser	*The Poetical Works of Edmund Spenser*. Ed. J. C. Smith and E. de Selincourt. 3 vols. Oxford: Clarendon Press, 1909–10.
Thomson	Thomson, James. *Poetical Works*. Ed. J. L. Robertson. London: Oxford Univ. Press, 1908.
Twickenham Pope	*The Twickenham Edition of Alexander Pope*. Ed. John Butt *et al.* 11 vols. London: Methuen; New Haven: Yale Univ. Press, 1939–69.
Wendorf and Ryskamp	*The Works of William Collins*. Ed. Richard Wendorf and Charles Ryskamp. Oxford: Clarendon Press, 1979.
Woodhouse	Woodhouse, A. S. P. "Collins and the Creative Imagination: A Study in the Critical Background of his Odes (1746)." *Studies in English by Members of University College, Toronto*. Ed. M. W. Wallace. Toronto: Univ. of Toronto Press, 1931, pp. 59–130.

Notes

Chapter 1. "Poor Collins" Reconsidered

1. Collins is quoted by Gilbert White, "Memoirs of the Life of William Collins, the Poet," *GM*, 51 (Jan. 1781), 12; the entire anecdote is quoted below in ch. 8. Alan D. McKillop, "The Romanticism of William Collins," *SP*, 20 (1923), 1–16, was the first to gather many of the more fanciful accounts of Collins that were published after his death.

2. *The Reminiscences of Alexander Dyce*, ed. Richard Schrader (Columbus, Ohio: Ohio State Univ. Press, 1972), p. 233.

3. *The Reaper*, No. 26.

4. *Poetical Calendar*, XII, 109.

5. *Ibid.*, XII, 111–12.

6. Sigworth, p. 55.

7. *Lives*, III, 338 n. (this definition is also pointed out by Patricia Meyer Spacks in her review of Sigworth's book, *PQ*, 45 [1966], 548). The word was often associated with diversion or amusement; cf. Boswell's journals of 1763-64.

8. See Wendorf and Ryskamp, pp. 200–01.

9. Collins's letter is printed by Wendorf and Ryskamp, p. 89.

10. *The Reaper*, No. 26.

11. *Ibid.*; Collins's letter has not survived.

12. *Ibid.*

13. *Ibid.* Leland D. Peterson, "The Spectral Hand in Swift's 'Day of Judgement,'" *PBSA*, 70 (1976), 209–10, speculates that Collins may have met Lord Chesterfield at Bath during this period, and thus have transcribed his copy of Swift's poem through this intermediary. But Peterson admits that he can produce no evidence to substantiate this possibility, and his entire argument has been seriously questioned by Sidney L. Gulick, "No 'Spectral Hand' in Swift's 'Day of Judgement,'" *PBSA*, 71 (1977), 333–36.

14. *Poetical Calendar*, XII, 112.

15. *The Letters of Samuel Johnson*, ed. R. W. Chapman (Oxford: Clarendon Press, 1952), I, 53. Hereafter cited as Chapman.

16. *The Reaper*, No. 26.

17. *Ibid.*

18. *GM*, 51 (Jan. 1781), 11.

19. *Boswell's Life of Johnson*, ed. G. B. Hill, rev. L. F. Powell (Oxford: Clarendon Press, 1934–64), I, 276 n. Boswell appends this note to one of Johnson's letters, dated 28 November 1754. Corroboration of this date is supplied by Mary Margaret Stewart, who points out that Gilbert White remained in Oxford from 14 October until 15 November 1754; see his account-book, reproduced in *The Natural History and Antiquities of Selborne, in the County of Southampton*, ed. Thomas Bell (1877), II, 344–45.

20. David Mallet, *Ballads and Songs*, ed. Frederick Dinsdale (1857), p. 54.

21. Chapman, I, 60, 90.

22. Johnson's "Life of Collins" adopts the 1756 date, but Johnson himself never specified an exact date for Collins's death. In his edition of *Johnson's Lives of the Poets* (Oxford: Oxford Univ. Press, 1971), p. 366, J. P. Hardy has reconstructed the process by which this error entered Johnson's "Life." Hampton's original "Account" "had simply read ' . . . where death at last came to his relief'. For the change the printer John Nichols was responsible, who wrote at the foot of a state of proof-sheets for this Life: 'There is no mention when Mr. Collins died. It was in 1756 at Chichester.' The misdating of Collins's death was therefore an error made by Nichols and not (as has been assumed) by Johnson." But Hampton's "Account" does include the mistaken date, and thus it seems likely that Nichols drew upon this source for his information. The proof-sheets Hardy refers to are in the Forster Collection of the Victoria and Albert Museum (Forster 298-48-D-56, 57). For a full discussion, see my article on "The Making of Johnson's 'Life of Collins,'" *PBSA*, 74 (1980), 95–115.

23. *An Essay on the Genius and Writings of Pope*, 5th edn. (1806), I, 182.

24. *Poetical Calendar*, XII, 109.

25. *The History of English Poetry*, rev. edn. (1824), III, 185 n. Warton also speaks of Collins's "memory failing in his last calamitous indisposition" (IV, 309). We cannot be certain, however, that Warton knew when Collins actually died, and thus it is possible that he meant to indicate their meetings in 1754. In a letter to Thomas Percy dated 1762, Warton specified that he had seen a book "about eight years ago [i.e., 1754] in the hands of a gentleman quite of your own Cast, Mr Collins of Chichester, who died soon afterwards" (*The Correspondence of Thomas Percy and Richard Farmer*, ed. Cleanth Brooks [Baton Rouge, La.: Louisiana State Univ. Press, 1946], pp. 45–46). Similarly, Joseph Warton noted in the Dyce Collection copy of the *Persian Eclogues* that "Mr Collins gave me this Copy with his own Hands when I & my Brother visited Him for the Last time at Chichester," which almost certainly refers to their meeting in September 1754. On the other hand, Thomas mentioned in his *History* (III, 185 n.) that many of Collins's scarce books "fell into my hands at his death," and this suggests that Warton would have known that Collins did not die before 1759. Joseph Warton's statement in his *Essay* indicates that one or both of the Wartons remained in touch with Collins after 1754. Oliver Goldsmith's reference to Collins in *An Enquiry into the Present State of Polite Learning in Europe* (1759) also suggests that some of Collins's friends knew that he was still alive: "The neglected author of the Persian eclogues, which, however inaccurate, excel any in our language, is still alive. Happy, if *insensible* of our neglect, not *raging* at our ingratitude" (*Collected Works*, ed. Arthur Friedman [Oxford: Clarendon Press, 1966], I, 315). But Goldsmith also entered the following marginal notation in his manuscript, which indicates that he was not in close touch with Collins: "Mr William Collins, author of some celebrated odes; now in a Mad-house" (I, 340).

26. *The Reaper*, No. 26; Shenton's letter is BL Add. MS. 42561, f. 129. For other accounts of these final years in Chichester, which are apparently indebted to Langhorne and Boswell, see Alexander Hay, *The History of Chichester* (Chichester, 1804), p. 528, and James Dallaway, *A History of the Western Division of the County of Sussex* (1815-30), I, 185.

27. BL Add. MS. 42561, f. 127.

28. *The Poems of William Collins*, ed. William Crowe (Bath, 1828), pp. ix-xi. Crowe writes that Smith repeated this story to Dr. Busby of Winchester College, who in turn retold it to an intimate friend of Crowe's. Smith's story is possibly apocryphal, and the date of their meeting is difficult to establish. Although traditionally considered a late occurrence in Collins's life, Smith's visit could have been made as early as 1753-54, when Collins first retired to Chichester.

29. *The Poems of William Collins*, ed. W. C. Bronson (Boston, 1898), p. xxvi.

30. *The Life of a Poet: A Biographical Sketch of William Collins* (London: Sidgwick and Jackson; New York: Horizon, 1967), p. 174.

31. "Madness and Poetry: A Note on Collins, Cowper, and Smart," *Bulletin of the New York Academy of Medicine*, 2nd ser., 46, no. 4 (April 1970), 213; rpt. in *Boswell's Clap and Other Essays: Medical Analyses of Literary Men's Afflictions* (Carbondale: Southern Illinois Univ. Press, 1979), pp. 137-92.

32. Sigworth, p. 53.

33. *TLS* (28 March 1975), p. 328.

34. See Walter Russell Brain, "The Illness of Dean Swift," *Irish Journal of Medical Science*, 6th ser., nos. 320-21 (1952), 337-45; Irvin Ehrenpreis, *The Personality of Jonathan Swift* (Cambridge, Mass.: Harvard Univ. Press, 1958), ch. 6; and Ida Macalpine and Richard Hunter, *George III and the Mad-Business* (London: Allen Lane, 1969).

35. *Lives*, III, 340.

36. Iolo A. Williams, *Seven XVIIIth Century Bibliographies* (London: Dulau, 1924), p. 102.

37. See *Lives*, III, 340-41: "The approaches of this dreadful malady he began to feel soon after his uncle's death, and, with the usual weakness of men so diseased, eagerly snatched that temporary relief with which the table and the bottle flatter and seduce." Collins's drinking seems here to be a result of his illness, not a cause. Cf. Chapman, I, 59 (a letter from Johnson to Thomas Warton, 21 December 1754): "I had lately the favour of a Letter from your Brother with some account of poor Collins for whom I am much concerned: I have a notion that by very great temperance or more properly abstinence he might yet recover."

38. *Lives*, III, 337; *A New Biographical Dictionary*, 2nd edn. (1796), s.v. "Collins."

39. *The Poetical Works of William Collins*, ed. W. Moy Thomas (1830), p. lxix.

40. *The Poetical Works of Goldsmith, Collins, and T. Warton* (Edinburgh, 1854), p. 73. Hereafter cited as Gilfillan.

41. *Ibid.*, p. 80.

42. *GM*, 65, Pt. 2 (Sept. 1795), 741.

43. *Ibid.*, p. 742.

44. The genesis of the monument is discussed by W. G. Constable, *John Flaxman 1755-1826* (London: Univ. of London Press, 1927), pp. 41-45.

45. Hagstrum, pp. 268-86 and plates.

46. *GM*, 51 (Jan. 1781), 11.

47. Langhorne, p. xiii; see also the *Encyclopaedia Britannica*, 3rd edn. (Edinburgh, 1797), V, 144.

48. *The Poetical Works of James Beattie, LL.D. and William Collins*, ed. Thomas Miller (1846), p. iv.

49. Gilfillan, p. 76.

50. *Ibid.*, p. 81.

51. *Ibid.*, p. 84.

52. *Boswell's Life of Johnson*, II, 106.

53. *The Poems of William Collins*, ed. Christopher Stone (London: Frowde, 1907), p. xix.

54. Moy Thomas's edn., p. xlv.

55. *Ibid.*, p. lvii.

56. *Calamities of Authors* (1812), II, 200-01.

57. *Ibid.*, II, 208.

58. *Ibid.*

59. Johnston, p. 336.

60. *The Poetical Works of William Wordsworth*, ed. E. de Selincourt, 2nd edn. (Oxford: Clarendon Press, 1952), II, 236.

61. Langhorne, pp. i-ii.

62. *Monthly Review*, 30 (Feb. 1764), 123.

63. Gilfillan, pp. 80-81; see also Charles Crocker's poem "The Lavant," in *The Vale of Obscurity, The Lavant, and Other Poems* (Chichester, 1830).

64. *Literary Hours* (Sudbury, 1798), p. 29.

65. *Ibid.*, p. 38.

66. D'Israeli, II, 202; see also Sir Egerton Brydges, *Censura Literaria* (1805-07), I, 354-55.

67. *Lives*, III, 337.

68. "Life of Savage," *Lives*, II, 321.

69. "The Name and Nature of Poetry" (1933), in *Selected Prose*, ed. John Carter (Cambridge: Cambridge Univ. Press, 1961), p. 188; see also F. L. Lucas, *The Decline and Fall of the Romantic Ideal* (Cambridge: Cambridge Univ. Press, 1936; rev. and rpt. 1963), p. 98. Housman also argues that the "elements of their nature were more or less insurgent against the centralised tyranny of the intellect, and their brains were not thrones on which the great usurper could sit secure." Northrop Frye takes a similar stand in *Fearful Symmetry: A Study of William Blake* (Princeton: Princeton Univ. Press, 1947), pp. 4-5: "Besides, if we look at some of the other poets of the second half of the eighteenth century—Smart, Cowper, Chatterton, Macpherson, Fergusson, Collins, Burns—we shall find the percentage of mental breakdowns and social maladjustments among them abnormally high. It is clear that the spiritual loneliness of Blake was not so much characteristic of him as of his age." But see Robert Brittain's refutation of such thinking in the introduction to *Poems by Christopher Smart* (Princeton: Princeton Univ. Press, 1950), pp. 3-4, and Donald Greene's interesting summary, "Smart, Berkeley, the Scientists and the Poets," *JHI*, 14 (1953), 327-52.

70. See Ober's review of the work of Josephine Miles and Patricia Meyer Spacks: "If we add to a passive, withdrawn diction the disjunctive, incoherent syntax and both of these to a poetic content expressing fear and anxiety as well as an inadequacy of affect, it is possible to outline a constellation of effects which, taken together, suggest depressive psychosis as that form of mental disturbance most likely to develop. . . . But such interpretations are subject to the caution that many poets wrote on melancholy, on thwarted love, on their fears and anxieties, and only a few developed clinical psychosis" (p. 220). Northrop Frye also attempts to link biographical material with the poets' technical accomplishments in "Towards Defining an Age of Sensibility," *ELH*, 23 (1956), 144-52; cf. Michèle Hammer, "A Propos D'Une Vie: William Collins," *Études Anglaises*, 23 (1970), 302-10.

71. *Complete Works*, ed. P. P. Howe (London: Dent, 1930), V, 118.

72. *Literary Hours*, pp. 38-39.

73. Freud notes the ability of the psychological novelist to split his ego into the different characters of his work, and this might be applied to the personification of emotions as well, both in "The Passions" and in the *Odes* as a whole. See "The Relation of the Poet to Day-Dreaming," *Collected Papers*, ed. Joan Riviere (London: Hogarth Press, 1925), IV, 180-81.

74. *Adventurer*, No. 57, quoted by Earl Wasserman, "The Inherent Values of Eighteenth-Century Personification," *PMLA*, 65, Pt. 2 (1950), 444. My discussion is also indebted to Bertrand Bronson, "Personification Reconsidered," in his *Facets of the Enlightenment*

(Berkeley and Los Angeles: Univ. of California Press, 1968), pp. 119-52, and to Chester F. Chapin, *Personification in Eighteenth-Century English Poetry* (New York: Columbia Univ. Press, 1955).

75. Wasserman, p. 441.

76. Quoted by Wasserman, p. 443.

77. *Ibid.*

78. *The Poetical Works of Mr. William Collins*, ed. Mrs. A. L. Barbauld (1797), p. vii.

79. Quoted by Martin Price, *To the Palace of Wisdom* (Garden City, N.Y.: Doubleday, 1964), p. 370.

80. See Fletcher, *Allegory: The Theory of a Symbolic Mode* (Ithaca: Cornell Univ. Press, 1964), p. 51 n., and Bloom, *The Anxiety of Influence* (New York: Oxford Univ. Press, 1973), ch. 4. Paul Sherwin indirectly raises the biographical problem without directly confronting it; see my review of *Precious Bane* in *MP*, 77 (1980), 440-44.

81. See Ralph Cohen, *The Unfolding of "The Seasons"* (London: Routledge and Kegan Paul, 1970), p. 172.

82. *The Anxiety of Influence*, p. 111.

83. *The Visionary Company: A Reading of English Romantic Poetry* (New York: Doubleday, 1961), p. 11.

84. *Odes on Various Subjects* (1746), pp. 5-11.

85. See, for example, Max Byrd, *Visits to Bedlam* (Columbia, S.C.: Univ. of South Carolina Press, 1974), ch. 5.

86. "Mourning and Melancholia," *Collected Papers*, IV, 152-70.

Chapter 2. The Poetical Character in the 1740s

1. For a discussion of the ode in the eighteenth century, see Woodhouse, "Collins and the Creative Imagination . . . ," pp. 95-96, and "The Poetry of Collins Reconsidered," in *From Sensibility to Romanticism: Essays Presented to Frederick A. Pottle*, ed. Frederick W. Hilles and Harold Bloom (New York: Oxford Univ. Press, 1965), pp. 118-19; John R. Sitter, "To *The Vanity of Human Wishes* through the 1740's," *SP*, 74 (1977), 451-52, 454-55; Norman Maclean, "From Action to Image: Theories of the Lyric in the Eighteenth Century," in *Critics and Criticism: Ancient and Modern*, ed. R. S. Crane (Chicago: Univ. of Chicago Press, 1952), pp. 408-60; George N. Shuster, *The English Ode from Milton to Keats* (New York: Columbia Univ. Press, 1940), ch. 7; and Paul H. Fry, *The Poet's Calling in the English Ode* (New Haven: Yale Univ. Press, 1980), esp. chs. 3-5.

2. Langhorne, pp. 137-46; see also Woodhouse, "The Poetry of Collins Reconsidered," pp. 112-13, and Maclean, p. 443 (and passim).

3. *Lives*, III, 341.

4. *Correspondence of Thomas Gray*, ed. Paget Toynbee and Leonard Whibley, rev. H. W. Starr (Oxford: Clarendon Press, 1971), I, 261.

5. For a full discussion, see Patricia Meyer Spacks, "Collins' Imagery," *SP*, 62 (1965), 719-36, rpt. in *The Poetry of Vision*, pp. 66-89.

6. See John E. Sitter, "Mother, Memory, Muse and Poetry after Pope," *ELH*, 44 (1977), 312, and "To *The Vanity of Human Wishes* through the 1740's," pp. 453-54; Bertrand Bronson, "The Pre-Romantic or Post-Augustan Mode," in *Facets of the Enlightenment*, pp. 159-72; and T. E. Blom, "Eighteenth-Century Reflexive Process Poetry," *ECS*, 10 (1976), 52-72.

7. All quotations from Warton's poetry are from the first edition of *Odes on Various Subjects* (1746). For a discussion of the publication of the *Odes* and Collins's relationship with the Warton family, see my introduction to the facsimile edition published by the Augustan Reprint Society (Los Angeles, 1979).

8. See Joan Pittock, *The Ascendancy of Taste* (London: Routledge and Kegan Paul, 1973), p. 127.

9. Hagstrum, p. 270.

10. *An Essay on the Genius and Writings of Pope*, 5th edn. (1806), II, 160. See also his analysis of Lucretius in "Reflections on Didactic Poetry," included in his edition of *The Works of Virgil, in Latin and English* (1753), I, 416-23.

11. Hagstrum, p. 286; see also Wasserman, "Collins' 'Ode on the Poetical Character,'" *ELH*, 34 (1967), 99-100.

12. See Geoffrey Hartman, "Romantic Poetry and the Genius Loci," in *Beyond Formalism* (New Haven: Yale Univ. Press, 1970), pp. 311-36. In this essay Hartman analyzes works by Collins and Thomas Warton, but not by Joseph.

13. Concerning the revisions, see Arthur Fenner, Jr., "The Wartons 'Romanticize' their Verse," *SP*, 53 (1956), 501-08; Julia Hysham, "Joseph Warton's Reputation as a Poet," *Studies in Romanticism*, 1 (1962), 229 n.; James G. Powers, "A Fact About Warton's 'Ode to Fancy,'" *NQ*, 215 (1970), 93; and Mary Margaret Stewart's reply, *NQ*, 217 (1972), 230-31.

14. BL Add. MS. 42560, f. 11 (no date, but probably late spring, 1746). Warton's unidentified correspondent is possibly Richard Tomkins, a fellow Wykehamist.

15. See Maclean, "From Action to Image . . . ," p. 436. Woodhouse also warns that the Wartons' "historical importance lies mainly in their tendency to combine one part of revolutionary doctrine with three of orthodox platitude, and thus commend the whole compound to the readers of their day" (Woodhouse, p. 88). Both Woodhouse, "The Poetry of Collins Reconsidered," p. 127 (n. 4), and Sitter, "To *The Vanity of Human Wishes* through the 1740's," p. 452, point out the didactic elements in Joseph Warton's odes.

16. David Fairer, "The Poems of Thomas Warton the Elder?" *RES*, NS 26 (1975), 401-02. Thomas's statement supports Woodhouse's conclusion that imaginative literature in the 1740s was meant to transcend the limits of actual experience: "With the Collins-Warton group, the imagination is to turn once more to what Bacon conceived to be her principal task, to create 'a more ample greatness, a more exact goodness, a more absolute variety that can be found in the nature of things' " (Woodhouse, p. 91).

17. Woodhouse, p. 91, and "The Poetry of Collins Reconsidered," p. 123.

18. BL Add. MS. 42560, f. 3 (no date, but probably early April 1745).

19. BL Add. MS. 42560, f. 4 (19 April [1745]); cf. Johnson's "Life of Akenside," *Lives*, III, 419-20.

20. Quotations from Akenside's *Odes* are from the first (quarto) edition; those from *The Pleasures of Imagination* are from the first edition, first issue.

21. Cf. the "Hymn to Chearfulness," ll. 93-94: "Let melancholy's plaintive tongue / Instruct the nightly strains of Y ―― ."

22. "On the Winter-Solstice, M.D.CC.XL.," ll. 55-57.

23. John L. Mahoney, "Addison and Akenside: The Impact of Psychological Criticism on Early English Romantic Poetry," *British Journal of Aesthetics*, 6 (1966), 269.

24. John Norton, "Akenside's *The Pleasures of Imagination*: An Exercise in Poetics," *ECS*, 3 (1970), 377.

25. For a full discussion of the critical theory Akenside and Collins draw upon, see Woodhouse, pp. 59-130.

26. This passage should be compared with *An Essay on Man* II.111-20, discussed below in ch. 4, sec. 3.

27. *Soliloquy or Advice to an Author* (1710), in Shaftesbury's *Characteristics*, ed. J. M. Robertson (London: Grant Richards, 1900), I, 136; quoted by Norton, p. 376.

28. Sitter, "Mother, Memory, Muse and Poetry after Pope," p. 324, also stresses Akenside's deification through sexuality: "Man and God are alike, at the close of *The Pleasures of Imagination*, because they are both in love with the same woman, Nature. . . ."

Much the same argument could be made concerning Collins's relationship with Fancy in the "Ode on the Poetical Character."

29. Sitter, "Mother, Memory, Muse and Poetry after Pope," p. 325, is a rare exception.

30. Collins's entire creation myth is in fact adapted from Akenside's "Hymn to Chearfulness," ll. 25-46.

31. For an interesting analysis of the poetical hierarchies within the poem, see Wasserman, "Collins' 'Ode on the Poetical Character,' " pp. 105-08.

32. *Ibid.,* pp. 101 n., 103.

33. *Ibid.,* pp. 101-05.

34. See Bloom, *The Visionary Company,* p. 6, and Thomas Weiskel, *The Romantic Sublime* (Baltimore: The Johns Hopkins Univ. Press, 1976), pp. 125–26.

35. See Wasserman, pp. 97, 99.

36. See Weiskel, pp. 127–28.

37. Wasserman, pp. 95, 97, 97 n.

38. *Fearful Symmetry,* p. 170.

39. Bloom, p. 10.

40. Weiskel, p. 128.

41. Bloom, p. 6.

42. See Alastair Fowler, *Triumphal Forms: Structural Patterns in Elizabethan Poetry* (Cambridge: Cambridge Univ. Press, 1970), pp. 23–24, for a discussion of the entrance of the sun, the sun-king, and Apollo in Elizabethan poetry, with which Collins was thoroughly familiar. I discuss Collins's use of symmetry in *An Epistle: Addrest to Sir Thomas Hanmer* in ch. 3, sec. 3, and his experiments with symmetry and chiasmus in the "Ode Occasion'd by the Death of Mr. Thomson" in ch. 7, sec. 1.

43. *Critical Essays of the Seventeenth Century,* ed. J. E. Spingarn (Oxford: Clarendon Press, 1908-09), III, 80.

44. See ch. 1, n. 74.

45. Lonsdale, p. 430 n.

46. See C. S. Lewis, *A Preface to Paradise Lost* (London: Oxford Univ. Press, 1942; rpt. 1974), pp. 49–51.

47. Weiskel, p. 130.

48. Music makes its auspicious appearance at the center of each stanza; cf. the "whisper'd Spell" of the strophe, and the music of the spheres and Fancy's notes in the mesode. For an analysis of Collins's musical odes, see ch. 6.

49. See Wasserman, p. 108, who also argues that the antistrophe "answers" the strophe; having first turned to appraise Spenser, the chorus finally turns to acclaim Milton, "the pivotal ground for the distinction lying in the mesode" (p. 106).

50. Bloom notes the poem's deliberate confusion (p. 4).

51. See Bloom, p. 4.

52. Woodhouse, p. 60.

53. *An Essay on Criticism,* ll. 679-80 (Pope is praising Longinus).

Chapter 3. Shaping a Career

1. See Lawrence Lipking, *The Life of the Poet* (Chicago: Univ. of Chicago Press, 1981), p. 69, who also discusses the authenticity of these lines.

2. *Observations, Anecdotes, and Characters of Books and Men,* ed. James M. Osborn (Oxford: Clarendon Press, 1966), I, 18, 21; Pope quotes Virgil's *Eclogues* VI.3-5. These "Observations" are cited by George Sherburn, *The Early Career of Alexander Pope* (Oxford: Clarendon Press, 1934; rpt. 1968), pp. 83, 85. See also John Paul Russo, *Alexander Pope:*

Tradition and Identity (Cambridge, Mass.: Harvard Univ. Press, 1972), especially ch. 1, for a discussion of Pope's imitation of Virgil.

3. In particular, see Sherwin's *Precious Bane*.

4. "Allusion: The Poet as Heir," in *Studies in the Eighteenth Century III: Papers Presented at the Third David Nichol Smith Memorial Seminar, Canberra 1973*, ed. R. F. Brissenden and J. C. Eade (Toronto: Univ. of Toronto Press, 1976), pp. 209-40.

5. *Rambler*, No. 154 (Johnson, V, 59).

6. For a history of their publication, see the head-notes to the poems in Wendorf and Ryskamp, pp. 99-101. "To Miss Aurelia C——r" is reintroduced as Collins's work in this edition.

7. John Middleton Murry, *Countries of the Mind* (New York: Dutton, 1922), p. 84.

8. Sigworth, p. 88.

9. First published in 1717, this poem was reprinted with revisions in Pope's *Works* (1736), III ("Consisting of Fables, Translations, and Imitations"). This edition would have made the imitations easily accessible to Collins in 1739.

10. Quoted from Cowley's *Poems*, ed. A. R. Waller (Cambridge: Cambridge Univ. Press, 1905), pp. 136-37.

11. For an explanation of the "baby," see *The Poems of Sir Philip Sidney*, ed. William A. Ringler, Jr. (Oxford: Clarendon Press, 1962), p. 465.

12. Twickenham Pope, VI, 12. The Twickenham editor, Norman Ault, states that Pope's are general imitations of Cowley and Waller, without specific models, but this is clearly not true of "Weeping."

13. *Poetical Calendar*, XII, 107.

14. Sigworth, p. 89.

15. *The Providence of Wit: Aspects of Form in Augustan Literature and the Arts* (Oxford: Clarendon Press, 1974), p. 61.

16. *Ibid.*, p. 64.

17. "A Discourse on Pastoral Poetry," Twickenham Pope, I, 25, 27.

18. Cicero, *Pro A. Licinio Archia Poeta Oratio* (VII, 16).

19. This was first suggested by W. C. Bronson in his edition (1898), p. 85 n.

20. Woodhouse, "The Poetry of Collins Reconsidered," p. 100.

21. Twickenham Pope, I, 27.

22. *The Works of Alexander Pope*, ed. Joseph Warton (1797), I, 61 n.

23. See Lonsdale, p. 387.

24. Lonsdale notes numerous revisions away from Pope in his edition; see especially ll. 25, 35-41.

25. See Crider, pp. 57-58.

26. Suggested by Arthur Johnston in *Selected Poems of Thomas Gray and William Collins* (London: Arnold, 1967; Columbia, S.C.: Univ. of South Carolina Press, 1970), pp. 131-32 n.

27. See Sherwin, pp. 39, 41; and Martha Collins, "The Self-Conscious Poet: The Case of William Collins," *ELH*, 42 (1975), 362-77, esp. 365.

28. For a discussion of structural symmetries, see Fowler, *Triumphal Forms*, pp. 23-124, and my comments below in ch. 7, sec. 1.

29. Sherwin, p. 41.

30. Hagstrum, pp. 281-82.

31. Lonsdale, pp. 388-89.

32. Hagstrum, p. 281.

33. *The Reaper*, No. 26.

34. These echoes are noted by Wendorf and Ryskamp, pp. 118-19, 121.

35. Johnston (*Selected Poems*, p. 123) stresses Collins's ability "to express some of the emotions which all men feel about death."

36. In our edition, Charles Ryskamp and I have followed Roger Lonsdale's ordering of the Drafts and Fragments, which, as Lonsdale admits, cannot be considered to be strictly chronological. It is possible that Collins wrote the seventh fragment at the same time he was writing the verse-epistles, even though the subject, diction, and stanzaic pattern of Fragment 7 seem far more mature. It is clear, however, that the seventh, eighth, and ninth fragments more closely resemble the *Odes* than they do the epistle to Hanmer, and thus they are considered to have been written after the verse-epistles.

37. Lonsdale, p. 534.

Chapter 4. The *Odes* of 1746

1. For an analysis of how epic elements made their way into the ode, see Maclean, "From Action to Image . . . ," pp. 419-23.

2. John Wooll, *Biographical Memoirs of the late Revd. Joseph Warton, D.D.* (1806), pp. 14-15 n.

3. For the correspondences between Warton's "To Fancy" and Collins's odes, see my introduction to Warton's *Odes on Various Subjects* (Los Angeles: Augustan Reprint Society, 1979).

4. Lonsdale provides a convincing explanation of Collins's relationship to Ross and Goddard in his edition, pp. 455-56.

5. For a full textual history see Wendorf and Ryskamp, pp. 142-44. Unless otherwise noted, the text and title of the version appearing in the *Odes* are quoted here.

6. John Butt has sensibly formulated the problem this fragment raises: "Collins's interest lay in discovering fit embodiment for his allegoric abstractions, implying their nature (for example) by the attitudes they strike, by the garb they wear, and by the places they haunt. In the draft of the 'Ode to Simplicity,' of which not a single line is carried over into the final version, there is but the faintest anticipation of this practice, and perhaps that is why the draft was discarded." See his review of the *Drafts and Fragments* in *RES*, NS 9 (1958), 221.

7. Crider, p. 63.

8. Crider suggests that Collins may have had in mind contemporary speculations on the first age of the world, and he quotes the *Guardian*, No. 22: "It was a State of Ease, Innocence and Contentment; where Plenty begot Pleasure, and Pleasure begot Singing, and Singing begot Poetry, and Poetry begot Pleasure again" (Crider, p. 66). This kind of formula was quite popular; see Hobbes's "Answer to Davenant," in *Critical Essays of the Seventeenth Century*, ed. Spingarn, II, 59.

9. Crider, p. 64.

10. *Ibid.*, pp. 66, 65.

11. *Ibid.*, pp. 63-64.

12. See Woodhouse, "The Poetry of Collins Reconsidered," p. 122, for a similar view. Maclean, "From Action to Image . . . ," pp. 428, 442-43, offers the fullest analysis of the structure of the ode in the eighteenth century; see also Hagstrum, p. 268.

13. For a discussion of this project, see Wendorf and Ryskamp, pp. 212-14.

14. See, for instance, Hagstrum, p. 268.

15. See Sigworth, pp. 100-01.

16. Johnston suggests this association, noting that the Samaritan had become "the type of human friendship and pity, as in Sterne's sermon on this text" (*Selected Poems*, p. 151 n.; the text is Luke X.33-34).

17. See Hagstrum, pp. 274-75, who quotes an appropriate passage from Ben Jonson's description of "Serenitas." Sherwin, on the other hand, points to the imprecise nature of Collins's visual descriptions in this ode by carefully analyzing Pity's "sky-worn Robes" (p. 11). I cannot, however, accept his comments on Collins's "visual and aural punning" here; see my review of *Precious Bane* in *MP*, 77 (1980), 443.

18. Crider, p. 59.

19. Hagstrum defines Pity's *signa* (p. 275); for a discussion of the age's preoccupation with the infancy of poets, see Benjamin Boyce, "Sounding Shells and Little Prattlers in the Mid-Eighteenth-Century English Ode," *ECS*, 8 (1975), 245–64.

20. See Hagstrum, p. 268, and Johnston, pp. 332-33.

21. Sherwin wonders why the southern wall should elicit such an enthusiastic response (p. 49), but Collins is probably drawing upon the conventional associations of the warmth (both physical and emotional) of southern climes; see his preface to the *Oriental Eclogues*, and Pope's description of his shrine's southern wall in *The Temple of Fame*.

22. See Johnston, p. 333.

23. Hagstrum (p. 270) considers Collins's odes to be "less objective than Milton's poems." Collins's poems are "prayers that breathe a kind of religious-lyrical awe present only occasionally and only for a limited purpose in the more brilliant but external moods and scenes of Milton's poetic twins." Collins's achievement, in other words, lies in the suggestive subjectivity of his poetry and in his successful use of personification to give that shadowy world a unified and recognizable form.

24. Crider, pp. 60, 62.

25. For other remarks concerning poetry that is "overheard," see Frye, "Towards Defining an Age of Sensibility," pp. 150–51, and Sitter, "To *The Vanity of Human Wishes* through the 1740's," p. 455.

26. "Absorption: A Master Theme in Eighteenth-Century French Painting and Criticism," *ECS*, 9 (1975–76), 139–77. Flaxman's monument to Collins suggests the kind of absorption that Fried describes (see Plate 1).

27. For a quite different discussion of *anagnorisis* in Collins's poetry, see Weiskel, *The Romantic Sublime*, pp. 107–24.

28. Related to this principle of dramatic recognition is Langhorne's suggestion that personifications are in fact "impersonators" (pp. 138, 145). This emphasis on "impersonation" strengthens the dramatic context of the poems, but it also implies that the personifications are not really what they seem to be, that they merely appear to us in a recognizable guise. For a discussion of the epistemological validity of this guise, see my remarks later in this section.

29. *The Poems of Sir Philip Sidney*, ed. Ringler, p. 145 ("Certain Sonnets," No. 16, ll. 1-4); Bronson supplies this reference (p. 119 n.). See also George E. Dimock, Jr., "The Name of Odysseus," *Hudson Review*, 9 (1956), 52–70, for a brilliant analysis of this principle in the *Odyssey*.

30. "The Inherent Values of Eighteenth-Century Personification," p. 453. See also Woodhouse's analysis of the validity of imagination in Collins's poetry: it bears "a relation to truth, and can seize on and present the 'idea' of things" ("The Poetry of Collins Reconsidered," p. 123).

31. Wasserman, p. 455.

32. Quoted by Wasserman, p. 456.

33. Edmund Burke, *A Philosophical Enquiry into the Origin of Our Ideas of the Sublime and Beautiful*, ed. James T. Boulton (London: Routledge and Kegan Paul, 1958; rpt. Notre Dame, Indiana: Univ. of Notre Dame Press, 1968), pp. 58–59. For a stimulating analysis of the sublime and the obscure, see Martin Price, "The Sublime Poem: Pictures and Powers," *Yale Review*, 58 (1968–69), 194–213.

34. Burke, pp. 60, 62.

35. *Ibid.*, p. 63.

36. See Jean H. Hagstrum, *Samuel Johnson's Literary Criticism* (Minneapolis: Univ. of Minnesota Press, 1952; rpt. Chicago: Univ. of Chicago Press, 1967), p. 100 and passim.

37. Bloom, *The Anxiety of Influence*, p. 111.

38. *The Poetical Works of Mr. William Collins*, ed. Barbauld, p. vii.

39. *Lives*, III, 338.

40. *Collins* (Oxford: Clarendon Press, 1928), p. 45.

41. S. Musgrove, "The Theme of Collins's Odes," *NQ*, 185 (1943), 214-17, 253-55.

42. "The Scheme of Collins's *Odes on Several . . . Subjects*," in *Restoration and Eighteenth-Century Literature*, ed. Carroll Camden (Chicago: Univ. of Chicago Press, 1963), pp. 371-80.

43. See Quintana, pp. 378-79; Lonsdale, p. 413; and Woodhouse, "The Poetry of Collins Reconsidered," p. 119.

44. In "The Manners," l. 16.

45. See my discussion of the "Ode to Pity" in the previous section and my comparison of the "Ode to Fear" with Thomson's "Summer" in ch. 1, sec. 3.

46. *The Philosophy of the Enlightenment*, trans. F. C. A. Koelln and J. P. Pettegrove (Princeton: Princeton Univ. Press, 1951), p. 107. One might compare this quotation with Johnson's remark on Richardson and Fielding: "There was as great a difference between them as between a man who knew how a watch was made, and a man who could tell the hour by looking on the dial-plate" (*Boswell's Life of Johnson*, II, 49).

47. Langhorne, p. 138.

48. Cf. Sherwin, p. 53, on Collins's obsession with wounding in the odes.

49. "Eighteenth-Century Poetry: The Teacher's Dilemma," *College English*, 23 (1962), 642-45.

50. Sigworth, p. 110.

51. *The Museum: Or, The Literary and Historical Register*, I, 117.

52. See Wendorf and Ryskamp, p. 137; the king pardoned one of the three noblemen.

53. Cf. Sherwin, p. 88: "Collins exhibits a rare confidence in his own capacity for imaginative enlightenment."

Chapter 5. Collins's Elusive Nature

1. *Poetical Calendar*, XII, 110. There is something of a paradox in Johnson's remark: these are "peculiar" habits of thought reconciled by "popular" traditions.

2. *The Art of Painting* (1744), p. 344. Collins mentions de Piles in Fragment 5.

3. Langhorne, p. 174.

4. See Wendorf and Ryskamp, pp. 149-50; Lonsdale, pp. 469-70; and Johnston, p. 339.

5. *An Essay Concerning Human Understanding*, ed. Peter H. Nidditch (Oxford: Clarendon Press, 1975), p. 47. Collins was obviously widely read in English as well as classical philosophy. Hobbes, for instance, had defined "opinion" and "doubt" in *Leviathan* (I, vii), and had provided a detailed description of the various passions (I, vi) as well as a definition of the manners (I, xi). Also of relevance to this poem is his account of the relationship between Fancy and the precepts of philosophy in his "Answer to Davenant": "But so far forth as the Fancy of Man has traced the ways of true Philosophy, so far it hath produced very marvellous effects to the benefit of mankinde"; but when the precepts of philosophy fail, "there the Architect, *Fancy*, must take the Philosophers part upon her self" (*Critical Essays of the Seventeenth Century*, ed. Spingarn, II, 60). In the same passage Hobbes envisions memory as a "looking glass" examined by Judgment and Fancy (II, 59).

6. For an account of the contemporary interest in the camera obscura, see Marjorie Hope Nicolson, *Newton Demands the Muse* (Princeton: Princeton Univ. Press, 1946), pp. 77-81. Nicolson points out the use Richard Savage made of this device in *The Wanderer* (1729), where the images are flashed on the walls of the hermit's cave. Collins may have had Savage's hermit in mind in ll. 37-58 of his own poem, which describe the moving pictures in Art's cell. He may also have been thinking of Pope's camera obscura in his grotto at Twickenham, one of the great tourist attractions of the 1740s; see Maynard Mack, *The Garden and the City* (Toronto and Buffalo: Univ. of Toronto Press, 1969), ch. 2.

7. *The Spectator*, ed. Donald F. Bond (Oxford: Clarendon Press, 1965), III, 550-51 (No. 414).

8. Lonsdale, p. 472 n. Sherwin (p. 46) asks whether these lessons are "Nature's or those of the Academy rejected in the exordium," but he provides no answer. Collins's lines are ambiguous, but his reference is apparently to the instruction of nature. Philosophy's lessons, which have been shown to be treacherous, have already been rejected; only nature, which is also the closest referent here, would provide a "safer Rule" than Art's "enchanted School."

9. It should at least be noted that even as Collins professes to leave Plato behind, his hermit's cell and flickering images suggest Plato's cave and Locke's dark room of the understanding (see Mack, *The Garden and the City*, p. 47).

10. William Collins, *Poems* (Colchester, 1796), p. 3.

11. *An Essay Towards Fixing the True Standards of Wit, Humour, Raillery, Satire, and Ridicule* (1744), p. 11; cited by Lonsdale, pp. 474-75 n.

12. Cf. Joseph Warton's "Ranelagh House: A Satire in Prose. In the Manner of Monsieur Le Sage" (*c.* 1744): Philomides, whose "favourite study is the knowledge of men and manners," is fond of reading "Le Sage, whose works he styles, The Mirror of Mankind" (John Wooll, *Biographical Memoirs of the late Revd. Joseph Warton, D.D.*, pp. 175-76). Johnson, in his analysis of prose fiction in the *Rambler*, No. 4 (31 March 1750), claimed that "If the world be promiscuously described, I cannot see of what use it can be to read the account; or why it may not be as safe to turn the eye immediately upon mankind, as upon a mirror which shows all that presents itself without discrimination" (Johnson, III, 22).

13. Ovid's preceding account of Perseus' adventures emphasizes other dangers of sight: "At the entrance to this place two sisters dwelt, both daughters of old Phorcys, who shared one eye between them. This eye by craft and stealth, while it was being passed from one sister to the other, Perseus stole away" (IV.774-77). Joseph Warton, some of whose *Odes on Various Subjects* Collins saw in 1746, wrote of Terror's "Gorgon-shield" in his ode "To Fancy."

14. *Newton Demands the Muse*, p. 81.

15. "The Grounds of Criticism in Tragedy," in *"Of Dramatic Poesy" and Other Critical Essays*, ed. George Watson (London: Dent, 1962), I, 248.

16. Hagstrum, p. 136.

17. Garrod (pp. 71-78) was the first critic to analyze the structure of the "Ode to Evening," but of his argument in general it is fair to say that "he cut away the deadwood without cultivating the green" (Henry Pettit, "Collins's 'Ode to Evening' and the Critics," *SEL*, 4 [1964], 363).

18. For interesting discussions of Collins's experimentation here, see Johnston, p. 335, and Sherwin, pp. 111-12.

19. Bronson, in his edition (pp. lxvii-lxviii), argues that "the absence of rhyme-emphasis at the ends of the lines favors the fusing of line into line, an effect which subtly harmonizes with the attempt to describe the dissolving appearances of twilight."

20. Hartman, "Romantic Poetry and the Genius Loci," in *Beyond Formalism*, p. 322, suggests that the conscious weaving in the poem resembles a dance of the Hours or the ritual of the marriage procession.

21. See Merle E. Brown, "On William Collins' 'Ode to Evening,'" *Essays in Criticism*, 11 (1961), 141-42, and Sherwin, pp. 113-14. I am indebted at several points to Brown's important discussion of the ode, even if I cannot accept it in its entirety.

22. Cf. Wordsworth's similarly complex use of the word in "Tintern Abbey," ll. 111-13: "Nor perchance, / If I were not thus taught, should I the more / Suffer my genial spirits to decay."

23. Hagstrum establishes the pictorial background for this passage (p. 278); for Collins's literary allusions here, see Lonsdale, pp. 464-65.

24. See Martin Price's analysis in *To the Palace of Wisdom*, p. 375.

25. Sherwin, p. 118.

26. Although this description of the seasons is thematically related to the lines that follow it, the full point at the end of l. 48 accentuates the manner in which Collins also attempts to set this passage apart and thus grant it resistance from the encroachment of time.

27. This is Brown's argument (p. 138): "The essence of Evening and the essence of Poetry . . . are identical." Hartman observes a sacred marriage "of the poet's genius with the genius loci" (p. 322), of one spirit with another, and I find this approach to their union more convincing.

28. See Hartman, p. 323, and Sherwin, pp. 121-22.

29. Northrop Frye, "Towards Defining an Age of Sensibility," *ELH*, 23 (1956), 144-52. Garrod is joined in his unsympathetic reading of the poem's conclusion by Hartman, p. 323, and Sherwin, p. 123. Alan D. McKillop, "Collins's *Ode to Evening*—Background and Structure," *Tennessee Studies in Literature*, 5 (1960), 73-83, provides a sound discussion of the role of personification in the poem.

Chapter 6. Words for Music

1. *GM*, 51 (Jan. 1781), 11.

2. See Wendorf and Ryskamp, pp. 193-94.

3. See *The Untuning of the Sky: Ideas of Music in English Poetry, 1500-1700* (Princeton: Princeton Univ. Press, 1961; rpt. New York: Norton, 1970). Throughout this section I am indebted to Hollander's work, as well as to the following studies: William Henry Husk, *An Account of the Musical Celebrations on St. Cecilia's Day* (1857); James Hutton, "Some English Poems in Praise of Music," *English Miscellany*, 2 (1951), 1-63; Herbert M. Schueller, "The Use and Decorum of Music as Described in British Literature, 1700 to 1780," *JHI*, 13 (1952), 73-93; James Kinsley, "Dryden and the *Encomium Musicae*," *RES*, NS 4 (1953), 263-67; Robert Manson Myers, *Handel, Dryden, & Milton* (London: Bowes & Bowes, 1956), pp. 17-62; Gretchen L. Finney, *Musical Backgrounds for English Literature: 1580-1650* (New Brunswick, N.J.: Rutgers Univ. Press, 1962); Bertrand Bronson, "Some Aspects of Music and Literature," in *Facets of the Enlightenment*, pp. 91-118; Rosamond McGuiness, *English Court Odes 1660-1820* (Oxford: Clarendon Press, 1971); and Oliver F. Sigworth, "A Way of Looking at Some Baroque Poems," in *Studies in Eighteenth-Century Culture*, vol. IV, ed. Harold E. Pagliaro (Madison: Univ. of Wisconsin Press, 1975), 31-41.

4. Hollander, p. 27.

5. *Ovid's Metamorphoses Englished, Mythologiz'd and Represented in Figures* (1632), p. 356; quoted by Hollander, pp. 172-73.

6. Hollander, pp. 406-07.

7. Quoted and translated by Elizabeth G. Holt, *A Documentary History of Art* (New York: Doubleday, 1958), II, 155-56.

8. A. Félibien, *Conferences de l'Academie Royale de Peinture et de Sculpture* (Paris, 1705), Preface; cited by Frances A. Yates, *The French Academies of the Sixteenth Century* (London: The Warburg Institute, 1947), p. 299.

9. *A Method to Learn to Design the Passions, Proposed in a Conference on their General and Particular Expression*, trans J. Williams (1734).

10. See Brewster Rogerson, "The Art of Painting the Passions," *JHI*, 14 (1953), 68–94, and Alan T. McKenzie, "The Countenance You Show Me: Reading the Passions in the Eighteenth Century," *Georgia Review*, 32 (1978), 758–73. Of more general interest is Bertrand A. Goldgar, "Pope's Theory of the Passions: The Background of Epistle II of the *Essay on Man*," *PQ*, 41 (1962), 730–43. It should be pointed out that the second part of Hume's *A Treatise of Human Nature* (entitled "Of the Passions") had been published in 1739, and that philosophical interest in the passions, which began with Hobbes, would therefore have been revived in the 1740s.

11. *Essays Upon Severall Moral Subjects*, 2nd edn. (1697), II, 22–23; quoted by Hollander, p. 175.

12. "The Strange Effects Reported of Musick in Former Times, Examined," *The Philosophical Transactions and Collections To the End of the Year 1700, Abridged*, ed. John Lowthorp and Henry Jones (1732), I, 619; quoted by D. T. Mace, "Musical Humanism, the Doctrine of Rhythmus, and the Saint Cecilia Odes of Dryden," *Journal of the Warburg and Courtauld Institutes*, 27 (1964), 258–59.

13. Quoted by Mace, p. 258.

14. *The Works of John Dryden*, vol. XV, ed. Earl Miner (Berkeley and Los Angeles: Univ. of California Press, 1976), 9–10.

15. Mace, pp. 261ff.

16. *Ibid.*, p. 263.

17. See Robert M. Myers, "Neo-Classical Criticism of the Ode for Music," *PMLA*, 62 (1947), 399–421.

18. For a discussion of Harris's work, see Robert Marsh, *Four Dialectical Theories of Poetry: An Aspect of English Neoclassical Criticism* (Chicago: Univ. of Chicago Press, 1965), ch. 5.

19. *Three Treatises. The First Concerning Art. The Second Concerning Music, Painting, and Poetry. The Third Concerning Happiness. By J. H.* (1744).

20. *Ibid.*, pp. 95–96.

21. *Ibid.*, pp. 99, 102.

22. *Ibid.*, p. 99 n.

23. *Ibid.*, p. 84.

24. Hagstrum, p. 276.

25. See Hollander, pp. 220–38.

26. *Ibid.*, pp. 148–50 and plates [4–6].

27. See Earl Miner, *Dryden's Poetry* (Bloomington, Ind.: Indiana Univ. Press, 1967), p. 275.

28. Pope's "Ode for Musick, on St. Cecilia's Day" (1708, published 1713) does not seem to have been a model for Collins; Pope strangely separates his description of the various instruments from his account of the passions. For an interesting analysis, see Earl Wasserman, "Pope's *Ode for Musick*," *ELH*, 28 (1961), 163–86.

29. See Hollander, p. 137.

30. *The Pleasures of Imagination* I.299–302.

31. For the metrical variations in the *Odes*, see Lonsdale, p. 413.

32. Hollander, p. 421.

33. Wendorf and Ryskamp, p. 89.

34. Sir James Thornhill (mentioned by Collins in Fragment 5) drafted a pen and ink sketch of "Ptolomy Giving Demetrius Directions to Build the Alexandrian Library"; see Robert R. Wark, *Early British Drawings in the Huntington Collection 1600-1750* (San

Marino, Calif.: The Huntington Library, 1969), p. 50. Wark lists two similar drawings by Thornhill, noting that the one in the British Museum is inscribed "Sr. Thos. Hanmer." Tantalizing as this information is, it seems unlikely that Collins would have been familiar with any of Thornhill's productions in Hanmer's possession.

35. Thomson had recently celebrated Greek music in *Liberty* (1735-36), II.272-74, 285-90.

36. See Ernest Walker, *A History of Music in England*, 3rd edn., rev. and ed. J. A. Westrup (Oxford: Clarendon Press, 1952), pp. 217-20; and Roger Fiske, *English Theatre Music in the Eighteenth Century* (London: Oxford Univ. Press, 1973), pp. 1-66.

37. "An Essay Upon the Ancient and Modern Learning," *Critical Essays of the Seventeenth Century*, ed. Spingarn, III, 56. See Herbert M. Schueller, "The Quarrel of the Ancients and the Moderns," *Music & Letters*, 41 (1960), 313-30.

38. *The Ordering of the Arts in Eighteenth-Century England* (Princeton: Princeton Univ. Press, 1970), p. 215.

39. Brown, p. 67.

40. *Ibid.*, p. 196.

41. *Ibid.*, p. 197.

42. *Ibid.*, p. 205.

43. *Ibid.*, p. 218.

44. *Ibid.*, p. 218 n.

45. *Ibid.*, pp. 234-35.

46. *Ibid.*, pp. 235-37.

47. J. A. Westrup, "The Nature of Recitative," *Proceedings of the British Academy*, 42 (1956), 31. See also Paul Henry Lang, *George Frideric Handel* (New York: Norton, 1966), pp. 612-15, and Winton Dean, *Handel and the Opera Seria* (Berkeley and Los Angeles: Univ. of California Press, 1969), ch. 9.

48. *The Passions, An Ode. Written by Mr. Collins. Set to Musick By Dr. Hayes* (Oxford, 1750), p. 9 ("Hayes A" in Wendorf and Ryskamp).

49. Mace, p. 291.

50. See Nan Cooke Carpenter, "The Place of Music in *L'Allegro* and *Il Penseroso*," *University of Toronto Quarterly*, 22 (1953), 354-67.

51. See Douglas Murray, "The Musical Structure of Dryden's 'Song for St. Cecilia's Day,'" *ECS*, 10 (1977), 326-34.

52. *The Letters and Writings of George Frideric Handel*, ed. Erich H. Müller (London: Cassell, 1935), pp. 10, 81; quoted by Schueller, "The Quarrel of the Ancients and the Moderns," p. 324.

53. Dean, *Handel and the Opera Seria*, p. 156.

54. See Bukofzer's discussion of "Audible Form and Inaudible Order" and the "architecture of keys" in *Music in the Baroque Era* (New York: Norton, 1947), pp. 365-69.

55. *The Classical Style: Haydn, Mozart, Beethoven* (New York: Norton, 1972), p. 168 (Rosen also compares baroque and classical structure in the first two chapters of his study).

56. *An Essay on the Genius and Writings of Pope* (1756), 5th edn. (1806), I, 38. R. D. Havens, *The Influence of Milton on English Poetry* (Cambridge, Mass.: Harvard Univ. Press, 1922), pp. 430-32, demonstrates that Warton's report of only "a few curious readers" is somewhat exaggerated; but it is clear that Milton's poems — as well as the two musical odes of Dryden — received considerable popularity as a result of Handel's settings.

57. Wilfrid Mellers, *Harmonious Meeting: A Study of the Relationship between English Music, Poetry and Theatre, c. 1600-1900* (London: Dennis Dobson, 1965), p. 258. I am also indebted to Lang, pp. 316-20, and Winton Dean, *Handel's Dramatic Oratorios and Masques* (London: Oxford Univ. Press, 1959), pp. 319-23. For a thorough discussion of

Handel's "interpretation" of Milton, see Michael O'Connell and John Powell, "Music and Sense in Handel's Setting of Milton's *L'Allegro* and *Il Penseroso*," *ECS*, 12 (1978), 16–46. O'Connell and Powell provide an analysis of the contrasting elements that Handel employed in his musical setting: keys, instrumentation, tonality, melodic line, rhythm, and the choice of different forms (e.g., the number of accompanying choruses in *L'Allegro*). They argue that "a system of opposition was necessary if he [Handel] was to achieve more than just approximation of emotional states" (p. 38).

58. Lang, p. 320.

59. Dean, *Handel's Dramatic Oratorios and Masques*, Appendix D, p. 640, lists numerous performances in London and Oxford but does not provide a yearly breakdown of his figures. The ode was performed nine times in Oxford during Handel's lifetime (i.e., between 1740 and 1759).

60. *A Method to Learn to Design the Passions*, pp. 36–46.

61. *A General History of Music*, ed. Frank Mercer (London: Foulis, 1935; rpt. New York: Dover, 1957), I, 85.

Chapter 7. Last Poems

1. *The Reaper*, No. 26.

2. Langhorne (p. 184) stated that "The ode on the death of Thomson seems to have been written in an excursion to Richmond by water," but no corroborating authority exists for his assertion. Wordsworth, however, entitled his own poem a "Remembrance of Collins, composed upon the Thames near Richmond" (1789).

3. The Loeb translation suggests "purify" our fields, but I believe the sense is rather "traverse" or "examine."

4. For another interpretation of these mottoes, see Lawrence Lipking's fine analysis of the ode in *The Life of the Poet*. Lipking places the poem within the tradition of the *tombeau*, comparing it with Jonson's elegy on Shakespeare and Auden's on Yeats.

5. For a full discussion of Collins's use of the word "Druid" see J. M. S. Tompkins, "'In Yonder Grave a Druid Lies,'" *RES*, 22 (1946), 1–16, and A. D. McKillop's review in *PQ*, 26 (1947), 113-14. It is at least possible that Collins also meant to imitate the druids' circular temples in the structure of his ode.

6. Collins's source for his description of the departure of the nymphs may have been Milton's hymn "On the Morning of Christ's Nativity": "The parting Genius is with sighing sent, / With flowre-inwov'n tresses torn / The Nimphs in twilight shade of tangled thickets mourn" (ll. 186-88). T. S. Eliot appears to have Collins's plaintive lines in mind (as well as Spenser's *Prothalamion*) in "The Fire Sermon" section of *The Waste Land*: "The nymphs are departed. / And their friends, the loitering heirs of city directors; / Departed, have left no addresses" (ll. 179-81). In Eliot's version, the nymphs have become "nymphos," as a later passage attests: "Highbury bore me. Richmond and Kew / Undid me. By Richmond I raised my knees / Supine on the floor of a narrow canoe" (ll. 293-95; his allusion here is also, of course, to the *Purgatorio*). See also the fragment entitled "Exequy" (which Eliot did not include in the published text of the poem), where the speaker envisions a different kind of ejaculation at his tomb. The fragment, and Pound's comment at one point that "This is Laforgue not XVIII," are printed in *The Waste Land: A Facsimile and Transcript of the Original Drafts*, ed. Valerie Eliot (New York: Harcourt, Brace, Jovanovich, 1971), pp. 100-03.

7. See E. M. W. Tillyard, "William Collins's 'Ode on the Death of Thomson,' " *A Review of English Literature (ARIEL)*, 1, No. 3 (1960), 36-37.

8. See Alastair Fowler, *Conceitful Thought: The Interpretation of English Renaissance Poems* (Edinburgh: Edinburgh Univ. Press, 1975), ch. 4.

9. See Fowler, *Triumphal Forms*, p. 23 and passim. Collins's selection of eleven stanzas was probably influenced by Milton's example in "Lycidas"; Fowler (p. 189 n.) characterizes eleven as the "number symbolizing mourning and the termination of mourning." Seven, however, is the number usually associated with elegies; cf. Pope's "Elegy to the Memory of an Unfortunate Lady," frequently echoed here and in Collins's earlier elegies. Interested as Collins was in symmetry and rhetorical structure, I do not believe that he was actually influenced by numerology. For an analysis of this distinction, see R. G. Peterson, "Critical Calculations: Measure and Symmetry in Literature," *PMLA*, 91 (1976), 367-75 (esp. p. 372).

10. Tillyard, p. 36.

11. See Nils Wilhelm Lund, *Chiasmus in the New Testament* (Chapel Hill: Univ. of North Carolina Press, 1942), pp. 31, 40-41.

12. *Lives*, III, 340.

13. *The Reaper*, No. 26.

14. For a full discussion of the ode's textual history, see Wendorf and Ryskamp, pp. 161-68.

15. For a discussion of Collins's use of "Genial," see ch. 5, n. 22.

16. Martin Martin, *A Description of the Western Islands of Scotland*, 2nd edn. (1716), p. 309.

17. Spacks, *The Poetry of Vision*, p. 82.

18. See Norman Maclean, "From Action to Image . . . ," pp. 408-60.

19. *Metamorphoses* XI.652-62.

20. *Observations on the Faerie Queene* (1754; rev. edn. 1762), II, 268; quoted by Arthur Johnston, *Enchanted Ground: The Study of Medieval Romance in the Eighteenth Century* (London: Athlone Press, 1964), p. 106.

21. For a discussion of the narrative frame, see Sherwin, p. 94. Spacks offers a penetrating analysis of the barriers—emotional and social—that separate Collins and Home from these primitive sources; see *The Insistence of Horror: Aspects of the Supernatural in Eighteenth-Century Poetry* (Cambridge, Mass.: Harvard Univ. Press, 1962), pp. 72-74.

22. Lonsdale (pp. 518-19) cites *Chevy Chase*, William Hamilton's "The Braes of Yarrow," and Pope's "Epistle to Dr. Arbuthnot."

23. Spacks, *The Poetry of Vision*, p. 78.

24. *Lives*, III, 337.

Chapter 8. Conclusion

1. Sherwin, p. 101. For other assessments of Collins's "failure," see Garrod, *Collins*, p. 8, and Bloom, *The Visionary Company*, p. 11.

2. *The Burden of the Past and the English Poet* (Cambridge, Mass.: Harvard Univ. Press, 1970), p. 4.

3. See Bate's *Samuel Johnson* (New York: Harcourt, Brace, Jovanovich, 1977); Mack, *The Garden and the City*, and "Pope: The Shape of the Man in his Work," *Yale Review*, 67 (1978), 493-516 (this essay forms part of Mack's work in progress on Pope's life); and Dustin H. Griffin, *Alexander Pope: The Poet in the Poems* (Princeton: Princeton Univ. Press, 1978). An entire study has recently been devoted to this problem; see *The Author in His Work: Essays on a Problem in Criticism*, ed. Louis L. Martz and Aubrey Williams (New Haven: Yale Univ. Press, 1978).

4. *GM*, 51 (Jan. 1781), 11.

5. *Ibid.*, pp. 11-12.

6. See Wendorf and Ryskamp, pp. 209-10.

7. *Lives*, III, 335.

8. Holt-White, p. 3.

9. *Ibid.*, p. 14.

10. *Lives*, III, 336.

11. *The Reaper*, No. 26.

12. For a discussion of these projects, see Wendorf and Ryskamp, pp. 210-12, 214-15.

13. *The Poems of William Collins*, ed. Crowe, pp. ix-xi.

14. Bronson presented this argument in a paper delivered at the 1975 meeting of the Modern Language Association; see also his essay, "Strange Relations: The Author and His Audience," in *Facets of the Enlightenment*, pp. 298-325, and John R. Sitter, "To *The Vanity of Human Wishes* through the 1740's," p. 453.

15. For a discussion of other characteristic changes in this period, see Sitter, "To *The Vanity of Human Wishes* through the 1740's," pp. 453-61. Martha Collins, "The Self-Conscious Poet: The Case of William Collins," *ELH*, 42 (1975), 362-77, also cites examples of self-consciousness in Collins's poetry, but she concludes (incorrectly, in my view) that Collins's self-consciousness was necessarily limiting. She fails to sense the ways in which Collins also transformed this restriction into a source of liberation (see my analysis in ch. 2, sec. 3, and in ch. 7).

16. *De Rerum Natura* III.1-3; *Metamorphoses* I.354-55.

Appendix

1. For their critical remarks, see *The Poetical Works of Mr. William Collins*, ed. John Langhorne (1765; rpt. 1771, 1776, 1781), pp. 105-84; and *The Poetical Works of Mr. William Collins*, ed. Mrs. A. L. Barbauld (1797; rpt. 1802), pp. iii-xlix.

2. I quote from "Collins," in *The Complete Works of Algernon Charles Swinburne*, ed. Sir Edmund Gosse and Thomas James Wise, IV (London: Heinemann; New York: Wells, 1926), 149-54.

3. *Collins* (Oxford: Clarendon Press, 1928).

4. "Collins and the Creative Imagination: A Study in the Critical Background of his Odes (1746)," in *Studies in English by Members of University College, Toronto*, ed. M. W. Wallace (Toronto: Univ. of Toronto Press, 1931), pp. 59-130.

5. "The Poetry of Collins Reconsidered," in *From Sensibility to Romanticism: Essays Presented to Frederick A. Pottle*, ed. Frederick W. Hilles and Harold Bloom (New York: Oxford Univ. Press, 1965), pp. 93-137.

6. *Poor Collins: His Life, His Art, and His Influence* (Ithaca: Cornell Univ. Press, 1937).

7. *William Collins* (New York: Twayne, 1965).

8. Hagstrum, *The Sister Arts: The Tradition of Literary Pictorialism and English Poetry from Dryden to Gray* (Chicago: Univ. of Chicago Press, 1958), ch. 10; Maclean, "From Action to Image: Theories of the Lyric in the Eighteenth Century," in *Critics and Criticism: Ancient and Modern*, ed. R. S. Crane (Chicago: Univ. of Chicago Press, 1952), pp. 408-60; and Spacks, *The Insistence of Horror: Aspects of the Supernatural in Eighteenth-Century Poetry* (Cambridge, Mass.: Harvard Univ. Press, 1962), pp. 70-74, and *The Poetry of Vision: Five Eighteenth-Century Poets* (Cambridge, Mass.: Harvard Univ. Press, 1967), pp. 78-82. Wallace Jackson, *The Probable and the Marvelous: Blake, Wordsworth, and the Eighteenth-Century Critical Tradition* (Athens, Ga.: Univ. of Georgia Press, 1978), pp. 39-61, offers a more recent discussion of the supernatural in Collins's poetry, but his analysis of individual poems is less valuable than his discussion of the transitional nature of much eighteenth-century poetry.

9. "To *The Vanity of Human Wishes* through the 1740's," *SP*, 74 (1977), 445-64;

"Mother, Memory, Muse and Poetry after Pope," *ELH*, 44 (1977), 312–36; and "Theodicy at Mid-century: Young, Akenside, and Hume," *ECS*, 12 (1978), 90–106.

10. Bloom, *The Anxiety of Influence* (New York: Oxford Univ. Press, 1973), ch. 4; Sherwin, *Precious Bane: Collins and the Miltonic Legacy* (Austin: Univ. of Texas Press, 1977).

11. Weiskel, *The Romantic Sublime: Studies in the Structure and Psychology of Transcendence* (Baltimore: Johns Hopkins Univ. Press, 1976), ch. 5; Fry, *The Poet's Calling in the English Ode* (New Haven: Yale Univ. Press, 1980), ch. 5. (Fry's study appeared too late for me to cite his comments on individual poems.)

12. Carver, *The Life of a Poet: A Biographical Sketch of William Collins* (London: Sidgwick and Jackson; New York: Horizon, 1967).

13. *Selected Poems of Thomas Gray and William Collins*, ed. Arthur Johnston (London: Arnold, 1967; Columbia, S.C.: Univ. of South Carolina Press, 1970).

14. *Thomas Gray and William Collins: Poetical Works*, ed. Roger Lonsdale (Oxford: Oxford Univ. Press, 1977). This is a completely revised version of the edition first published by Oxford in 1917 and subsequently revised in 1927 and 1937.

15. *The Poems of Thomas Gray, William Collins and Oliver Goldsmith*, ed. Roger Lonsdale (London: Longman, 1969).

16. *The Works of William Collins*, ed. Richard Wendorf and Charles Ryskamp (Oxford: Clarendon Press, 1979).

Index

Index

Richard Wendorf is associate professor of English at Northwestern University. He is the editor, with Charles Ryskamp, of *The Works of William Collins* (Oxford: Clarendon Press, 1979), and editor of *Examining the Sister Arts: Essays on English Art and Literature from Hogarth to Tennyson* (forthcoming).